Ricœur and the Negation of Happiness

Ricœur and the Negation of Happiness

ALISON SCOTT-BAUMANN

B L O O M S B U R Y
LONDON • NEW DELHI • NEW YORK • SYDNEY

Bloomsbury Academic
An imprint of Bloomsbury Publishing Plc

50 Bedford Square
London
WC1B 3DP
UK

1385 Broadway
New York
NY 10018
USA

www.bloomsbury.com

Bloomsbury is a registered trade mark of Bloomsbury Publishing Plc

First published 2013

British Library Cataloguing-in-Publication Data
A catalogue record for this book is available from the British Library.

ISBN: HB: 978-1-7809-3605-5
PB: 978-1-7809-3636-9
ePDF: 978-1-7809-3771-7
ePub: 978-1-7809-3797-7

Library of Congress Cataloging-in-Publication Data
Scott-Baumann, Alison.
Ricœur and the negation of happiness / Alison Scott-Baumann.
pages cm
Includes bibliographical references and index.
ISBN 978-1-78093-636-9 (pbk.) – ISBN 978-1-78093-605-5 (hardcover) – ISBN 978-1-78093-797-7 (ebook (epub)) – ISBN 978-1-78093-771-7 (ebook (pdf))
1. Ricœur, Paul. 2. Negativity (Philosophy) 3. Happiness. I. Title.
B2430.R554S36 2013
194–dc23
2013015416

Typeset by Deanta Global Publishing Services, Chennai, India
Printed and bound in India

CONTENTS

ACKNOWLEDGEMENTS

Mike, James, Lizzie and Benjie made this book possible with their love and support.

I thank the Conseil Scientifique of the Fonds Ricœur for supporting me in my interest in working on Ricœur's archive. In particular I have been fortunate to work with Professor Olivier Abel, President of Fonds Ricœur, Mme Catherine Goldenstein, Chief Archivist and Curator at Fonds Ricœur and Professor Nicola Stricker, Director of the Fonds Ricœur. The Conseil Scientifique have been supportive and patient and I am very grateful to them for that understanding: Corina Combet- Galland, Marc de Launay, Mireille Delbraccio, François Dosse, Michael Foessel, Daniel Frey, Jérôme Gramont, Jean Leclercq, Sabina Loriga, Johann Michel, Jean- Claude Monod, Jérôme Porée, Myriam Revault d'Allonnes, Gilbert Vincent and Heinz Wismann.

I thank the Leverhulme Trust for the generous Fellowship that has made it possible for me to finish a five-year programme of research and also to make a contribution to the archives of transcriptions and translations of some Ricœur papers (2012–13). I also thank the Economic and Social Research Council (ESRC) for funding my colleague Dr Sariya Cheruvallil-Contractor and me to run a 'follow-on' project (2012–13). This is to facilitate dissemination of research findings that are the culmination of fifteen years of work on social justice issues with British Muslim groups, which often become the 'other' of modern media mythologies. There is a strong reciprocal influence between my philosophy work and my social justice work.

I thank those who have invited me to talk on this subject in Canterbury, Lisbon, Paris, Moscow, Bath, Lecce, Cheltenham, Strasbourg, Valencia and London over the last five years. Family, many friends and colleagues have supported me with this writing: Manuel Barbeito, Marco Busacci, Mehmet Dikerdem, Astrid Dret, Tom Grimwood, Ana-Maria Isliwa, Hiroko Kawanami, John Lotherington, Gonçalo Marcelo, Kris Mason O'Connor, Terry O'Connor, Shuruq Naguib, Chris Norris, Liz Ramshaw, James and Elizabeth Scott-Baumann, Mike Sohn, Alison Stone, Joy Sullivan, Benjie Way and especially Simone Roberts for textual guidance and editing support. I thank also Olivier Villemot and Gonçalo Marcelo for working with me on Ricœur archival texts as part of the Leverhulme project.

ABBREVIATIONS AND BIBLIOGRAPHIC NOTE

I have provided two dates for many books and papers, including Ricœur's, that have been translated; the year of first publication in the original language, usually French, followed by the year of publication in English. Vansina's 2008 Ricœur bibliography is the most comprehensive, especially for tracking the many different sites, languages and dates of publication.

Archival items: the full referencing system as developed by Mme Catherine Goldenstein, Chief Archivist at Fonds Ricœur is as follows:

Archives Ricœur, Fonds Ricœur – Bibliothèque de l'I.P.T. – Paris, Inventaire 1, dossier 96 La Négation. Cours (c. 1952–68) feuillets 8479–80.

I have abbreviated this for ease of use to: AR/FR, Bib. IPT: Inv. 1, d96 La Négation, Cours, (c. 1952–68) feuillets 8479–80.

http://www.fondsricœur.fr/photo/Editorial%20Guidelines.pdf.

Books

A Key to Edmund Husserl's Ideas 1950/1996

Philosophy of the Will 1
The Voluntary and the Involuntary: Freedom and Nature 1950/1966

Philosophy of the Will 2
Finitude and Culpability: Fallible Man 1960/1965
Finitude and Culpability: Symbolism of Evil 1960/ 1967

History and Truth 1955/1965

Freud and Philosophy: an Essay on Interpretation 1965/1970

Husserl. An Analysis of his Phenomenology (English 1967), essays published separately in French 1949–57

The Conflict of Interpretations: Essays in Hermeneutics 1969/1974

Political And Social Essays, essays published separately in French 1956–73

Biblical Hermeneutics. 1975

Interpretation Theory: Discourse and the Surplus of Meaning 1976 English only

The Rule of Metaphor 1975/1977

The Philosophy of Paul Ricœur eds. Reagan and Stewart 1978

Hermeneutics and the Human Sciences 1981

Time and Narrative. 3 Volumes. 1983, 1985, 1985/1984, 1985, 1988

Lectures on Ideology and Utopia. 1986/1997

Critique and Conviction 1995/1998

From Text To Action: Essays in Hermeneutics II 1986/1991

Oneself As Another 1990/1992

Figuring The Sacred: Religion, Narrative and Imagination 1997

Love and Justice 1995/2008

The Just 1995/2000

Thinking Biblically 1998/1998

Memory, History, Forgetting 2000/2004

The Course of Recognition 2004/2005

On Translation 2004/2006

Reflections on The Just 2001/2007

What Makes Us Think? A Neuroscientist and a Philosopher argue about Ethics, Human Nature and the Brain (with J-P Changeux) 1998/2000

Vivant jusqu'à la mort 2007

PROLOGUE

Being an archive

Paul Ricœur (1913–2005) can be seen in faded black and white photographs as a teenager and young man with a quiff in his hair, round owl-like black-framed spectacles and an earnest, steady expression. He and his bride Simone appear young, fragile and hopeful on their wedding day. They had five children, one of whom, Olivier, committed suicide. Ricœur's personal and academic life was marked indelibly by major events of the twentieth century: losing his father in battle in the World War I, being a prisoner of war in the World War II, opposing fascism to support Eastern bloc intellectuals in the cold war, protesting against the colonial war waged by France in Algeria, attempting to set up a new sort of university at Nanterre while invoking the wrath of students like Daniel Cohn Bendit in the era of 1968 student protests, and sitting on government commissions about immigration and health as well as working on women's issues. He taught at Strasbourg University, at the Sorbonne and Nanterre and spent several months of each year, in the second half of his university career, at Chicago and other US universities. Ricœur became a famous philosopher and travelled a great deal.

In the 1950s–60s, the major span of this book, he was passionately interested in existentialism, phenomenology and then hermeneutics. He also studied and wrote about ethics, historiography, law, linguistics, literature, politics, psychoanalysis, psychology, science and theology. As a practising Protestant Christian brought up in a Roman Catholic country he felt isolated because of his faith and always sought to develop ideas that would facilitate engagement with those of other faiths and of none. Ricœur's significant contributions to mainstream philosophy outnumber his religious writings, yet both those of faith and of none seek to claim him for their own. He was not part of the fashionable set of Parisian philosophers and psychoanalysts of the 1950s–80s, and yet he wrote incisively and brilliantly about Freud, about structuralism and about British rational analytic and ordinary language philosophy. He can be relied upon to carry out a unique deconstruction of text that is of forensic detail and remorseless in seeking internal inconsistencies. However, he only worked on text with which he felt some common ground, some empathy and where he could discern some moral value. This meant that he remained silent on many so-called postmodern writers; however, such silence also forms part of the negation debate.

Ricœur was interested in leading a better life and his work gives us hope, while also exacting a high price: he insisted upon the likely failure of philosophy to provide satisfactory answers and he developed dialectical juxtaposition that kept a debate provisional and tentative for as long as possible, to facilitate exploration , uncertainty and conjecture. His published work will now, little by little, be augmented by the newly opened archives like a palimpsest of the twentieth century and all its hopes, fears and fatal flaws that play themselves out in the twenty-first century.

Near the catacombs in the Boulevard Arago where skulls and thigh bones lie together underground, the archives are housed in a purpose-built library floor at the Protestant Theological College of Paris.[1] We enter the archives through the electronic library security gate, a portal, an *arkhe* such as the one through which the maidens led Parmenides, having persuaded Dike, the goddess of Justice, to let them leave and pass into the outside world; *arkhe* which means an archway, a portal and also a principle, a conviction with which to 'frame' thought, like an archway through which one's ideas must pass in order to become organized. We enter through an archway that means to convey that this is an archive of significance, the end of a journey and the beginning of a quest. At the end of his journey, Parmenides abandons the maidens in order to be with Alethiea, the goddess of knowledge who says she will teach him about truth.

This museum of words and paper in Paris contains page after page of the extremely spidery writing, the physical history of Ricœur's thought. The physicality of the archive's contents is revealing. He kept nearly everything, starting with notes taken as a teenager, notes made on paper the size of postcards, A6 (paper being a luxury in the war years and afterwards) then graduating to the luxury of A5, notes made on Strasbourg University paper, on Paris Sorbonne paper, on US university paper, on ripped up school notebooks with tiny squares and finally (for the negation papers at least) A4 plain paper at Nanterre, sometimes with the Nanterre letterhead. He sometimes added sections to his notes with snippets of paper cut and sellotaped into place between or over previous notes. His handwriting changed from the pre-war to the post-war period, becoming much harder to read after the war when fountain pen gave way to ballpoint biro. Everywhere he went he wrote – and the writing's necessity was to go backwards and forwards, back to the Pre-Socratics, forward to Hegel, back to Kant, back again and again to Aristotle; always apparently wary of Hegel and post-Hegelian philosophy and always keeping several sometimes contradictory projects running in parallel. The dialectical approach is clearly demonstrated in his working patterns as well as in his thought: combine, counterbalance, return and develop. He wrote the lecture notes on which this project is focused for communicating directly and clearly with his students and they represent a form of limited publication: he made them available in the public domain by delivering them at French state universities. All these lecture notes are now officially archived and available, with an online catalogue at www.fondsricœur.fr.

But, archives are odd things. Who decides what an archive is and who decides about access? I see it as a place for living debate and discussion, where Ricœur's work can be made accessible to scholars to whom he was talking even if they were not yet born, and indeed it has been established in this spirit of intent. Derrida's *Archive Fever* is a seminal text, often cited, and when analysing the passion of archival pursuit we also think of Foucault and also more recently Groys, with his commentary on the ways in which archival collections are sequestered, kept apart and protected in ways that enhance their apparent importance and police the access that would interrogate this perceived importance.[2] Foucault uses the term archive to describe the unwritten rules that govern permissibility: what is and is not acceptable in societal tendencies. Hence, Deleuze, in his book on Foucault, in relation to Foucault as 'a new archivist', draws attention to distinctions between archaeology and genealogy, where genealogy demonstrates the hidden ideas that govern society. Whether we take Foucault's very big definition of archive or the more customary one as favoured by librarians, there is here a paradox that archives impose impersonal order on the most personal objects, and do so in order to reveal, precisely, the personal and idiosyncratic nature of a scholar's mind, and habits. There is the seduction of being so close to the mind of another and the covetousness this intimacy can engender.

Indeed for these reasons, archives should be well protected,[3] and yet we also require – and the archives deserve – an element of democratized access; perhaps this democratization may come with digitization. Still, we must always accept the possibility that such a volume of material, if digitized, would be visually accessible but not necessarily more within our comprehending grasp, despite all the talk of portals, real and virtual. Touching the folders, holding the papers, seeing the way the ink marks the paper, all this is real history.

In fact, some sanitization has already taken place in the Fonds Ricœur: the archiving process has apparently necessitated cleaning up, removal of some folders to fit materials into their new boxes. Through a French government-funded project, 2011–13, courses given by Ricœur that were printed into *polycopiés*, the student handbooks, are being digitized. Will it help us to understand Ricœur better or open up philosophy in new ways? Will these faint ballpoint, ink pen or pencil marks on old paper retain a stable identity as archival matter when they are digitized? Groys asks us what we are left with if a page, a paragraph, a line, is taken away from the whole during the process of making the text virtual. And if it is all virtual, it ceases to be 'real'. I can look at some of the papers on my computer, but they are not really there and that special new access does not necessarily foster a closer understanding. Nothing can replace the physicality of the papers themselves and the bond of affection for papers pored over and puzzled over. However, although I mistrust the digitization programme, I very much wish for it to happen so that papers I and others have worked on can be made accessible to those far away. A more dispersed, yet more democratic access will give a more present, positive and real understanding of Ricœur, by virtue of being shared.

With his ideas about the new, Groys reminds us of the academic conveyor belt of innovation: we need new ideas in order to be intellectually stimulated, to avoid boredom and also for our careers, and thus the desire to discover something 'new' can force itself upon us in a Deleuzean repetitiveness of frenzied archival diggings. These papers of Ricœur's become, then, through no material change on their part, aspects of a new narrative that those still living will create. In the process of questioning these searches for innovation and the attendant positions of legitimization and authority, I want to maintain both a lightness of touch that sees these papers as living words and texts with both a history and many possible futures. I also hope to communicate a close attention to philosophical detail about his developing thought on the negative, and the intricacies of the papers that will allow others to follow what I have read and how I have understood it.

The archive, for Foucault, is an organized body of statements that result from archaeological investigations of material; in this sense we can argue that it is in fact Ricœur's published *oeuvre*, his 26 or so major texts that comprise the Ricœur archive. In the Anglophone world of philosophy, Ricœur scholars pore over Ricœur's dense, rich prose in his published works almost as if it were rare manuscript.[4] This has happened because he argues very tightly and in a complex manner, with an extraordinary attention to detail and exegetical depth of analysis, drawing on very large numbers of texts. He also communicates to us his desire that his works will help us, his readers to live better. One must follow carefully in order to avoid misrepresenting him, and some of his ideas may be lost or changed in translation.[5] Of course, we will misunderstand any author we read, at some point, but reading such complex text in translation is to read an interpretation of the text by the translator. Bibliographic anomalies can also arise as a result of translation into a different philosophical culture: I have noticed that when Ricœur mentions the Encyclopaedia (by which he means the *Encyclopaedia Logic*, the shorter version of Hegel's *Science of Logic*), it is often not referenced in translation. Hence, the tendency to see the published works as sacrosanct and the archival works as sketches is an artificial polarization, possibly influenced by those in the publishing world.

Now, thanks to archivist Mme Catherine Goldenstein, Chief Archivist and Conservator and Prof Olivier Abel, President of the Fonds Ricœur, the academic community has inherited great quantities of work by Ricœur, that most people close to him did not know about when he was alive. That which Ricœur in life did not destroy, but sorted, filed and catalogued has now become (potentially) accessible in Paris. We call it an archive because it has aspirations to be one, but it has not *become* one yet because it is not yet being much read and understood, nor yet seen alongside the published works in some sort of conversational companionship, complementarity and maybe even contradiction and conflict. Opening an archive to the scholarly world is a very complex undertaking, with reputations and issues of authority to deal with. Whose opinion is accepted on chronology and the relationship among different sections of papers? How do we, Ricœur scholars or the board of the Fonds Ricœur, establish accuracy or plausibility of the organization we impose on Ricœur's papers? To do so, after all, is to make a portrait of the man over which he has no control, to which he cannot respond.

Carolyn Steedman's *Dust* (2002) is a partial response to Derrida's *Archive Fever* and takes the historian's view that archives contain that which will not go away: in archives our interpretation of the past will be held within certain parameters set by the archive's managers, yet this does not preclude us from making mistakes in dating papers or distorting evidence deliberately or by mistake: this is forensic work that requires obsessive attention to detail, careful recoding and checking and long hours of reading, sifting, conjecturing, checking and checking again.[6] We must constantly review our understanding of how to approach the past because, like de Certeau's 'other', we will disrupt what we touch. This is especially true in the case of a scholar's archive. Our extrinsic ordering must interfere with the papers' intrinsic order (however purposeful or dishevelled that may have been). In a way, we are editing another person's mind when we work in archives.

It is Osborne who offers a temporary cooling to the feverish debate around our relationship with archives, with three archiving principles: publicity, singularity and mundanity.[7] A principle of publicity makes archival material available to some or other kind of public, a principle of singularity focuses archival reason upon questions of detail and a principle of mundanity makes the commonplace dimension of everyday life into the privileged focus of archival reason, by which he makes reference to Foucault and Tocqueville.

Why would any of this matter? I hope it will prove to be intrinsically interesting as an aspect of Ricœur's thought; his critique of modern philosophy is controversial and his working methods as well as his ideas provide demanding analyses of the real world. No archive should become like catacombs, with the skulls of thinkers ranged neatly and symmetrically, useless except as a bank of memories to be respected and revered. Of course, there is no earth, no dirt, no darkness here, but there are many dangers; what is it about archives that is so seductively attractive: the cream ribbon bows and grey boxes, the calm and tranquillity, the secret possibility of finding a new and wonderful commentary by Ricœur. Caution is the byword of all archival researchers. How wonderful the possibility of archival revelation can be – literally a revealing of material never before considered, an innovation that invites us to look anew at Ricœur, his way of working and his hitherto unseen material; the solitude, the companionship of soft, fragile, aged paper, the dialogue with one dead who seems to be speaking to me. It is a glamour, a magic one must guard against. The risk of hubris, the possibility of misunderstanding and the Hegelian temptation to desire the ultimate interpretative solution: the archival scholar risks claiming to know the author's mind. Origins feel near. But, Barthes warned us. The author is dead. Sense must be made from traces left behind. And Derrida also warned us: origins are bad infinities. Groys identifies suspicion around the very idea of an archive, every archive that Derrida identified as needing to be 'sheltered, and as sheltered, to conceal itself.'[8] For Groys it is also this suspicion that leads to innovation, open-mindedness, movement towards new formulations, because the suspicion acts as a self-interrogating irritant as well as a doubting of others, in line with Ricœur's understanding of suspicion.[9]

Working in an archive is also a reckoning with oneself, with one's tolerance for the tedium involved: archival work is long and slow and necessitates painstaking attention to detail. When the detail is revealed for further analysis by others and the chronologies are agreed upon, many months and years of work seem small and insignificant.

Ricœur's own archive

What were Ricœur's papers, lectures, and plans on the negative to which he took this variety of different approaches? I believe it is fair to say that his conversation with his students on negation was a long discussion between himself and Hegel, Sartre and then Kant. He produced, kept and archived several separate versions of his lectures on negation and several lecture series that analyse the history of negation, while publishing very little on the subject. These lecture notes show Ricœur tracing the negative and negation right through the Pre-Socratics, Plato and Aristotle, Plotinus, Hegel, Nietzsche, Kierkegaard, Heidegger and Kant. The lectures develop over a working period of 20 years during which structuralism emerged as the dominant French school and as Ricœur was building up to his own linguistic turn. As in his published work of this period, we see in the negation lectures his enduring interest in the problems of evil, guilt and infinity.

What is the form of this work that Ricœur requested not be published unless it already had been at least a *polycopié*? The negation lectures are listed as a *polycopié* (students' handbook) in 1962, in the Sorbonne list of *polycopiés* that was managed, typed up and printed by a co-operative of students; however, Ricœur never prepared it fully for publication. After working in the archive for 3 years, I recommend that they can be read and we can treat them with the following contextual notes in mind. Ricœur established his own archive of lecture notes and scripts – scripts is an appropriate term as he read the lectures (which he called 'lessons' in a teacherly way) from carefully prepared, often typed, prose texts (which he termed 'chapters' as if they were to become books, which some of them did). I believe both style and content assure us that they were designed expressly for this purpose, that is, to be spoken out loud for students, and not simply academic texts that he read out. The prose is often syntactically less complex than the prose in his published works. He often gives his students explicit advice about what to read, and he often makes reference to his publications in a cognate field in the margins of his own lectures. Syntactical simplicity does not, however, mean the lectures are easy to understand, as he is dealing with levels of abstraction as complex as those dealt with in Plato's dialogues. However, he often uses the syntactical simplicity to express arguments of great complexity and subtlety precisely because they are subtle and difficult to keep track of while listening. These lectures do not make easy reading either, but they are enlightening to those who want to fully understand his thinking. Many were handwritten in full and then typed up by his wife Simone or by students or friends from text or from audiotapes. It is possible to tell from some errors of transcription that some of the lectures were typed from recordings. He often makes additional notes that require scrupulous tracking in the margins in order that they are understood accurately as supplements to the main argument. Most importantly, we can see how he analysed, reordered and reanalysed the themes, the paradoxes and the – to him – insoluble aspects of ancient and modern philosophy. While the feathers were flying all around him in the 1950s and 60s, Ricœur considered the explosion of thinking in the negative, which pervaded modern philosophy since Hegel, and attempted to develop a philosophy of negation.

The notes as we receive them are as Ricœur archived his own work, on negation, work that spans more than twenty years of study, starting with teenage notes and ending with his Nanterre lecture notes and his handwritten lecture notes on Kant. He created a file of his lectures in a different sequence to the order in which he delivered them. Through his own archival work of organizing his papers and storing them in the metal filing cabinet at Châtenay Malabry, we can see clearly the shape for a five-part plan, in five folders.[10] Through reading the archival material, I have read his published works with more awareness of the negative. Ricœur's personal library of books also proved invaluable for considering how he studied, how he consulted ancient Greek texts in the original and in translation and how he read secondary literature. With the notes, the lectures, the chronology of their delivery and the re-ordering in Ricœur's own archive, his annotated volumes provide nearly unrepresentable understanding of the multidimensionality of Ricœur's scholarly process. Archives do afford a scholar a more textured and multidimensional knowledge of another scholar's thought.

Being in an archive

There is a limitrophal quality to this project and its artefacts. It is easy to feel like a frontier troop, kept in the borderlands by being allowed only restricted access to the archives: yet even restricted access is very time consuming and not to everyone's taste, requiring archival research that combines obsession and vision. Such an experience reflects Ricœur's sojourn into the negative, to and fro mapping an older territory in a new way. The archives themselves have a paradoxical quality; they have their own floor in a library and are being cared for by attentive experts, but there is also still this limitrophal quality to the papers themselves: on the edge of Ricœur scholarship because still unresearched, and their value alongside the published works is an unexplored question. There is discussion among the archive's managers about their importance and about how they relate to his published works. Catherine Goldenstein, as archivist and curator of the archives, sees them as having three purposes: first, for verification of historical fact: for example, Ricœur's position on the Algerian civil war. Secondly, the archives safe-keep his taught course material, not to be published but to be available for scholars to consult. And thirdly, they preserve these unpublished works in order to facilitate a deeper understanding of the internal structure of his published and unpublished works. In a situation of such clear rules for use and so much new and unexplored material, it is difficult to know that the rules can always stand. An archive is a kind of new territory, and that mapping requires a heightened alertness. It's difficult to know in advance what matters.

Archival study must painstakingly demonstrate the fabric, content and form of material and I believe that the researcher should also make available the ways in which she drew her conclusions. Methodology for my work included consulting Mme Catherine Goldenstein for her unparalleled expertise in dating the papers and in teaching me how to recognize the signs of each era and how to decipher Ricœur's handwriting. My excel spread sheet of his personal archive on negation will be placed on the Fonds Ricœur website to coincide with the publication of this book. This will provide an annotated map of the papers on which I have been working and make them accessible, which they were not before.

I believe that Ricœur's work on negation in his published *oeuvre* is a neglected area in need of research, and his unpublished lectures on the subject illuminate the published work on this theme. Negation is seldom if ever referenced in the indexes of his books, yet he brought the theme into more than one published text. It was a kind of substrate to his work in the 1950s and 1960s. My close textual analysis of his early published works shows a great deal of discussion of negation, but editors make little or no mention of it in the indexes of his books, and negation/negativity do not appear in Vansina's index of Ricœur's works. If we treat negation as if it were breadcrumb trails in his published works, rather than little stones to lead us through his early work, then we fail to take account of the negative to the extent that he clearly had done. More, we lose one of the few, maybe the only, tracing of the history of negation in philosophy. We would be negating the negative in his work, and losing a chance to understand the often erased *arkhe* of the negative in thought, to which the unpublished work can sensitize us.

When we pass through the *arkhe*, the portal, as Parmenides did in search of true knowledge, we need to consider the importance of sharing what we find, in a co-operative spirit of discovery, unlike Parmenides, who abandoned the girls after they helped him to find the goddess of truth, *Alethiea*. This book is an attempt to share.

INTRODUCTION

Many social commentators characterize the twenty-first century as a world of instant gratification and scepticism, arguing that we are increasingly less able to deal with not having what we want, with not being someone different or not understanding what's happening to us (Baudrillard, Bauman, Foucault). This makes it easy to negate the value of the things we cannot have, the person we cannot be or the ideas we cannot understand. Eventually, for certain modern thinkers, this death of meaning may be replaced by something even worse; the end of the birth of ideas, that deprives us of the ability to generate new positives and negatives (Schopenhauer, Kierkegaard, Adorno). This can lead to certain postmodern trends, upon which Roger Scruton passes judgement as follows:

> This arrest of the soul in the posture of negation is worthy of study, since it is at the root of much that passes for philosophy in a modern university . . . the proof that there is no source of law, no value and no meaning.[1]

Ricœur (1913–2005) was an outstanding French philosopher, a Protestant thinker who developed both hermeneutical and phenomenological techniques. His extensive and unpublished work on negation will demonstrate how we can challenge Scruton's analysis and also live more companionably with these negative aspects of life.

Throughout the centuries in western philosophy, there has been a great debate about not-ness; at one extreme, the negative could be death and at another extreme it may be a holistic vision of unified oneness that denies not-ness entirely. However, there are other tangential understandings; what about nothingness? Is that only death or can it be the exquisite lightness of being that may be possible when one has surrendered completely to a spiritual innocence, an apophatic way of knowing nothing that is a sort of knowing everything? A difficulty with the negative/negation is that difference is at work in its meanings. We note that where there is *not*, there also *is,* so it is necessary to look at the binaries that go from the Pre-Socratics, through Aristotle's law of the excluded middle, to Kant's antinomies and Hegel's dialectic. Hegel of course added a third element and if we want to find different structures from those in this list we would need to look to eastern philosophy – where many of the patterns will become visible in different guises. That is another project: in this book I will focus on Ricœur's early thought and his seemingly erratic path along the *via negativa*.

Ricœur was perplexed by the fear of finitude, nothingness, nihilism, pessimism and decay that he saw reflected in modern philosophy and looked everywhere he could think of in the ancient and modern world for the sources of these aversions, asking himself repeatedly whether they count as negative and whether the negative is 'bad'. What if we found that we should accept the negative as an integral component of our daily lives and that, in fact, this would not cost us as much effort as we might think and could in fact help us to live better?

Ricœur lectured and wrote for over 20 years on negation ('do I understand something better if I know what it is *not*, and what is *not-ness*?') and never published his extensive writings on this subject. This book draws on his early published work and previously unavailable archival material. Ricœur concluded that there are multiple sources for negation; it can, for example, be *the other person* (Plato), it can be *the included opposite* (Hegel), it can be *apophatic spirituality* (not being able to know God) and it can be *existential nothingness* (Sartre) and it can be the operations of psychological denial. He concluded that the negative as a theme, and negation as a method in thought, are not self-identical or consistent in the history of thought. I propose that his work on negation creates deep subterranean springs that nourish his subsequent development of dialectics. He also found his study of negation in Greek philosophy to be valuable for demonstrating his belief that much modern and postmodern philosophy and structuralism is shallow and dry. Ricœur's search to understand humans and help us to improve our lives is suffused with the conviction that negation is necessary but not sufficient; what is also required is some sort of affirmation that we know we are split by contradictions and nevertheless try to overcome them.

Eventually, he seems to have decided that negation is a mechanism that is integral to human existence and that its multiple forms are better taken account of in *ethical action* rather than *philosophical form*. This is Ricœur the existentialist providing a Marcelian basis for his response. Most importantly, and perhaps as a template for much of his dialectical work, the negative aspect is not only balanced against but also with itself: the negative element in all phenomena must be acknowledged and faced in a sort of Hegelian doubling. He subsequently found a resting place for negation, albeit unstable, impermanent and provisional within his dialectical model and his ambitious expectations of metaphor as an ethical force.

If negation, for Ricœur in the late 40s, was bipolar: willed and suffered, by the mid-50s negation was the dark side of an act that he argued must also demonstrate its bright side, hence much more integrated into the person's power to act and an explicit challenge to Sartre's dark vision.[2]

By the early 60s, negation was definitely channelled into various clearly incompatible paths: the fault as possibility, the symbolism of evil, psychoanalytic mourning. His demand? That there should be progression, not *stuckness*.

By the late 60s and the 70s, negation was integrated into a clear statement about linguistic patterning, structuralism and the need for a critical philosophy on the one hand to challenge reason and on the other hand to accept the need for belief systems. At this time, he cautioned us about Adorno's *Negative Dialectics*, which he saw as, in part, an expression of Enlightenment thinking that tips over into excessive negativity, that is, an attack on itself: faith is an integral part of Enlightenment thought. It does not constitute the opposite of reason, so a part of emancipated thought will be destroyed if faith is rejected. Similarly, the positive is only so because it contains negative features, so the negative cannot be rejected or it will destroy the positive too.

Ricœur worked on the understanding that critical philosophy will be negative because reason must stand over against reality in a highly critical matter, so as to prevent easy reconciliation between the individual and society, between belief and knowledge. Yet always this will be a clear desire to do honour to the different ways of being a human, including our inclination to faith. If we continue to ignore the role that negation plays in early Ricœur, we risk doing what he counselled against in philosophy and indeed in our own thinking; that is, paying too little attention to negation.

I am motivated to undertake this project by three major concerns: one of my major interests is to create a small, indicative archive of one self-limiting aspect of Ricœur's work: negation. It influenced his published work and is not known about. His many lectures on negation are completely unknown. He based them on Heraclitus and Parmenides and also on Plato, Aristotle and Plotinus. He also used these ancient thinkers to resolve his concerns about Kant, Hegel, Kierkegaard, Nietzsche, Sartre and modern philosophy's negative turn.

Secondly, I wish to show how archival work can be used to contextualize Ricœur's work alongside that of more popular contemporaneous philosophers. In the Anglophone philosophical world, Ricœur is seldom considered as seriously as many of his contemporaries, the subjects of many texts to which he forms a footnote. I believe this is a grave omission and therefore I will introduce his ideas on negation as he traced and retraced them through thinkers from Parmenides to Deleuze: he lectured a lot on Parmenides and not at all on Deleuze. This gives me the opportunity to measure Ricœur's philosophy of negation against these great thinkers' views on the negative. I regret the dominance of dead white men and will rectify that in my next book.

Thirdly, I am passionate about applying Ricœur's work to real-life problems: his work on negation resonates strongly with many current issues of great importance in the areas of race and society, mental health care and education. In the Western world, there is an apparent resurgence of racism, whereby we negate the 'other'. This social and psychological negation affects our politics, which in turn affects our collective civil life right down to the languages that are offered in the education system. In mental health care, we show a tendency to revert to an almost Cartesian dualism, such that many illnesses are misdiagnosed as purely physical; we negate the mind's role in influencing the body. In education, we seek to deploy a consumerist model of pleasure and consumption and are distressed if children fail or experience frustration as part of the learning process. An overwhelming desire seems to have possessed us to avoid failure, pain and ambiguity, and it becomes correspondingly more and more difficult to talk about the negative aspects of living without seeming puritanical or sado-masochistic, or just weak. There are several case studies to illustrate these issues (ADHD, pedagogy, ME, racism and sexism). I also make some use of literature: Kafka and Murdoch.

The negation papers form only a very small part of Ricœur's archive. My intention is to offer some of what I found in them as an indication of the magnificent and fascinating materials kept in the Fonds Ricœur and as the basis for this study of Ricœur on the negative and negation. Importantly, the negation papers should not be studied in isolation, so I draw from the several different groups of papers I have looked closely at detail, and hope to place those readings on the history of negation in philosophy within the context of Ricœur's published work.

There are many questions that this research raises, such as why there is such a major discrepancy between the negation lectures and his publications on negation: he published very little on negation, he never completed the *polycopié* that he was asked to produce for printing and distributing to students, and he kept publicly aloof from the long running debate about, for example, Plato and Aristotle, nothingness and the negative. Yet, he lectured repeatedly on negation and with great attention to the interaction of various different arguments about negation. His major concern was not necessarily publishing. In the lectures and unpublished papers, we can sense the great pleasure that he took in teaching and the way in which he developed his ideas as a result of teaching a similar sequence of topics in different order and with different emphases and interpretations. He wanted to resolve intellectual and real-life problems and keep the two always in relation, even if or perhaps especially if, they prove irresolvable.

Ricœur's negation papers mainly span the early 1950s to the late 1960s and comprise various different groups: there are several lecture series given in French in Strasbourg, Paris, Nanterre and elsewhere, and several lecture series given in English in the United States. Some of the material has been typed, much is handwritten. Some lectures are present in both handwritten and typed forms, some are missing.

Ricœur also developed a small, personal archive of papers that he drew from different parts of his lectures on negation and arranged them separately in five labelled folders as a set. This material has all been catalogued by Catherine Goldenstein, Chief Archivist, as an integral part of the Ricœur archives. There is clear justification for taking seriously the ordering of these papers that he kept and organized, even those that are only a few pages long or incomplete; all were retained and ordered by Ricœur for some unexecuted purpose. He clearly valued his teaching materials, although he stipulated that those that had not already been, must not be published. Throughout this book, I will propose some ways in which these sequences on negation can be seen to resonate with his published work, and contextualized within his other work around evil, morals, nothingness, finitude and infinity. There are also resonances with other major fields of study explored by Ricœur, such as existentialism, psychoanalysis, structuralism and major philosophical fields including the ancient Greeks, phenomenology, hermeneutics and analytic approaches.

Negation is complex and has been considered a problem by Western philosophical thinkers from Heraclitus to Sartre. Ricœur is not considered among them as he published very little on this subject. Yet, for about 20 years he lectured not only on negation but also on related themes such as finitude and infinity, nothingness and apophatic theology. My research in the Ricœur archives demonstrates that, as a young philosopher, he consulted combinations of thinkers; for example, thinking about Kant's negative while fully acknowledging his debt to Hegel, the modern father of the negative. Ricœur also made practical efforts to free himself from the Hegelian legacy. With the project of this book, I hope Ricœur scholars and philosophers interested in negation can develop a heightened awareness of his fascination with the negative, and we can use that fresh sensitivity to trace the negative impulse in some of his significant works in ways that are currently not appreciated.[3]

Ricœur eventually abandoned his initial quest to develop a philosophy of negation, yet I will show how he incorporated the negative impulse into his later ideas – metaphor, dialectic and personal identity.

This is a young archive, bequeathed by Ricœur to his family and placed in the care of the Protestant Institute of Paris. Under the leadership of Prof Olivier Abel, the Fonds Ricœur is now housed in a purpose-built top floor added to the Institute's existing library. Under the leadership of Catherine Goldenstein, Chief Archivist, the archive is now catalogued and searchable online.

This work therefore cannot avoid important issues about archiving, as raised by Derrida, Foucault, Groys and others. What is an archive? How can we help one another to explore such an enormous collection? Should there be an obligation upon academics to make accessible the materials that have shaped their thought processes? I believe so, which is why I have worked with the Conseil Scientifique of the Fonds Ricœur. Much more can be achieved by those who wish to study the papers that I have transcribed and translated to be placed on the Fonds Ricœur website, to accompany the excel spread sheet of the negation papers.

Ricœur started by looking at an idea: the negative at the core of the human spirit and character. I will show how our desire to deny this negative has crept into our daily lives in most unwelcome forms, such as the innocence of the ignorant school child who is allowed to avoid learning, or the decision on the part of some caring professions to ignore research evidence. Yet, it is both exciting and necessary to seek evidence for Ricœur's hopes. We can accomodate the negative in a strong and creative way into new ways of achieving this acceptance of our own complexity. In the current climate of consumerism, in which we *seem* able to buy happiness, it is also useful to look at whether we have developed excessive expectations of happiness, not least perhaps because we think we can use it to eliminate the negative.

CHAPTER ONE

Reading Ricœur on negation

I hesitate precisely because the world is an ironic question: and you, what will you do? Each tentative project is like a stammering response whose progress is delineated by an outline of closed and open roads, of obstacles and implements, of openings and blank walls. But this response is immediately overshadowed by another one. The unease of indecision contrasts a definite anticipation and an uncertain decision. The world moves on while I mark time. (Freedom and Nature)[1]

Here is a statement by Ricœur that is full of negatives, of stammering, uneasy indecision from a chapter on hesitation and choice. It takes the form of an extended metaphor: it is a little episode based around a symbol for evil, deviation from the path of the journey.[2] The passage also contains a rich use of language that includes a sketched Hegelian type of dialectical pattern, simile, metaphor and symbol, and almost has the feel of a miniature parable. Indeed much of his philosophy became an explicit analysis of language such as metaphor and parable for existential support, personal enrichment and moral guidance, (even though his philosophical style of writing became less rich in imagery). Ricœur later developed and elaborated a picture of human living that asserts the necessity of attestation, of living by one's faith and of living for the other, using not only language but, also among other disciplines, politics, psychoanalysis, social theory, theology, history and, of course, philosophy.

I believe it is to Hegel that Ricœur was speaking much of the time in this negation work; Hegel was highly influential for French thinkers at this time, proved difficult to get rid of, and could be addressed partially through engaging with Sartre. Yet although he tackled Sartre, the negatives presented here by Ricœur in 1950 in *Freedom and Nature* stayed with him and demanded a response. In his unpublished lectures on negation (c. 1952–68), he worked intensively on the key issues contained in this passage: is there a negative impulse at the core of the human being? There must be that possibility, or else why would I even imagine that there could be a problem with which road to take? And what about the road I do not take? Why would I be motivated by desire that I cannot satisfy (a definite anticipation and an uncertain decision) and do I suffer because of the discrepancy between what I can achieve and the surrounding environment – the world is insolently ironic and moves on while I mark time? In answer to this dilemma Ricœur evolved a philosophy that worked within yet constantly struggled against an oppositional or contradictory logic and that takes its inspiration from Spinoza to an extent: 'all determination is negation'. If we interpret this as meaning (as Melamed does), that finite things are determination of the maximally determinate infinite being that is God, then in an existentialist world without God (as it was for Sartre) we can gesture towards the decision that is an analogue of Spinoza: when I take one road, I cannot take any other, the infinite possibilities of action are curtailed.[3] However, I will argue that because it is more manageable, we narrow down our decisions into binaries; either this path or that path. Ricœur often used positive/ negative as shorthand for these options, as we all do, yet I propose that he developed linguistic structures of negation such as neither/ nor, perhaps because they impose an added negativity upon a negative/positive dialectic that is already unstable. He also used either/or and I hope to show that these are not mutually contradictory, yet nor are they conducive to stability.

However, the neither/nor structure of oppositional thought does not have a strong identity in western philosophy except in the theological and philosophical debates of those such as Plotinus (AD 204–270) and the apophatic approach to God – the nothingness of not knowing as a potent force for good. The neither/nor has the benefit of opening up the possibility of a third phenomenon, that, unlike with Hegel's dialectic, does not necessarily need to be closely related to the first two opposing elements. It bears some resemblance to that of Nishida Kitaro and other Eastern thinkers, but Ricœur sought other solutions in preference and I will explore these as well as set them in the context of modern life.[4] As demonstrated in Ricœur's extended metaphor above, we tend to feel burdened by the need to deal with negative options, and one of our responses is to name a phenomenon as negative and, having categorized it as negative, give ourselves the privilege of vilifying it and avoiding it (axiology gone wrong). One of the examples of this that I will work through in more detail is our response to people of a different skin colour or eye shape from our own: I will argue that it is plain wrong to use skin or eyes as predicates for judging a person and that this is a stable, rational argument.[5] A less stable argument would be that surrounding use of mind-altering, psychotropic drugs. Despite advances in contemporary neuroscience that settle the fact that mind and body work together much more closely than previously imagined, I believe that profit-driven pharmaceutical corporations are presenting us with powerful concoctions that assume a Cartesian dualism: changing the brain will heal the mind and reduce individual differences by negating even healthy mental characteristics. This instability can be seen in the diagnosis and treatment of ME: myalgic encephalopathy or chronic fatigue syndrome; a condition which I suggest has dualist aetiology, being based upon a dualist negation of the influence of mind upon body. If we do this in order to privilege body, it becomes more difficult to diagnose – yet psychiatrists may take a Cartesian view too, just that it is one in the opposite direction, privileging mind over body. Either binary choice will hamper treatment of a condition that may have both physical and emotional components.

I will use these and other examples to show how powerful the mechanism is for creating a kind of dualist, binary model of nearly everything, naming one half of it negative and refusing to consider other evidence. This provides us with a naive axiology – a philosophy of values that we are well pleased with as we can constantly compare and contrast dualities and find satisfaction in their differences. I propose to use axiology in this context of dualistic value judgements. Ricœur went back to the roots of western thought to explore the nature of negation, looking at fallibility, guilt and sin, and seeking an existentialism that would neither crush us as reprobates with predestination nor cast us loose into a free market of infinite choice and despair – of course it is easy to use these contrasting negatives as I have just done: choice – despair – I make the argument seem more dramatic by polarizing the alternatives.

Negation is a challenge to the way we think, and may indeed constitute a Ryle – type category mistake, that is, misnamed because misunderstood: often we use the term 'negative' to describe phenomena that make us unhappy, that we do not like or do not understand and that we seek to dismiss by calling them negative. Life is also at least partly about dealing with the variations between personal identity and that which is different from me. At a broader, historical level, understanding negation may also be the way to understand identity and difference, as when one examines the chronology of western philosophy, in which the self has gradually peeled itself away from its identification with God. I will also argue that dichotomy could often signal complementarity, not opposite and bad, and complementarity may, in a Hegelian sense, be necessary for living in a balanced way, as we see, for example, with the mind: body dualism argument, which seems to me to be coming back to haunt us.

Of course, there are contexts in which the negative is part of a pair and such oppositions can be very useful; in literature, for example, that philosophises. As Cervantes realized, the master and his servant can give us great pleasure as they travel, argue and disagree fundamentally, and in a manner that is less full of foreboding than Ricœur's extended metaphor of the journey through life – Diderot followed this positive: negative pattern with Jacques the fatalist and his master, and our lives are littered with many other examples of positive: negative patterns such as male/female, good/evil, friend/enemy. Derrida showed us how we privilege one of the pair. The negative is much more subtle than simple opposition, but we tell ourselves that the distinction we are drawing is oppositional and value laden, while also denying that we do this – rather reminiscent of Nietzsche pointing out that modern Western culture has killed God while denying that we have done so. The strength of Cervantes and Diderot is that they use conversational dialectic structures, to tell the reader what they are playing at, but we often refuse to explain ourselves while deciding upon our pet polarities.

I hope to show that Ricœur moved this discussion away from vexatious and insoluble human habits regarding the use of the term 'negative' and its multifarious meanings and towards a pragmatic harnessing of the negative impulse inside linguistic structures about negation – from a debate that *used* language to the potential *inside* linguistic structures themselves such as metaphor, parable, dialectic and narrative. I will show that this sensitivity to the form and structure of language as a reflection of meaning was not a structuralist move in the usual sense, because Ricœur's tracing – or construction – of this movement contained at all times a desire to show how language can be used to express the meaning of life, ontologically to reflect and support the human spirit and its struggles to be good. My other main aim is to contextualize Ricœur's work on negation within his early thought (of which negation forms a part) and, to an extent, within a comparative frame of other philosophers who have also considered negation. This is the beginning of a longer process, as the connections need to be built carefully, given that Ricœur did not enter into the debate about negation as others understood it.

On the one hand, Ricœur was both fascinated and repulsed by the French revival in Hegel studies that started with Kojève in the 1930s and entailed interest in binary structures of debate and dialectical tensions between positive and negative, such as Kojève's famed emphasis on Hegel's master: slave dialectic. On the other hand, he felt challenged by Sartre's emphasis on negation in *Being and Nothingness*, which in many ways comprised a response to Hegel and what seemed a much more pessimistic approach to human existence. In tandem with Hegel and Sartre, who functioned initially for Ricœur as two book ends for his debate about negation, there are many books in between which Ricœur reads in order to address himself periodically to Heraclitus and Parmenides and follows right through to Kierkegaard and Nietzsche, as well as Plato, Aristotle and Plotinus, among others. Ricœur's avowed aim was to find the source of the negative. He hoped that at its core he would find affirmation of the human spirit *by* the human spirit. He was also perplexed by the idea of nothingness; is it a 'bad' thing to be denied, as Parmenides thought, or is it a good thing as Plotinus saw in the powerful humility of the apophatic way to God. Or, is the negative an inevitability of existence and to be managed as best we can, as Sartre saw it? Or, is it simply our fear of pain and death?

By the mid-1950s, Ricœur had dropped Sartre as one bookend from his phenomenological exploration and Hegel remained. Kant was always in the room, waiting. For Ricœur this was an opportunity to look at the problem in a different way, now that it had become unbalanced by his dismissal of Sartre, and by the late 1950s Ricœur was considering what he briefly called four 'fathers' and four 'sons' as providing the genealogy of negation: Hegel, Marx, Kierkegaard and Nietzsche as fathers; and Jaspers, Marcel, Heidegger and Sartre as sons. By the early 1960s the 'sons' also proved inadequate to the task and enabled Ricœur to critique the concept of existentialism as a unitary entity. He was also beginning to make his so-called 'linguistic turn', and here we see a change of direction: given the lack of clarity around the term 'negation', I believe Ricœur returned to strands that he had already explored in the 1950s and which now gave rise to work on language, narrative and hermeneutical philosophy. Here we see the intent to identify negation and its role in language and meaning, as in *Semeia* on metaphor and parable and by demonstrating creatively how it can be done, as in *The Rule of Metaphor*.

Hegel was not easy to get rid of and in fact Ricœur concluded, unlike his peer Deleuze who believed it was possible to be free of Hegel, that it could not be done: Hegel was an integral part of French thought and had to be accepted as such. As I discuss in Chapter 4, Hegel was far less important at that time in Britain – Iris Murdoch (1919–99) commented in her 1957 essay ('Hegel in Modern Dress') on Sartre's *Being and Nothingness*, 'It is almost mysterious how little Hegel is esteemed in this country'.[6] For Ricœur at this time Hegel was very present, and Aristotle remained as a constant and useful companion, yet by the late 1960s Ricœur was no longer pursuing Aristotle's attempts in the *Physics* to explain change in nature. However, Ricœur retained the original sense from Aristotle that negation is either willed or suffered, in consonance with Aristotle's views about agency, and Ricœur *combined* willing and suffering to demonstrate his original hope that the affirmation of will is at the core of the negative. If this is so, then the negative is crucial to our self-realization and it is through such sequences as Kant's philosophy of limits that we understand the necessity of the negative in us, for showing us our limitations and, thereby, our potential. Negation becomes both limitation and possibility, and as such, it is through inescapable tropes such as metaphor and parable that Ricœur continues his interest in the negative, not least because of the distinction Hegel drew between logical and real negation. If we were to follow Aristotle on this, as Ricœur had attempted in the 1950s, we would find Aristotle's attempt to prove that nature is characterized by unbroken, natural conformities, yet this, as Ricœur concluded, would eliminate the negative in the human experience, both as a defined term and as an existential state.

If we become sensitized to the theme of negation in Ricœur's published work, we will find sections where he discusses it explicitly, initially to interrogate it, then to attempt provisional definitions using classical and modern figures and subsequently to revert to using it in an everyday way. We will also see that he continued to use terms like negative and positive in an everyday sense; that is, with implicit value judgements about bad and good and an implied binary, which Derrida had already analysed. This sort of dualism permits one to set up an initial positional debate, but also leaves unsaid and unresolved many issues, the nebulous existence of which had triggered the initial exploration.

So what does it mean: the negative? There are different word forms, of course: 'negativity' may imply a generalized state of mind, whereas 'negation' can be used to suggest the act of saying no. But what does that mean? I am not concerned here with the many rich terms we can use to communicate negative emotion or intent, such as to amputate, to deride, to erase, to shatter, but with the overuse of terms that have the root 'neg': negative, negate, negativity. The linguistic lack of clarity remains as an insoluble problem since we cannot alter our daily tendency to say; 'I have a negative reaction to that, or, on the negative side. . . . While on the positive side that. . . .'. I believe that in due course Ricœur moved *inside* language structures, with the self-conscious awareness that, for example, metaphor describes what something is by telling us what it is not. He also developed a more open dialectical debating structure than that of Hegel, presenting the potency of, for example, narrative structure and then negating its power to do much more than manage problems, without being able to initiate debate or formulate the existential philosophical questions.

How could such an alternative be developed in the western philosophical tradition in which failure to master ideas and concepts is not favoured? Ricœur studied philosophy like a time traveller seeking answers to the meaning of life while roaming freely without regard for chronologies. Sequencing through time does not always imply causal development: during his lifelong journey through ideas, Ricœur moved backwards and forwards in deliberate defiance of chronology, such as back from Hegel to Kant, from Plato to Heraclitus and skipping to Aristotle. To complicate matters he also worked on many divergent projects simultaneously, where he showed that many non-chronological connections can be made. He enjoyed showing how many glaring, known and unknown, contradictions can coexist once one moves through the tradition. Many of the texts described briefly here will be discussed again in other chapters in the context of Ricœur's projects that relate to negation and to the thinkers he engages on negation.

Starting to explore negation: The published work

Ricœur's intellectual struggle was developing in the midst of a horror of wars and their aftermaths: the World War I, The Spanish Civil War and the World War II. There were great optimistic hopes for a better future. There was also the doubt, suspicion and depression that beset much of

Europe, which was strongly reflected in much contemporary art, such as that of Picasso's *Guernica*, Valéry's 'negative philosophy', James Joyce's hallucinogenic *Finnegan's Wake*, Sartre's *Huis Clos* and Samuel Beckett's darkly witty vision of lack, loss and despair, in *Waiting for Godot* or Beckett's *Not I* (now there we have the real horror of negation in a literary work). The intellectual backdrop to Ricœur's work was complex: existentialism was a significant development in France, and there was also much else at stake for French thought, with a Stalinist form of communism and also strong Christian groupings. Ricœur was keenly tuned to the optimism and the pessimism of the century.

There was much going on, especially in Paris. Another element in this heady mix was Hegel. In the middle third of the twentieth century, a grand revival of Hegel's thought was underway in France; initiated by Kojève, prepared for publication by Queneau, continued by Hyppolite and adopted by many, from Beckett, to Diès to Deleuze. Hegel, as the master of dialectical negation, proved to be an invaluable yet ultimately disappointing companion for Ricœur, because of Hegel's totalizing tendencies, bringing the negative into a grand scheme that removed its power to subvert. Heidegger also came to occupy a special place in much French intellectual thought, and Ricœur's admiration for him would become tempered by exasperation with the short cuts and omissions that he believed Heidegger made in his analysis of human experiences. Ricœur was attracted to Husserl's phenomenology and this early phase of his philosophy (broadly speaking 1950–70) was characterized by concentrating on consciousness as a source of direct experience. Phenomenology was the way in to developing his own ideas for Ricœur. In the late 1950s and 1960s, structuralism was a dominant force in French philosophy, with its conviction that it is the deep structural forms of language that provide meaning – not the humans who utter them. Phenomenology, with its reliance upon personal sensitivity to meaning, came under fire from structuralism, and this forms part of Ricœur's problem too, as he perceived structuralism to, in effect, be negating personal responsibility for the language we utter. However, he distinguished between structuralism as a methodology (vital) and structuralism as the basis for philosophical structures (arid). In the 1960s, he developed a more hermeneutical turn, looking more actively for meaning. He also considered the theological manifestations of the negative, with Plotinus' apophatic way to God. Over a 20-year period Ricœur sought to trace the roots of negation in all these phenomena of human thought.

There were initially three particular intellectual strands influencing Ricœur's views of the negative. One comes from the grounding in sceptical thought that he had received from Dalbiez and others during his early education. He attended lectures in his teens on Pyrrhonism, Aenesidemus and the notion of suspending judgement. Another strand is the dominant Hegelian discourse in twentieth-century France between the two world wars. Kojève's Heideggerean interpretation of Hegel 1932–38, presented in lectures in Paris attended by Merleau-Ponty, Lacan, Levinas, Bataille, Aaron, Henri and Queneau, come to influence much French thought. Twenty years later, Ricœur reviewed Hyppolite's attempt to present a different view of Hegel, not the Marxist vision of Kojève. Such academic learning was taking place in a Europe full of blood, betrayal, dilemmas and death: and thirdly Ricœur also lectured on Sartre, which played a role in his critique of the structuralist denial both of history and of the personal voice.

In 1950, 7 years after Sartre published *Being and Nothingness*, a strong statement about the negativity of human existence, Ricœur published *Freedom and Nature*, the first part of his never finished *Philosophy of the Will*.[7] Towards the end of the book, he developed an extended lament about the negative characteristics of life. He employed many grim images to describe a phenomenon that he called negation and that he found demonstrated in such images as the arbitrary nature of birth, the ravages of time in ageing, a sting, a scratched wound, suffering, amputation, pain, forced choice and freedom. World War II was not long over, and this imagery is startling for its overwhelmingly painful symbolism and existentialist tone. In addition, he overlaid the imagery in his text with dialectical patterns; binaries and reciprocities with terms such as conscious and unconscious, willed and suffered, being and non-being, freedom and negated freedom. He described existential negation as being bipolar: on the one hand, a willed, active negation of freedom and, on the other hand, a suffered, passive denial of the self.

'To choose means to exclude, man assumes appearance and form in a series of amputations' and not surprisingly 'this kills the unity of the self'.[8]

When Ricœur published *Freedom and Nature* in 1950 he was already endeavouring to develop a philosophy of negation, predicated upon his emerging belief that negative thought is a powerful force with several different origins. He was also concerned about the finite and the infinite, about Hegel's Absolute Spirit and by nihilism. In this early phenomenological text *Freedom and Nature*, in the tradition of concentrating on a consciousness as a form of direct experience, he addresses the complexity of a negation that may be more productive than existential nothingness or nihilism:

> The idea of nothing is an inexhaustible source of error. As it is, negation already has an important place in fundamental ontology: lack or need, the gaping hole of possibility opened by a project, the refusal inaugurating all voluntary affirmation, the negativity of finitude, the impotence indicated by death and even birth itself. But this negation must be set apart from the Nothing of vanity, which complicates it and perverts it.[9]

This passage is extraordinary, full of awful contradictions, encapsulating the start of his experiment with negation by seeing it in several different manifestations: yet negation/the negative is seldom discussed in modern scholarly literature on Ricœur and rarely referenced in indexes to Ricœur texts. He addresses the negative in several of his phenomenological texts, and then appears to abandon it. Meanwhile, he continued to lecture on negation until the late 1960s. Husserl was the major influence who enabled Ricœur to develop a counterbalance to the powerful negation of Hegel, not least because Husserl did not engage with the negative. He sought clarity about what exists, not what does not exist. At the time Ricœur published *Freedom and Nature* in 1950, he was still strongly phenomenological and Husserlian. He had not yet developed his Hegelian model fully, only using Hegel's model of negation in relation to the struggle between consciousness and habit:

> Habit is a way of shrinking away into the negative labour in which Hegel recognised an escape from consciousness.[10]

Hegel's bulky frame was almost impossible to get past and in the process of acting as an antidote to Hegel's mass, Husserl's phenomenology had a great deal of its lightness squeezed out of it. Husserl refused to countenance negativity: it heralds the end of phenomenology by forcing a transition from the ideal into the real-seeming contraries of dialectic. For Husserl, this transition damages beyond repair the possibility of being true to one's perceptions in a non-contradictory way, by imposing external categories. With *epoché*, Husserl brackets 'naturalistic' approaches to knowledge grounded in facts and uncovers the primordiality of consciousness. *Epoché* is Husserl's attempt to remove distracting phenomena from the consciousness and focus on the true ability of the conscious mind to differentiate between our many superficial responses and our significant perceptions. Husserl's purism involves a form of phenomenological negation, denial of superficiality, that rejects attempts at creating order when they resemble an Aristotelian mode of categorizing the material world into hierarchies, but Husserl would not understand this process as a negative force, and Ricœur finds Hegel much more useful in this respect. In effect, Hegel's development of the dialectical negative introduced a new logic of perceptions (if this is this, it is not that, yet by contrasting these two I can see a third form which can harness the fact that the two original phenomena share some of each other's characteristics). This categorization destroyed the possibilities of phenomenological thinking by insisting that we sort things into lists and categories that tend to become hierarchies and value judgements related to real and ideal characteristics, reverting in a sense to Aristotle's dichotomizing. Husserl's writing did not engage in such ideas and could not help to dispel this, so Ricœur had to think differently from phenomenology at this point in his development.[11]

Soon he already seemed to have become more upbeat, as witnessed by a paper published in 1951, 'The Unity of the Voluntary and the Involuntary'.[12] However, I believe it would be facile to assume that the paper was necessarily written after the book, as Ricœur was fully aware of the complexity of such arguments, and often took competing positions in different papers in order to explore a range of arguments. Moreover, the 1951 paper still expresses the frustration of what it feels like when we grasp how limited we are:

> Consent to necessity is never achieved. Who can accept himself without qualification, concretely, daily?[13]

And even in 1950 in *Freedom and Nature*, Ricœur showed that he had a gritty understanding of the possibly intractable problem he had set himself to resolve – dualism cannot be easily resolved as it is an integral part of our thinking:

> Dualism is not simply demanded by understanding; it is, in its way, a daily reality: *Homo simplex in vitalitate duplex in humanitate*, as Maine de Biran loved to say.[14]

Within *Freedom and Nature* (1950), it almost seems as if he had clambered into the existential distress of Sartre's *Being and Nothingness* (1943). Yet he approached the task with a pragmatic verve and stubborn determination to interrupt and alter the rhythm of dualist thought that he saw in modern (i.e. post-Hegelian) philosophy. Ricœur wanted to change how and why we negate, hoping to persuade us that to negate can also mean to acknowledge and to create, not simply to erase.

Hegel and negation

Hegel's work has never exercised the influence over Anglophone philosophy and culture that it has enjoyed in Continental thought, yet there is a renaissance of interest and recent reinterpretations of interest in him, as we see with Pippin and Pinkard who take Hegel more as a Kantian and place less value to metaphysics, and Beiser and Houlgate who concentrate more on the *Logic*. Hegel revolutionized our understanding of the negative by placing it at the very heart of his thinking. Through him we see that the physical negative is part of the process of being mortal, the finitude of human life. We have not the power to live forever, and our desire to be invincible must come up against our acceptance that we are limited mortals which is our foundational experience of the negative and must lead to a further discovery of a new, more productive attempt on our part to make a better job of being finite: such effort necessitates a reworking of the physical negative as a dialectical one. Developing the new is a way of delaying the end; begetting children, creating works of art, making accessible 'new' material in an archive. In its turn, this reworked Hegelian version of making a big job of living will make us aware of a different tenor of negation and will necessitate another reworking of our positions and approach to life. Allocating this pole position to the negative is helpful because Hegel recasts the dialectical negative as a contradiction that is simply an integral part of our development and one that engages us in a struggle to become. It is problematic because in his *Logic* he develops several different forms of negation that cannot easily be translated into our daily lives, yet seem that they must be necessary, if we believe Hegel. For example, we may not all or not always decide to problem-solve by thinking first of an abstract idea or a code of values, then deriving from that a negative example, and from that pairing deduce a positive outcome. Yet Hegel pits two value codes against each other, such as state and family, in order to show the need to go beyond determinate negation and seek a new synthesis. Indeed Hegel believes that this struggle to identify, accept and grapple with the negative generates in us the energy to carry on living and to accept dying. The physical negative of death is the source of our preciousness and a spur to the dialectical negative which is creative.

Hegel puts his dialectical ideas to work to illuminate our lack of self-understanding. His sense of us as fallible is persuasive and seems sensible: as finite beings who are both weak and destined to die, we do form part of a greater whole that is the world we inhabit and that repeats our finitude as part of a huge pattern of being. According to Hegel, our finitude is held by a force that he calls *Geist* or Spirit which creates the mechanism for understanding that we are one finite part of a great pattern of being that represents the *in*finitude of being. We contribute individually to an idea that is 'the human', although each of us will perish.

In the article, 'Negativity and Primary Affirmation', in *History and Truth*, Ricœur opposed Hegel and Sartre to each other as using negation immoderately and incompatibly, seeking to use this critique as a springboard to ask whether I, the ordinary person, am negativity incarnate because I have the power to say no and whether this power makes me negate the possibility of the complete person I might otherwise be. In other words, do both Hegel and Sartre invite me to abandon the struggle to make myself a better person, by their emphasis upon their own respective forms of determinism?

Ricœur's evolving view of Hegel

In due course, Ricœur identified Hegel as being of paramount importance when considering the negative. In order to explore Ricœur's approach to Hegel and the negative, I want to sketch the content and sequence of some of Ricœur's most significant published papers on Hegel, of which the first was in 1955, entitled 'Philosophie et Ontologie'. This was a review of Hyppolite's 1953 *Logic and Existence*, and Ricœur's review became known by its subtitled 'Retour à Hegel'. In 1954, Gilles Deleuze, a close contemporary of Ricœur but not a friend or even acquaintance, had also reviewed Hyppolite's book on Hegel – *Logic and Existence* – finding an opportunity for the first time to propose the ontology of pure difference that he found in Hyppolite's first section. In Ricœur's review, he indirectly criticizes Kojève for his Marxist, atheist and master-slave heroics in Kojève's 1947 analysis of Hegel's *Phenomenology of Spirit* in *Introduction to the Reading of Hegel*. Hyppolite's approach can then be seen as very different to that of Kojève: Hyppolite critiqued Kojève and concentrated on Hegel's *Logic*. For Ricœur, Hyppolite showed 'brilliantly' that dialectical negation cannot be dismissed as a false problem, nor as being surmountable as Kojève believed it to be. Negation differentiates objects one from another and, even more spectacularly, reverses the creative momentum to recognize positive aspects of negation. We cannot restrict ourselves to using contradiction as a sign of error, or as in the *Critique of Pure Reason* by paralogisms and antinomies. It is the mere setting in opposition, or worse the imposition of naive axiology, that is the mistake. In the sense that much philosophy does not give negation a satisfactory status, Hegel must be admired. Yet Ricœur found excessive Hyppolite's assertion that we are all and have always been Hegelian, in our thought, identity and history. Ricœur also baulked at Hyppolite's assertion that ordinary language can encompass the universal – and yet within 10 years he himself was moving towards language, ordinary language philosophy and, I will argue, the investigation of linguistic tropes as creative instances of the negative impulse. Ricœur even commented that he preferred Kantian sobriety and calmness to Hegelian inebriation and excessive language style, yet we will see in the Kant chapter how Ricœur later used Hegel to tease out of Kant the risk-taking *noumenon* that insists upon cognitive and perceptual failure as a sort of moral success.[15]

Ricœur argued in his review of Hyppolite that negation embodies in fact a very special sort of problem: not only does negation function as a practical device for identifying one object as different from another (the whale is not a fish), but it also has a character that sets it apart from the very power of affirmation that it makes possible (i.e. the statement 'it must be something else' is not regulated by the negative impulse that caused us to make the statement). For Ricœur, this meant that logical negation can legislate for features in reality, by saying what they are not, but negation has no say over their identity because it cannot say what they are; only what they are not. We can go further and consider our everyday experiences of being denied something: this emphasis on process that Ricœur identified – being told 'no' or failing, which is a form of 'no' – can have potency completely separate from the actual event of denial, potency that is not only about facts but can also affect self-perception, confidence and attitude. All forms of negatives can resonate beyond the instance of their occurrence.

As commented upon earlier, part of Ricœur's evolving view of Hegel was the fact that Husserl's philosophy was unable to withstand the onslaught of Hegelian negative. In his 1957 Husserl essay 'Existential Phenomenology', Ricœur demonstrates how Hegel's version of phenomenology destroyed Husserl's phenomenology because 'Hegel introduced into the field of phenomenological analysis the 'negative' experiences of disappearance, contradiction, struggle and frustration which impart the tragic tone to his phenomenology'.[16]

In the 1960s and 1970s, Ricœur deploys dialectic to develop dissonances between Freud and Hegel. Hegel and Freud dance together for Ricœur, Hegel appearing in Ricœur's book *Freud and Philosophy: an essay on interpretation* (1965–70), especially the last two chapters, book III, Chapters 3 and 4. Hegel and Freud also partner each other in the collection of essays, *The conflict of interpretations* (1969–74). They function as a dialectical pair, with Ricœur balancing against and with each other the archaeology of Freud's childhood memories and the teleology of Hegel's Absolute Spirit's history. In *The Conflict of Interpretations*, both are worked upon with surgical precision, such that the unconscious is excised from Freud's thought and the Absolute Idea is excised from Hegel's thought. (*The Conflict of Interpretations* was published later than *Freud and Philosophy* but not necessarily written later – as we see in the essay 'Conscious and Unconscious', that was given as a talk in 1960 at Bonneval). Ultimately, Hegel tends to dominate, because in spite of Hegel's inability, in Ricœur's view, to create a satisfying and systematic philosophical unity, he does offer a dialectical model that can create a rhythmic energy out of the diversity of experience and reality.

In *From Text to Action*, containing essays written in the 1970s, the essay 'Husserl and Hegel on Intersubjectivity' shows us a definitive critique on Hegel in a concluding paragraph.[17] Describing Hegel's often used 'strategy of productive contradictions', as relying upon the 'extraordinary polysemy of the term *negativity*', Ricœur then questions whether this profusion is excessive and perhaps masks the 'inconsistency of a nebulous concept of dialectic' and comments on the campaign waged against it by English-language analytic philosophy. He suggests that we should move away from the negative and use different strategies of explanation, such as decision-making theory and game theory. He also commends Husserl for his use of *Auslegung* (literally setting out or laying out, a strong form of interpretation) because this facilitates more possibilities than dualism. It is Husserl's ability to analyse phenomena at their unique level of originality and set out their rich threads of connection to each other that is more useful than Hegel's insistence upon turning ideas into objects that become huge and dominant, which post-Hegelians found to be ripe sources for state apparatus or huge ideological positions. Instead of Hegel's objective spirit, we can choose Husserl's insistence upon individual agents, responsible for their own actions and able to account for themselves. This seems to be a reasonably definitive renunciation of Hegelian dialectic.

In his later essay called 'Should we renounce Hegel' in *Time and Narrative, 3*, 1985/66, we see Ricœur no longer preoccupied with different forms of negativity, but more concerned that Hegel's view of history, especially European history, has been destroyed by more recent historical events, and the special horror of the twentieth century nullifies Hegel's view of history as being an ineluctable movement towards Absolute Spirit. Hegel's attempt to demonstrate that the passage of time will be a unifying, developing manifestation of the Absolute has also been shown by events in real time to be wrong: I see Francis Fukuyama's 'end of history' thesis as a misguided Hegelian attempt, via Kojève, to tell us that we had reached the pinnacle of civilization with democratic capitalism. However, Ricœur settles for a compromise; the task now is to think *after* Hegel, as it would be impossible to think *without* Hegel. In his attempt to renounce Hegel and move on to think differently, Ricœur cites one reason for moving away being Hegel's rebuttal of the separation between a formal system based on ideas and an empirical system based on facts.[18]

In his penultimate book, *Memory, History, Forgetting*, 2004, Ricœur uses Hegel more as a historical witness about methods and sources, no longer chastizing Hegel for failing us with excessively optimistic historical models. This may contribute to the tone of the book, where one feels that the opportunity for denunciation has been allowed to subside. In his last major published work, *The Course of Recognition* (2004/2005), Hegel again plays a major part, mainly in the second half of the book and mainly as part of an analysis of Honneth's work on recognition. Here, Ricœur was happy to rely upon Kojève's master-slave analysis and studied the *Realphilosophie* from Hegel's philosophy of Spirit. After Kojève's powerful Marxist interpretation of Hegel, Hyppolite offered a different approach, an ontological negative, and there is more discussion of Hegel's negative in Chapter 4.

Negation resurfaces constantly in deciding how to define things, (by this manner of defining what they are not), in a strange inversion of creative power. If negation as a force cannot explain what something is, but only what it is not, this makes social negation a strange process indeed, devoid of identity or meaning yet highly potent and, as we know from our daily usage of it, circumscribed by our own often deliberately careless shorthand to imply something adverse, bad or difficult. Deleuze attacks this negative aspect of social and physical negation of our will in *Difference and Repetition*. Deleuze rejected the negative as depriving us of the ability to discern positively, and characterizes the negative as all that is shadowy and bad, and difference as all that is vibrant and good. For Ricœur, however, this inverted, strange sort of potency in the negative impulse denies us the right to call negation an error, because negation is not a mistake, it is the vitally important counterweight to balance the creative powers that allow us to describe and understand our world. It is interesting to note at this point how Ricœur was moving towards something like the ideas he later came to admire – and then reject – in Kant's 'Negative Magnitudes', of which more in the chapter on Kant.[19] Ricœur came to find useful Kant's later integration of the negative impulse with the paralogisms and the antinomies, yet ultimately he rejected them.

Kant, Hegel and Sartre on negation

For Kant, speculative reason can think ultimate reality, yet not cognize it, that is, fully understand it – this is the difference between faulty and strong thought. We have no real cognitive access to the world. In the first critique, Kant explored what he saw as the declining scope of metaphysics. In the second critique, he focused on the moral aspects of his thought and in the third on the general and aesthetic aspects. In his essay on Kant and Husserl (1954), Ricœur showed how he believed that this work by Kant provided the limits and foundation of phenomenology by demonstrating that practical reason can think about the intelligible world but not feel or intuit its way into it. This real world can only be entered by complying with it respectfully – so the only sense in which I exist *is* as a member of a 'practical and ethical totality'; I will not be able to understand the other person except as a phenomenon to be respected; the Other as an idea made manifest. This respect does not arise because I have learnt to respect that person but because each and every human deserves my respect: this must be understood negatively, in the sense that I 'should' never act against that person – they are an end in themselves. In an elegant and playful way, Derrida disrupts this respectful approach in his delightful essay 'Parergon'.[20]

Kant had no phenomenology of the Other, and this contrasts starkly with Sartre's feverish sense of the other, in whose gaze Sartre felt that he lost his agency as a subject and became an object. Clearly, Sartre assumed that his 'other', his hostile freedom, had not read Kant. Ricœur's work on the negative in Sartre and Kant is of considerable importance in its own right, demonstrating Ricœur as a great twentieth-century thinker: he contrasts Kant – integrating the negative and positive in different ways into critical philosophy – with Sartre who demonstrated the modern sadness of an easily meaningless freedom of choice that has no limits. At this early stage, 1950s, Ricœur was also conducting a conversation with Sartre, but it seemed rather one way, action coming from Ricœur.[21] In his 1957 essay, *Existential Phenomenology*, Ricœur explored what the choice could be, for Sartre, between a freedom of being truly alive and being, in effect, lifeless. Sartre introduced the idea that 'existing consists in being its own nothingness'.[22] This is freedom for Sartre and he used it to weaken phenomenology. As a result of 'this bath in negativity' that Sartre gives Husserl, the latter's intentionality becomes different. Negativity creates distance, it becomes a stepping away from oneself, a distancing from oneself, ontology of nothingness that the phenomenologist of a Husserlian type cannot do, and Ricœur felt that it is a philosopher of a different sort – like himself? who has to do it.[23] Ricœur becomes this philosopher and later, he publishes on Sartre and Ryle and the imagination (1981). Ricœur's later work on imagination raises the issue of whether Kant's use of the negative as a limiting feature was fatally flawed because there is no place in it for the human who thinks and who thinks new things, no possibility in his negation for creation, only for limits set to our capacities.

Ricœur was keen to give credit to Hegel for being the first philosopher to give a satisfactory *status* to negation, but attributed to Hegel less *success* in this than Plato – in Ricœur's habit of ascribing foresight with disregard for chronology, Plato's preference for difference already seems opposed to Hegelian contradiction. For Ricœur, there was an ineffable strangeness about the absolute in Hegel; it both creates itself through negation and unmakes itself through negation, so whether it exists or not, the absolute is pervasive. This is a nearly intolerable paradox, unless we radically rethink negation. We will discuss this more in the next chapter – for now I want to keep up the momentum of what Ricœur wanted to do about the difficulty of negation. One solution he found inescapable was the need to explore Hegel in more depth and he resolved this in several different ways; by studying Hegel directly (mostly emphasizing *Phenomenology of Spirit* and much less on the *Logic*); by studying Hegel indirectly through those he influenced, like Kierkegaard; and thirdly, by sometimes ignoring Hegel almost completely.[24]

Ricœur's published writings on negation discuss how to try and think beyond Hegel and live more companionably with the negative aspects of life, such as our potential for failure, by accepting their existence and yet also by avoiding simplistic binaries. I will explore some of these negatives later. However, this will only be possible, for Ricœur, if we face up to the horrors of which we are capable. In *Freedom and Nature, Fallible Man, Symbolism of Evil*, increasingly Kantian texts, Ricœur looked at the possibility and actuality of evil. These three texts represent some of the strongest aspects of Ricœur's phenomenological phase, that is, using consciousness as the trigger for finding meaning. As he moved towards hermeneutics, that is, using textual interpretation to interpret life as a text and action as text, Ricœur wrote *Freud and Philosophy* as an approving critique of psychoanalysis, in which he used the best of Freud's hermeneutics of suspicion. Ricœur considered the tragedy of childhood suffering, fate and the tragedy of repetition, the ineluctable pulling backwards to the beginning:

> The return of the repressed, the libido's tendency to return to such surpassed positions, the difficult of the work of mourning, and in general the decathexis of censored energy and the absence of libidinal mobility[25]

Thus, Ricœur showed us our paradoxes: we often define our state of mind by what we lack or lose, by what we desire or believe we need, rather than by the positives of what we have, who we are, what we achieve. He concluded *Freud and Philosophy* with problems that he then addressed more in terms of text as a way of transforming action into a meaningful impulse, in *From Text to Action*. At the end of *Freud and Philosophy* therefore he suggested that on the one hand 'the unconscious ought to be assigned another place than the categories of reflective philosophy and that, on the other hand, hope is destined to open what system tends to close up'.[26] Hope is what we need, and it is less easy to write about than desire, or violence or duplicity, and very difficult to think about. Yet Ricœur found a combination of love and justice that he believed could provide some grounds for hope. In a late essay of which he was very fond, called *Love and Justice*, he suggested that there is a secret discordance between the perceived equilibrium achieved by balancing the logic of superabundance (love) and the logic of equivalence (justice).[27] He recommended that Kant's golden rule of loving the other as yourself can contain a utilitarian tendency of doing as you would be done by, yet can avoid a utilitarian drift if it incorporates justice and here he was harking back to *Oneself as Another*, in which he proposed that we only learn about ourselves properly through attempting to understand the other. These are almost impossibly difficult recommendations to follow, and they all rest upon keen awareness of our negative potential, yet I wish to illustrate with case studies how it can be done. We can live a life that draws on Ricœur's philosophy and that helps us to answer the ironic question: 'and you – what will you do?'.

The relevance of negation in the world

As a philosopher-activist, I work in areas that require me to think differently about ordinary aspects of life and I believe there are three areas in particular that can benefit from Ricœurian insights derived from the negative: the current obsession with happiness, social justice issues that involve ethnic distinctions, and the pressing health issues of the aged. To point the discussion in such a direction requires a different register from that of pure philosophy, and I will attempt this, even with the risks attached, because I will show how we need philosophy in order to think clearly about practical issues. There will be difficulties with this, as Parmenides and others were not interested in mental health, they were interested in infinity, eternity and abstract thought . . . although one could argue that such topics could have impaired their mental health, if only they had noticed.

Happiness, well-being and education

Happiness is a phenomenon of great interest in policy circles; there are now major research programmes investigating happiness, contentment, well-being and a common perception that the human race (particularly in the developed world) is in a negative frame of mind. The illogical corollary that now makes politicians demand a happiness quotient is the idea that we should all be happy, that we are entitled to be happy and that we *can* and will be happy, as in Richard Layard's book *Happiness, Lessons from a new science*. Barbara Ehrenreich challenges this approach: in describing the aggressively 'happy' therapy she received during treatment for cancer, she tells us there are also powerful fashions for positive thinking that are now coming under critical scrutiny, and at a personal level, she challenges this credo: that we must not be sad or depressed, even if that is natural, because these are negative emotions and they are sure to help the cancer to grow and multiply.[28] Ehrenreich does not 'embrace' the idea of happiness, she insists upon the negative as being real and honest and an integral part of the human being.

I will also explore the strange resurgence of the deficit model that I see in modern child psychology practices (defining children by what they cannot do rather than by what they can, and medicating them towards a norm) and the counterproductive desire in school pedagogies to prevent children making mistakes (with the argument that errorless learning removes failure and makes children happy).

Regarding the so-called happiness debate, I will draw our attention to the prevalent rhetoric of political discourse and in positive pedagogy about eliminating all potentially negative experiences.[29]

Social justice

I use Ricœur's writings on negation for my work on social justice, to study people's negativity towards others. Since the demise of the capitalist–communist dichotomy so beloved of politicians in the mid-twentieth century, the West–East divide has proved useful for media and politics. Ricœur's work can be valuable when applied to such issues of social justice, most significantly, the tensions within secular societies and the place of those with religious beliefs, the most stridently debated being Muslims. The customary 'othering' of the Muslim performs a valuable function for some sectors of the Western media and for certain governments: in the media we see how the Muslim as 'other' can be negated, denied humanity and made to be a receptacle for those features of human life that are perceived as bad. Because I have undertaken work with the British government, I have had to decide whether it is acceptable to undertake research that may be contaminated by policies regarding the so-called 'war on terror'. I have also had to face my own perceptions of Islam from the perspective of a liberal white Western feminist. There are, furthermore, remarkable facts that demonstrate how ideology can determine policy: currently, the British government is recommending that modern languages should be taught in primary schools: the list of languages includes Latin and Greek, French, German and Mandarin Chinese, but not Arabic. My research on the Arabic language suggests to me that this is an example of 'othering', as a very good case can in fact be made for teaching Arabic in Britain. If, as Ricœur has argued consistently, the best and indeed only way to learn about yourself is through learning about others, then we deny ourselves when we negate others.[30]

Health issues

Ricœur's middle and late work has been providing impetus for new applied work in medicine, education and race relations for over 30 years. I believe this new research on negation from his early work has the potential to provide renewed impetus and vigour for enhancing good practice in applied fields, for analysing and resolving issues such as doctors' empathy for others, denial of illness, rejection of other ethnic groups and the relentless pursuit of happiness as an entitlement.[31] Here, I will focus on the use of Ricœur's ideas in the care of the sick.

Shapiro, a Professor of Family Medicine, reports that many young doctors have less empathy with patients several years into practice than when they started their training and she is concerned to address the perceived failings in medical training.[32] She argues, most specifically, that Ricœur's writings (such as *Oneself As Another*) can influence trainee doctors by facilitating empathy, emphasizing their own vulnerability and facing their own fear of disease and suffering; what she calls an ethics of imperfection.

It is worth asking whether this crossing over from idea to action can be strengthened as Shapiro hopes it can:

> An ethics of imperfection would likely draw heavily on the insights of philosophers such as Ricœur, whose philosophical theories could provide a foundation from which humane and empathetic behaviours might emerge, not just as checklist behaviours, but as deeply felt moral imperatives (2008).

Perhaps this new work on negation can help here; it may be necessary to train young doctors to be consciously negative (aware of their own prejudices towards the old) and also objective (attempting to be factual about the clinical necessities for each patient, regardless of whether they smell or not) *as well as* empathetic so that they may face their own negative thoughts.

Negation challenges the way we think, and may even be a Ryle – type category mistake, miscategorized because misunderstood. It is certainly usually the less favoured of a pair, and the ensuing dualism can provide structure or confusion; either way such binaries are very difficult to avoid. Ricœur published one essay in 1956 on negation, concerned with analysing Hegel's effect on modern philosophy, up to and including Sartre. Here, he described negation as bipolar, both willed and suffered. For Ricœur, this gave negation an inverted, strange power and demonstrates that the negative impulse is very real. From Plato onwards the other has been a sort of negative, as we can never fully understand others. This and other aspects of the negative became of such interest to Ricœur, and particularly in terms of his approach to Hegel, that he initiated a series of lectures on negation in the early 50s. Central to his focus was a critique of the Absolute and he developed in due course a philosophy of limits that incorporated negation into linguistic usage.

I will push further than Ricœur on this and argue that negation may indeed be both real and a mistake; we use it deliberately, and deliberately wrongly: it is a daily event that is vitally important for balancing our creative powers and for dealing with our discomfort at being at odds with ourselves and with others. I will plead for something more like Keats' 'negative capability', our often untried capacity to be receptive rather than to impose categories.

CHAPTER TWO

The negation papers

Ricœur kept all his lecture notes in boxes and in filing cabinets in his home at Châtenay Malabry. Within this extensive personal archive, Ricœur also set up a small archive called *La Négation*. This is preserved in the Fonds Ricœur in the order he gave it with eight folders (mostly orange, some green), originally inside a large yellow folder, labelled by hand by Ricœur with variations upon '*La Négation I-V*'. I see no significance to the colours except that some of the orange ones are from a Sorbonne student co-operative that created copies of lecture note for students. They are all now in grey boxes anyway. It is clear from the lecture notes in the Fonds Ricœur (many handwritten, many typed in preparation for a student handbook, many rewritten) that he rearranged the material many times and yet there is a consistency of focus on key figures, from 1954 onwards: Parmenides – oneness of the universe and the inevitable influence of people's sensory-based misconceptions; Heraclitus – contradiction as integral to life and a precursor to dialectical thought; Aristotle – creating a new force of negation in time and movement; Plato – the other and difference rather than negation; Plotinus – apophatic way to God, seeking affirmation at the heart of negation, not knowing God; Kant – negation as a form of limit, a way of making critique possible; Hegel – arguing for *an und für sich* self-containing forms of negation.[1] Ricœur describes himself in these lectures as responding to the post-Hegelian explosion of Marx, Kierkegaard, Nietzsche, Heidegger and Sartre and attendant issues of modernity: the putative final section of the negation papers, apparently only ever handwritten, is 38 densely written pages on *Kant et la négation* from the Nanterre period in the late 60s and early 70s, which take us back to lectures that Ricœur attended as a young man in 1933 on *Kant et le problème de la négation*. At that time, the early 1930s, Kojève was lecturing on Hegel in Paris and although Ricœur was not in Paris, he acknowledged the influence of Kojève. So, how did these 20 years of activity on negation develop in the shadow of French Hegel studies?

Throughout this book, I will attempt to paint, albeit with broad brush strokes, the context in which Ricœur wrote. I will allude to various fashions in interpretation, including some of the varied sources on the negative of which Ricœur availed himself. I will also, on relevant occasions, attempt to conjure up the atmosphere of French post-war philosophy, especially in Paris; some of the strutting cockerels, the arguments and the loud silences (such as that between Deleuze and Ricœur).[2]

In the early 1950s, Paul Ricœur began to lecture in Strasbourg on a philosophy of negation, and then gave versions of these lectures when he moved to the Sorbonne in Paris and finally at Nanterre also, with periodic lectures in the United States during his many visits there – work on negation spanning two decades.[3] Ricœur presented several different series of lectures in the 1950s and 60s on negation. He planned a *polycopié*, the student handbook to accompany lectures, but only three lectures from it were ever typed up, possibly by students for approval by Ricœur before distribution to students. However, Ricœur established his own archive of negation materials, in which I will show that he was clearly planning a final form of argument that was different from the sequence of lectures that he gave over 20 years, because those lectures contained very little reference to Kant. Kant appears to arrive late at the party, but it is as if he were there all along, as Ricœur, quite late, in the Nanterre period of the late 60s onwards, placed his lectures on Kant and negation in the position of the fifth and final chapter of a text on negation.

He proposed that the negative is crucial to the positive, and hoped to demonstrate that there should in fact be an affirmative core at the heart of all negation. He wanted to challenge those manifestations of the negative that he believed to lack this affirmative impulse, most notably in Sartre's existentialist philosophy. Ricœur also became perplexed about what the referents might be of the term 'negative' – and the term 'positive' for that matter. From an early point in his work, he sought to reject the polarization of negative/positive as some sort of evil/good dichotomy, but he found it dominant and foundational in our thinking and difficult to separate out from everyday language use. We have organized our systems of meaning around antinomies and the negative plays a vital yet obscure role in this. I will expand on the rhetorical use of negation in later chapters: as an interim working definition, I wish to indicate the rich connotations generated by the term 'negation'. It is difficult to explain; it has few synonyms and while we often use it as one half of a perceived polarity, of which it is the less approved part, we also use it frequently to simply *imply* something that is not good. It gestures at the unthinkable, at evil, at contradiction, at difference, at unpleasantness, at total annihilation, at our human inadequacy to taking on our freedom; but it also gestures towards confrontation, commingling, interaction, synergy, possibility and creation – depending on the hands of the philosopher working it. Either because or in spite of the richness of the vein he struck, Ricœur seemed to stop working on the negative in the 1970s and published very little of his extensive research on this subject.

As we explored in the first chapter, he made some commentary on negation in his first major text, *Freedom and Nature* and then again in his collection of essays, *History and Truth*, in the second edition of which (1965) he published an essay about negation published in French in 1956.[4] The essay in *History and Truth*, called 'Negativity and primary affirmation', is in fact the only text he published that deals with negation explicitly and as a major focus. In his lectures, however, he followed that term and its analogues through his time travels in philosophy. This book is now an attempt to initiate work on his unknown lecture notes on negation, which are held in the Fonds Ricœur archives in Paris.

The archival collections have been assembled and archived into grey boxes, tied with bows of cream ribbon and stored in a purpose-built library with a security system. They represent a treasure trove in several senses; they are unique, extensive and also a challenge to explore – over 60,000 pages of densely handwritten notes by Ricœur or typewritten scripts, notes of his philosophical reading starting in the early 1930s when he was still at school and, even more interesting, lecture notes and preparatory material for published texts from the 1940s to the 1990s. The archives also include journal papers by Ricœur that are hard to locate, newspaper articles about him and by him, correspondence with other philosophers and theologians and commentaries about Ricœur. The archive papers now comprise part of the big Ricœur collection, retained in its entirety as the property of his family and entrusted to the Fonds Ricœur, to be kept in the Institut Protestant de Théologie.

In order to set the scene for my analysis of Ricœur's negation, I will present three broad phases in his work on the negative, and I will return to this material throughout this book to demonstrate his repeated tanglings with five themes. I add the full catalogue details in endnotes, so readers may find the material in the archives, should you wish to pass through the *arkhe*, the gateway of principles and submit yourself to Dike and Alethiea.

In general terms, he wished to analyse modern philosophy and the problems he thought it faced, by mapping a history of negation and relating that to the issues of modern philosophy; in 1952–53 and then 1953–54 he taught two different aspects of this – classical and modern – all that remains of this are his planned headings for those 2 years, addressing the problems of negativity in modern philosophy, and we can already see the problem he faces about the origins of negation: in 1952–53 he analysed the ancient Greeks, and in 1953–54 he analysed modern philosophy, that is, from Hegel onwards. The two areas are kept separate, although he wished to use each to clarify the other, and this pattern will become a back-and-forth movement that repeats itself for two decades (c.1950–70). I believe Ricœur moved through philosophy this way because he concluded that there is a fundamental incompatibility between negation in the ancient world and negation from Hegel onwards, even as Hegel, Heidegger and other modern philosophers proclaim their lineage from Heraclitus and Parmenides and other ancients.

There is also, I believe and argue in this book, a fundamental inability on the part of modern culture to deal with negation properly, openly, accessibly. There is a difference between negativity as a general attitude of hopelessness or desperation, and negation as an act of will, a rejection or contradiction, often expressed in language rather than through physical action. Ricœur also wanted to control the reflux of Hegel into classical philosophy and interpret the ancient thinkers in his own way, at his own discretion, without undue influence from Hegel whenever possible. As I indicate later, Hegel's influence upon French thought was more significant than upon British thought. The dominance of Hegel in French philosophy will, I believe, provide at least part of the answer for why Ricœur picked up and then later abandoned the negation project, in order to transform it into a different approach.

PHASE 1: At the time of Ricœur's *Husserl. An Analysis of His Phenomenology* (1967) which comprises papers from 1949 to 1957, *A Key to Edmund Husserl's Ideas* (1950/1996), the *Voluntary and the Involuntary: Freedom and Nature* (1950/1966) and *History and Truth* (1956/65) (major published work).

During a phase of early negation work in Strasbourg that dates from 1952 to 1956, in an early lecture written in clear yet stilted English, Ricœur began to refine his ideas. In attempting to get to grips with what he perceived as a predominantly negative cast of mind in Western philosophers since Hegel, Ricœur began to analyse this change of tone: he decided at this stage to differentiate between political dilemmas, psychological states and individuals' crises, so initially he focused on Marxism, psychoanalysis and existentialism. Naturally, he took Marx, Freud and Nietzsche as well as Sartre as key figures of these three movements. We do not have lecture notes from this exploration, just a summary of lectures given, which show two distinct pathways: negation in ancient philosophy and the problems of modern philosophy, including nothingness, evil and guilt. He adopted these three lines of enquiry – Marxism, psychoanalysis and existentialism – to work on from 1952 to 1956 while teaching at Strasbourg in the context of his desire to develop a philosophy of negation. In the 1950s, he lectured at Haverford College in the United States in a lecture entitled 'The origin of negation and the human experience'. He spoke in English and told his audience that he was looking at a philosophy of negation:

> if we admit that transcendence of thought is a genuine source of negation, it is enough for building a coherent philosophy of negation. But can it be enough to build a coherent philosophy of negation — therefore I leave this other question: is the negation implied in 'mediation' (Hegel) implied in 'transcendentalism' (Hegel)–to speak in Hegelian terms — an ultimate negation or is it only the reverse side of some higher affirmation?[5]

Quite soon (we will see this explicitly stated by Ricœur when he lectures in the United States in 1958) he lets Marx drop, not out of lack of respect, but because he believes that Marx applied negation to the class struggle in a way that became rather formulaic – the dialectic between the manager class and the worker class.[6] At this stage, the 1950s, Ricœur was more interested in the negative that can become nothingness, or that creates a crisis of feeling guilty, and that can be read more broadly as the problem of evil or human inadequacy. The term 'negation' seemed to mean to him an act of saying no at some level to something we find not good, and the term 'negativity' seemed to convey a general state of mind of feeling negative – and it is both phenomena that he wished to understand and explain.

Each of these sources of negation – Marx, Freud, existentialism – takes him away from Husserlian phenomenology by making Ricœur accept the negative aspects of perception and thought: that there are things we do not experience because we do not know about them and things we refuse to experience through choice or inability to understand them easily. Our experience is limited by situations and by our own shortcomings. This approach introduces a more existentially limiting manner than Husserl's model, which had been suffused with the desire to locate the glowing essence of reality through shedding the irrelevant. Ricœur had continued to work on Husserl since translating Husserl's *Ideas* in the margin of the German copy he had as a prisoner of war, and his text *Husserl* brings together essays from 1949 to 1957. He analyses Husserl's progressive abandonment of the idealism in the *Cartesian Meditations* towards 'the totality formed by the ego and the surrounding world in which it is engaged'. He would later critique Sartre's views on God as unsuitably tackled by Sartre with a philosophy of ego. Here, Ricœur emphasized the stark differences between Husserl's world as 'a totality inaccessible to doubt' and Nietzsche's, Kierkegaard's and Sartre's world that is riven by doubt and worse.[7] What we have here in a roughly contemporaneous lecture given by Ricœur in English in the United States should make us feel uncomfortable about these differences:

> first, 'the *otherness* implied in the objective distinction between something and something else'; secondly 'the *lessening of existence*, implied in the subjective experience of need, of regret, of sorrow, of anxiety etc. and thirdly *transcendentalism* is a third sort of negation, as the transcendental negation. I am not what I am; it is to say, I am not, as thought and freedom, what I am as finite point of view and as limited power of life.'[8]

These three manifestations of the negative (otherness, lessening of existence and transcendentalism) represent a '*not* – Husserlian' existentialist approach to the negative, seeing the negative as a necessary force that presses upon the individual. I believe these three distinctions are at the locus of confusion, the place where we make our category mistakes. A little earlier, in 1952/53, in a set of lectures entitled *The ideas of nothingness and decay in modern philosophy*, Ricœur had explored the 'negativity specific to humans: not being God' and considers the influence of Greek tragedy upon the Christian ideas of fault and of the fall from grace, which can only be resolved by transcendence from the real world.[9]

Later, Ricœur would also add to this fallen state of not being one with God, the Hegelian idealism with its assertion that we exist in order to sacrifice ourselves in the end for the great Idea that is humanity's ever improving destiny. According to Hegel, we represent his great idea while alive, and therefore we must accept that each of us must perish – the ultimate negation – in order that the definitive essence of humanity can persist. We are part of Hegel's idea of Spirit, an all-encompassing teleologically focused force. However, Ricœur later used Kant also to explore whether there is a twist because we misunderstand the negative as saying no, rather than as showing us, with Kant's *noumenon*, that we cannot know. This approach to negation is a more austere, more humbling idea than the grand spiralling upward of the Hegelian dialectic that we could see (according to Hegel) if we decided to. What Ricœur seeks in his negation project is an understanding of negation as affirmative, but not as negation swallowed up in dialectic, as may be with Hegel:

> As I move to transcend my own limitations, in a movement paradoxically always bound up with my coming to be, my being-in-the-world, am I in some fundamental way defined by my power to say no? Am I negativity? Is my being the nullity of the complete individual, the being-there?[10]

Here I believe that Ricœur is gesturing to Plotinus, of whom more later, with this sense of negation as a facilitating impulse that will bring me nearer to understanding God and myself. However, this quotation also shows how delicate the balance is: maybe if I have no God I can fall easily into Sartrean anxiety that could immobilize me. As early as the 1950s, Ricœur felt that he was faced with different kinds of negative and that the ones he was looking at were potentially contradictory and incompatible, from Heraclitus and Parmenides, through Plotinus to Hegel, Heidegger and Sartre, (to name a few of the major figures he considered in this context). He also wondered which is more 'negative' within some models of negation: finitude as a statement of mortality or infinitude as an assertion of the unreachable. While seeking to disentangle them from themselves and from each other he was still seeking an affirmative core to them all, influenced more by Gabriel Marcel's existentialism than that of Jean Paul Sartre.[11] For Marcel and Ricœur, the 'me' is racked by doubt and is able nevertheless to find comfort in thinking about human nature as a force for creating good:

> The different functions of negation are not connected directly in any way, except by the power of affirmation that constantly creates these functions.[12]

Thus, the young academic Ricœur took an existentialist and pheno-menological position, considering the Hegelian unhappy consciousness as reflective of our personal unease, because we are constrained by physical and mental limitations from being the person we want to be and doing what we want to do. We will see him then attempting to decode this state of mind by exploring the pre-Socratic world that emphasizes the life of the natural world and the individual as somehow in harmony with it; rather than the life of the individual as being at odds with the world, as seen in existentialism.[13] Ricœur explored pre-Socratic philosophers, mainly Heraclitus and Parmenides, to see if he could uncover whether there was a *logos*, the deep meaning to human existence, before the logical structures of Aristotle imposed binary orders, that followed the either/ or model of argument. Aristotle's individual is mortal, a scientist, and therefore more easily identifiable than Parmenides' human who has the characteristics of a perfectly balanced sphere; Aristotle is in control of the world in the sense that he understands it as a measurable, predictable laboratory and one that he can explain by developing laws and then using them to legislate for nature's moves.

In this first phase (which of course is neither precise nor hermetically sealed, as Ricœur constantly moved back and forth in his searching), I see his phenomenological thinking as dominant. He was publishing on Husserl, and the 1957 essay 'Existential Phenomenology' shows his interest in Husserl's collision course towards existentialism as an assertion of the negative, trapped, fearful and even despairing human. The crash would diminish significantly Husserl's phenomenology, not least because Husserl 'lost the key' to the negative that Hegel appropriated so masterfully. This Hegelian negative furnished modern existentialism from Kierkegaard onwards with the 'negative proof of being, the empty ontology of lost being' that, Ricœur feared, could not be incorporated into modern philosophy unless the negative could be understood as an integral, necessary and even productive component of our being.[14] However, we see in the second phase of the lectures that such a model of the negative might find a place in neo-Platonic models of apophatic thought with Plotinus.[15]

PHASE 2: At the time of Ricœur's *Political and Social Essays* (1974) (essays published separately in French from 1956 to 1973) *Finitude and culpability: Fallible Man* (1960/65) and *Finitude and Culpability: the Symbolism of Evil* (1960/67).

This Phase 2 includes the bulk of his lectures on negation in classical philosophy, where he consolidated his earlier planning and lectured in the mid-1950s on pre-Socratics up to Plotinus, a phase that actually lasted until the late 1960s.[16]

In this second and middle phase of studying negation, Ricœur returned to classical philosophy to apply what he had learnt about negation in the classical world to modern philosophy.

The ordering goes like this:

Part I *Parmenides and Parricide, Heraclitus*
Part II *Negation in a philosophy of language and discourse*
Part III *The enigma of movement,* and *Time, movement, negation*
Part IV *Negation and the apophatic way (Heraclitus)*
Part V *Kant and Negation*

His classical lectures started either with 'Parmenides and interminable exorcism' (exorcism of the many) or with 'Heraclitus and originary contradiction' (a model of negation). Among many other debates that he set up between Plato and Heraclitus and Plato and Parmenides, he then demonstrated Plato's other as functioning like a negative, and Aristotle's attempts to develop a sense of movement that would not disrupt the categorical definitions of the subject. To this end, Aristotle denied the negative in nature. This sequence of lectures was called 'Negation in a philosophy of language' or 'Negation in discourse' and 'Negation in a philosophy of movement and time' or 'Time, movement, potential'. Ricœur also presented Plotinus as the neo-Platonist who brought the negative to its pinnacle at this point in philosophy, because of his use of the negative in a positive way. In these lectures, he made a few references to Kant, Hegel and Heidegger (of which more later), thereby tending to keep the two threads – classical and modern – separate and letting them cross over and intertwine occasionally.

In 1958, while lecturing in English at Union Theological Seminary in the United States, Ricœur focused on the moderns who for him, in the context of Sartre's negative, meant Hegel onwards. He entitled these 8 2-hour lectures 'Anthropology and Religion in the Philosophy of Existence'. He listed eight aspects of what he called 'the modern philosophy of negativity' and attached each epithet in order to Hegel, Kierkegaard, Nietzsche, Marx, Jaspers, Marcel, Heidegger and Sartre:

> unhappy consciousness, dread and despair, upsetting the table of values, the struggle of classes, the challenge of unhappiness, unhope, Being towards death, freedom as separation and breaking as annihilation.[17]

In this list, Sartre has the dubious honour of two epithets, the last two: 'freedom as separation and breaking as annihilation'.[18] Ricœur called Hegel, Kierkegaard, Nietzsche and Marx, the fathers of existentialism and was exploring the possibility of a family tree of negative thought, with the aforementioned 'fathers' spawning four 'sons': Heidegger, Jaspers, Marcel and Sartre. He was clear in his lectures that Marx took a rather formulaic view of negation as opposition between social classes and that he would therefore not give a 2-hour lecture on Marx; it is not clear from the notes whether the workers were given that lecture off or not. He retained Hegel, Nietzsche and Kierkegaard as fathers of negation and of existentialism at this point, however. In 1957, in the published essay 'Existential Phenomenology', Ricœur had also explored the possibility of familial similarities between Hegel, Nietzsche and Kierkegaard and their use of the negative, arguing that Hegel's use of the negative weakened Husserl's phenomenology beyond repair.[19] By 1963, in the two companion papers on Kierkegaard, Ricœur openly and explicitly abandoned the idea of labelling these eight thinkers existentialists, because he found them so disparate in their work. He commented in the first of the two 1963 papers that 'To-day, the breaking apart of this group, if it ever existed elsewhere than in our handbooks, is evident', which may indeed be a reference to his detailed development of the idea of the eight existential figures, four fathers, four sons from his 1958 lecture notes and is an interesting pivotal point in the 'work of the negative', as Hegel called it. The 1957 essay seems to me to function as the pivot point for this phase.[20]

The 1957 Husserl paper, the 1958 Union lectures and the two 1963 Kierkegaard essays show clearly how, between 1957 and the early 1960s, Ricœur had replaced the Husserlian influenced phenomenological approach from *Freedom and Nature* (1950) with a strong Hegelian model of negation as 'disappearance, contradiction, struggle and frustration' in order to try and understand what had happened to western secular thought between Hegel and Sartre.[21] The content is different in the United States of America; Ricœur presents Hegel historically as well as negatively and positively for an audience whom he knew – at the time in the 1950s – were not as steeped in Hegel as the Europeans were. Ricœur provided them with the understanding of Hegel that covered the negative experiences to consider the impossible human desire to be different, to struggle with master and slave relationships and generally to be an unhappy consciousness.[22]

Back in France, Ricœur was exploring another way of tackling Hegel; through Plotinus' way of analysing the mystical negative of loving God who is nothing yet everything, and the human soul which strives for that unity with God, yet is inevitably nothing, merely mortal. As I show in the chapter on Deleuze, Sartre and Nietzsche, Plotinus is significant early on in Ricœur's linguistic turn.

The linguistic turn

There is a difference between the chronology of the *lectures* as he originally gave them in the 1950s and early 60s and the sequencing of *ideas* that he established in the late 1960s. A shift in focus takes place in Ricœur's thought at some point between Phase 1 and 2, and there is dated lecture material from the late 1960s and 1970s to show some of his thinking. The five sections of his original 1950s' lectures sustain a significant alteration in Part II. Part I is Parmenides and Heraclitus. Part II was originally negation in a philosophy of language and discourse. Part III is Time, movement, negation with Aristotle. Part IV is Negation and the apophatic way, with Heraclitus and Part V is Kant and negation (which he added later, in what I call Phase 3). It is Part II of the lecture series that changes significantly, with additions to the original Strasbourg structure of Paris: Sorbonne and Paris: Nanterre lectures. Part II is the only section of the lectures to contain these three time periods of Strasbourg, Sorbonne and Nanterre, and the content is significantly influenced by structuralist thinking and linguistics: Benveniste, Chomsky, Godel, Martinet, Saussure and others. Ricœur also lectures in collaboration with Madame Granier on Negation and Subjectivity; he comments in planning notes that *he* will teach negation, *she* will teach subjectivity, the latter with an emphasis on negation as a doxic operation, which he explains as related to belief as opinion, not belief as faith. By making this distinction, I believe Ricœur is signposting the way towards his own attempt to address the theology of negation in ways that make it accessible to a more 'secular' reader, a reader who might not understand the mystical tone of Plotinus' metaphorical turns. The promise of Plotinus' metaphorical form will indeed become accessible in 1975/1977 in *The Rule of Metaphor*, wherein metaphorical structure is a moral compass needle that shifts backwards and forwards between limits and finally settles upon approximate understanding based upon the tension between what something is and what it is not. He achieves the same feat in 1975 in 'Biblical Hermeneutics' with the parable as heuristic device interpreted and better understood by means of metaphorical structures. We see also in *Oneself as Another* the development of this 'push me-pull you' between ourselves and others, to facilitate better understanding through similarities and differences. It is also interesting to note the position of this Part II: it comes immediately after the Pre-Socratics and before Aristotle, thereby giving Ricœur an opportunity to develop his exploration of language and thought at a time before the negative was strictly managed by Aristotle in structures of opposition that led to contradiction and the either/or structure that seems to me to require Ricœur's and our attention.[23]

PHASE 3: At the time of Ricœur's *Freud and Philosophy: An Essay in Interpretation* (1965/1970) and *The Conflict of Interpretations: Essays in Hermeneutics* (1969/1974) (major published works).

During the early to the late 1960s, Ricœur had concluded that there are in fact multiple sources and kinds of negation and that they are indeed incompatible and potentially overwhelming for modern philosophy.[24] This third and final phase of his exploration centred on Kant, hoping that Kant's antinomies and other forms of the negative could make it possible for negation to become a central and integral part of critical thought, rather than being one category among others that causes unbearable tension as a chameleon-like free radical – different forms of negation. The Kantian antinomies have their own structure: they are binary and mutually contradictory, characterized by two speculative lines of argument that cannot be held together because of their contradictory nature. They contain a negative impulse that provides a critical possibility for thought and represent Kant's riposte to the abuses of metaphysical reasoning: he was critical of arguments such as there must be a limit, but what is beyond that limit? There must be a beginning, but what came before that beginning? I will trace a succession of reworkings by Kant of ideas about the negative, from his early essay on 'Negative Magnitudes', through the *Critique of Pure Reason* to the *Critique of Practical Reason* and ending in the sublime of the *Critique of Judgment*. I will show how Kant performed a vital function for Ricœur in being 'positive' about the negative, and also in folding it into his first Critique, yet did not succeed at escaping from the dualist model that was and is still so dominant in human thought. Ricœur wrote much on Kant throughout his career, yet never integrated his lectures on Kant and negation within the main body of his work, although it is clear from archival evidence that he planned to add them to his negation project. This evidence can be seen in the folders he labelled himself as La Négation, I, II, III, IV and V, of which folder V is labelled *Kant et la négation*.

Ricœur used Kant's thinking to understand Kant's philosophy as a philosophy of limits. Kant rejected the ancient Greek legacy of argument and logic, both Epicurean and Stoic, yet he could do no other than to think within these classical frameworks that were an integral part of his culture. Kant inherited the Western tradition of Aristotle's laws of contradiction and of the excluded middle, whereby there is a tendency to define phenomena by contradiction, or by what they are not: A is not B. This is a pervasive response and separated from living examples. Kant found it wanting, as did Leibniz and Wolff, yet he went further than they did, as they were still attached to the idea of a unified world of thought and action. Kant asked himself how B can exist if it is not A, and is not contained within A, and is therefore not accounted for by the law of contradiction. (Of course, Hegel later juggled with A and not-A to make a related point in a different way). In reaction against this logical pattern, Kant developed a startling assertion that the negative is a positive and subsequently attempted to integrate the positivity of the negative into his developing model of human thought. He developed this idea in an early essay on 'Negative Magnitudes' and then altered it in order to apply it to the *noumenon* and the phenomenon in the *Critique of Pure Reason*.

These three broad time phases are characterized, I believe, by five themes that are not of the same order of things: ancient Greek philosophy, an apophatic way to God and/or to self, Hegel, language, Kant. We can also see possible confusions: even early Ricœur is characterized by Hegelian triple sequences; if everything is developed in Hegelian threes, it may become confusing or tedious and it may appear that Hegel is blocking our view by forcing us to think in his way. Indeed this was a perennial issue for Ricœur, who developed his own more open, tentative and provisional form of dialectical argument. However, we will see a pattern emerging; Ricœur tended to go backwards more than forwards, and refused to adhere to strict chronologies, being interested more in *problems* than in strict time lines. For example, he concentrated on Hegel in the three Louvain lectures of 1955, and several years later (1958–59) he was working assiduously on Heraclitus and Parmenides with Hegel in the background. By the later 1960s at Nanterre, he was lecturing both on negation within language and on negation in the Pre-Socratics and Aristotle and Plato.

He found himself grappling with the three major forms of negation I described above – otherness, lessening of existence and transcendentalism – appearing in different combinations and different forms. He saw them manifested in these five thematic typologies that are different in kind from one another: ancient Greek philosophy, an apophatic way to God and /or to self, Hegel, language and Kant. The problem for him was how and even whether to reconcile the three forms of negation with the five typologies or the five with the three: he repeatedly rearranged the sequence, reorganized the subordination and the nesting of one idea within another and experimented with the origins and end points of these negative moments. The origins and outcomes of negation were so problematic for him that he produced more lectures about the middle of his notional sequence (Phase II) than he did the beginnings and endings.

Ricœur's exploration of negation is a deliberate and long-term project, which he clearly enjoyed, living, through himself, his tenet that consciousness is a task not a given, into which he drew his students willingly. In his lecture notes, he reminded them about how he handled a topic the year before and how he planned to develop a topic very differently next year. They are his confederates. They know from him how provisional these debates are, and yet that there are certain core issues to which they must return together. With Ricœur, they tackle first the idea that thought has changed: for the ancient philosophers, negation was to do with the nature of reality, whereas in the modern era negative thinking challenges our knowledge and our self-perception. Ricœur's students looked also, with him, at the tension between a philosophy of unity and a philosophy of mediation. A third issue is the perceived deceptive nature of modern philosophy. Ricœur described modern philosophy as being full of camouflaged lures or snares, which he found difficult to critique because he could not find them.

Sartre as another

Sartre functioned for Ricœur a little like Hume did for Kant, except that Ricœur had not 'slumbered' dogmatically for 6 years in his prisoner of war camp, he had translated Husserl's *Ideas*. Sartre's 1943 *Being and Nothingness* seemed in a way to Ricœur like a culmination of the preoccupation with the negative that he felt Hegel had initiated. Ricœur wrote about Sartre in *Freedom and Nature* and in *History and Truth* and he lectured from 1952 to 1960 on Sartre's plays, including *The Flies* and *The Devil and the Good God*, both at Strasbourg and at the Sorbonne. He also lectured on Sartre in 1958 at the Union Theological Seminary, on the fathers and sons of negation (an approach he abandoned soon after, yet interesting for its ideas).[25] He sets the frame as being the role of negation, of nothingness, of non-being – which he sees summed up by the problem of negative thinking. He describes how since Hegel, the experience of nothingness has been used to emphasize the meaning of existence: in Hegel's *Phenomenology of Spirit,* there is 'a certain annihilation of mystical consciousness before God'. Whether this is the true relation between man and god or not, it is one moment in Hegel's dialectic, a transitory phase, on the way to absolute being – yet when Kierkegaard came along, Ricœur detected that modern philosophy became stuck in this transitory moment, such that the relation between the self and God became a tragically excessive relationship between the self and itself. Humility and the experience of alienation became tragically altered as they entered modern philosophy. So, the Nothingness that, let us say, Plotinus depicted as such a special state of innocence with God, has now become despair. Sartre's philosophy was the extreme point of this development that started with Hegel.

In 1958 Ricœur describes to his American audience how difficult it is to grasp the actual Sartrean philosophy because Sartre was so fashionable, and comments also that Sartre's philosophy has grown out of the crisis of modern Europe; a crisis of bourgeois ethics, of faith and atheism, of democracy and communism. He sees in Sartre's *Being and Nothingness* a neo-stoic filiation from Heidegger (analysis of dread as our structural relation with this world) and to Kierkegaard (tied to the identity between dread and freedom). He sees Sartre attempting to continue the tradition of Hegel, Husserl and Heidegger, which Ricœur describes as the twofold failure of realism and idealism. Here, Sartre's negation is related to nothingness and to the problem of negative thinking. Sartre interiorized the Kierkegaardian anxiety – relation to oneself equals extreme nothingness. This is freedom as decompression, as Sartre says. Things exist. I have to be and I am therefore not, because my existence is an accident and my freedom is nothing; no-thing, 'the ultimate triumph of the Hegelian unhappy consciousness'. Ricœur explains how negativity became the actual movement of freedom as a lasting distanciation from oneself.

Ricœur also comments on atheism in Sartre: he is taking into account the interests in theology that he shares with his audience in these Union Theological Seminary lectures of 1958. He describes the principles of the philosophy that sees God as a contradictory concept; in-itself and for-itself, a synthesis of nothing and thing, but he insists that this contradictory concept is not a philosophical fancy but is, on the contrary, rooted in the human condition: God is the irrealizable ideal which haunts the project of myself in the world and of myself faced with the other.[26] This atheism justifies Sartre's understanding of responsibility: I am responsible for the world because there is no god to take that responsibility. In an entirely negative way I am condemned to freedom and forced to justify my own existence. Ricœur wonders whether there is not here an inconsistency and that this negation was not, as it claims, mere nullification, but an effort to present an image of the human as a being who *can* act almost like the god whom he finds absent, with freedom functioning as a free possibility. Yet the avowed core of Sartre's philosophy is negation as the structure of human existence, with man construing himself as a self-negating being. Ricœur stresses that this process of self-negation functions as man's enactment of 'nothing', which, he warns, equates to an escape from causality and a denial of responsibility for one's past. Ricœur also sees here an incompatibility: he believes the problem of God cannot be put into a philosophy of the Ego. There it encounters only the god which I cannot be, which Sartre calls being haunted by the longed for ideal of in-itself at one with for-itself, desiring that, in preference to becoming impotent under the gaze of the other. This haunting is the contrary of a revelation, but Ricœur is not convinced by it as an argument for the existence of freedom as such. Ricœur wonders why Sartre's freedom is not merely negation, but *also* a dream, an ideal, even what Sartre calls a haunting, and Ricœur concludes that it is partly to do with Sartre constructing a God that is for Ricœur false, the notion of God as *causa sui*, a God made by himself. Ricœur rejects the device of *causa sui* because this theological principle can also be used to suggest determinism or meta-logical-rationalistic arguments. Thus, for Ricœur, Sartre's image of the God he rejects is itself to be rejected: it has only excluded the false God that man cannot become. I think part of this is because Ricœur would see God as living in us.

In these unpublished lectures, Ricœur concludes that Sartre develops a highly interiorized form of Kierkegaardian anxiety, in which one's relation to oneself becomes an extreme form of nothingness par excellence, and asserts that Kierkegaard's concept of despair is the atheist's moment of faith – but he does not see Sartre taking the final plunge and going beyond anxiety into the depths of Kierkegaard's despair, hoping that therefore Sartre's philosophy is not closed and may still be available to look in a different way at the problems of guilt, sin, existence; possibly with Sartre's notion of *contingency*. Sartre explains how a meeting between two people is contingent, yet it is also of course a fact. However, the risk is that if contingency is an integral part of me, this can lead to determinism, which can serve to exaggerate the fear, shame and enslaving subjugation that I experience in the gaze of the other. As with Sartre's use of Kafka's *The Trial* and *The Castle*, Ricœur sees how existence would then depend on a 'plot of unknown initiatives', in which I am controlled by the other. Ricœur analyses Sartre's study of the other and the look of the other, that makes me an object, objectified, no longer an acting subject, and that contrasts starkly with Hegel's depicted satisfaction of self-recognition and mutual recognition, even between slave and master.

Sartre adopts an unrelentingly negative view of human existence, if we define 'negative' as an existential state of anxiety about not knowing how to act, not being autonomous, feeling powerless to act well and yet having to act because there is no God to act on our behalf. Ricœur notes that Sartre actually needs to abandon the language of negation when it becomes self-contradictory, as a result of mingling *thing* with *being* and *nothing* with *not being*.

While giving these lectures in the United States of America, Ricœur was also investigating ancient Greek ideas of negation. Thus, his study of Hegel and his impact on modern philosophy was reflected in parallel by an attempt to look back and see whether he could detect the lineage of Hegel's negative.

Developing an archival commentary

Ricœur developed a series of different levels for analysing his thought and developing new ideas: his courses and lectures function to create commentaries on texts, providing a vehicle for close textual analysis and exegesis and contributing to his published oeuvre. Many of his lectures on other topics led to published works. I do not know why he did not publish the *polycopié* or make more of negation in his written work, but I will conjecture about this as we proceed. It is very important throughout to consider the nature of these lectures and I draw on Skinner and Ganeri for developing a commentary about the nature of these lectures, their place in the archives and their importance in the Ricœur oeuvre.

Ricœur took account of many factors when he lectured, including the philosophical background of his students, their position on a spectrum of religious literacy and personal faith and his own requirements as an academic and intellectual. Ricœur identified various problems within Kant's, Hegel's and Heidegger's thought and ideas and then analysed classical texts to see if they could help. This followed his earlier study of the thinkers in the ancient world when he was a teenage student, (see 1933–38 materials) and led him to detailed exegesis of the Pre-Socratics and later writers, in his attempt to disentangle the causes of the negative turn in modern philosophy and his use of the ancient Greek canon to address new problems in new ways. He wrote and delivered several other lecture series on related topics; one such was on Sartre's plays *(Théâtre et Philosophie)* and another was on Horkheimer's and Adorno's *Negative Dialectics*. He also wrote and delivered a three-part lecture series on *Finitude, Négativité, Affirmation* (1955), and lectured often on *Le Néant, Le fini, Fini et infini, Hegel et la négation, Hegel et la Négativité, Nietzsche et la Négativité* etc.

Ricœur's commentary mediates between past and present by creating a dialogue that he wrote for his students and presented to different groups on many and repeated occasions. He read Aristotle more philosophically than historically and created new ways of thinking about canonical texts. The approach he used and the conclusions he drew are different from those of his contemporaries and his predecessors, whom he read and referred to: he read and referenced Ross, Cornford, Kirk and key continental thinkers such as Diès, Wahl and Wundt. He used the German Diels-Kranz collection of ancient Greek texts as source material, which was standard practice at that time. He intervened in the existing stream of academic discourse and analysis for his own intellectual development and to give his students a fresh view, yet in this context (negation) he did not publish his views. What are we to make of this? We can assume that he was not interested in publishing these lectures, in which he makes detailed textual exegesis, general interpretations of classical thinkers and extrapolations of their views to his analysis of modern thinkers. However, it is true that his other lecture series often became *polycopiés* (student handbooks) for his students and subsequently often became books or papers. I show later how I believe he negotiated a different place for negation, deep inside language.

How can we consider what purpose the negation lectures served, if they were not published nor even made into a full *polycopié*? Quentin Skinner proposes that we analyse texts according to the illocutionary model developed by J. L. Austin, and recommends that we use historical context and fact to judge what the writer meant and intended. Skinner argues that we can only use clearly evidenced fact as a basis for exegetical arguments when studying writers' texts. Jonardon Ganeri, in his wonderful work on early modern Indian philosophical manuscripts, partly agrees, and also challenges Skinner. Ganeri issues a caution about 'fact' and develops a new model of illocutionary intertextual interpretation, arguing that we must also consider the texts with which the writer is in conversation, indirectly or directly, in order to understand his work.

Ganeri adds that by assuming an element of prolepsis we may read better: the thinker may well be engaged in conversation with those not yet born, not yet listening (Ganeri 2011). In Ricœur's case, we can endorse and enhance the profound relevance of Skinner's choice of 'illocution', as these lectures were indeed spoken communications. I suggest that Ricœur's illocutionary gestures of giving his lectures can now, in written form, have perlocutionary effects that are new and that permit us to benefit from his original illocution. He is addressing future readers in ways that invite us to make a commitment to understanding him now. Ricœur himself comments in 1985 that:

> Because philosophical discourse is a discourse, it is ultimately addressed by someone to someone else; this illocutionary character entails strategies of persuasion inseparable from the demonstrative strategies of the system considered as a great monologue.[27]

If we make a commitment to understanding Ricœur, we need to consider categorizing these lectures in order to understand the nature of these written texts; what sort of lectures were they and what function did they fulfil if they were not to be published? Clearly, the North American ones (e.g. 1958) fulfilled a different function from the Paris ones: his English was good, albeit stilted at this early stage, but even more importantly he was communicating with students and scholars who were not steeped in the heady Parisian atmosphere of Sartre, Camus, Beckett and Deleuze, Foucault, Derrida and

Levinas, nor were they necessarily under the sway of Hegel, as the French arguably still were.

The Strasbourg series (1952–57) is completely different from his American lectures: it demonstrates the classical core of his typically French higher education, from studying the classics at school, and also reading Heidegger and others like Ross, Cornford and Kirk, all of whom wrote commentaries on the ancient Greek writers. In its turn, the Strasbourg series influenced the Paris series, which then shows us that Ricœur himself was very much an activist philosopher and a subtle thinker; he opposed the French war in Algeria, yet also refused to advise French soldiers to desert, he lectured on Sartre's new plays with interest while criticizing Sartre's philosophy of negation very strongly and he supported Eastern European philosophers when they were oppressed for their ideas. Yet, as an aside, we can note that he very seldom created new terms or new ways of using language, such as we see in Derrida and Deleuze.

As a man of faith, a devout Protestant, he believed that he had a different relationship with language from that of the better known philosophers, one based upon a belief in its restorative powers. He also gave different emphases depending on the more or less theological or secular views of his audiences: we see this when he delivered small sets of papers to a theologically active audience, as in Leeuven 1955 (these were entitled: *Finitude, négativité, affirmation* and took a Hegelian approach).

There are therefore clearly differences between these various lecture series in content, language, audience and range. Do we need to develop a technical language to explain this aspect of the archives? A technical language must be able to facilitate quantification; in this case Catherine Goldenstein's work has created a frame of codes for naming, listing and categorizing the papers and these are invaluable for mapping pathways through the archives. However, the task is still yet to be done of quantifying the value and importance of these lectures, because there are thousands of pages in the archives, as yet not analysed in detail. One way of seeking to map such changes and repetitions involves following Ganeri and categorizing the lectures into types, in order that a typology will facilitate chronology, quantification and evaluation. These are some of the variations: the level and scope of textual exegesis and analysis, time span in the history of philosophy, diversity of ideas and the scope of assertions made. These different levels are apparent across the 20 years of negation papers as well as often within one lecture.

Ricœur's lectures function as commentary upon the primary texts and also a commentary upon that which he had not yet written or was in the process of writing: in the first major Aristotle paper, he commented on future pathways; perhaps he did not even know at that point that these would be three major themes in his work.[28] They are as follows: he drew a first pathway that would lead to language and discourse, negation and logos, the meaning of logos and the branching off from the Megarics, via Plato's Sophist to Aristotle's Organon, and dealing with Aristotle's major distinction between contradiction and contrariety. This resonates for me with *The Rule of Metaphor* and 'Biblical Hermeneutics', because these later works analyse the heuristic and ethical value of language forms such as metaphor, parable and narrative. The second pathway he outlines will start at the Eleatics, and then move to Aristotle's physics rooted in nature, where Aristotle seems to provide a sense of movement in narrative, with – when Ricœur turned to other Aristotle texts, mainly the Poetics – the negative at its core. Here, we sense the work that led to the books *Time and Narrative* and *Memory, History, Forgetting*. Thirdly, he hopes to reach the place of originary beginnings, with the Semata, the symbols of Parmenides' poem, Anaximander's unlimited, apeiron, and the Good of Plato, with arrival at Plotinus, for whom The Unity is notness. This is about the impossibility of envisaging God in any way whatsoever, and that impossibility makes him divine; so here we have meontology and ontology together: nothing and something come together into a profound analysis of meaning. He would conclude in texts like *Oneself as Another* that nothingness has an immeasurably important existential significance: our relationship with others can only be fully realized when we understand ourselves through the other and reflected in the other and I believe that this may require something akin to Iris Murdoch's 'unselfing', in which the ego becomes as nothing in order to be able to facilitate happiness in others – which is the only way to be fully happy oneself.[29] This mapping of three major themes, logos, nature and narrative and transcendence through the other that coincide with later work, a form of prolepsis that provides his own prediction of how he wishes to develop his ideas, all show how deeply Ricœur's later interests were already embedded in his early work as well as how he focused on others in order to gain distance from Hegel.[30]

We witness this aversion from and attraction to Hegel clearly in 1955 when he travelled to Leeuven and gave three lectures on consecutive days entitled, in a very Hegelian manner, *Finitude, Négativité, Affirmation*. He was based in Strasbourg at that time and these three lectures come 5 years after *Freedom and Nature* and 3 years before the several negation series of 1958–59. Hegel plays a significant role in these three lectures. Some of the text from these three Leeuven lectures was used by Ricœur in 'Negativity and Primary Affirmation'. It seems therefore that the Leeuven trilogy and the essay 'Negativity and Primary Affirmation' are closely related. In 1956, he set down clearly what he had been working on and why he chose Hegel to investigate the complex nature of negation, in 'Negativity and Primary Affirmation', which became the last essay of the second edition of *History and Truth*, published in that collection in 1964. Here, he stated his two current interests in negation: why has philosophy since Hegel 'made negation the proper activity of reflection' and secondly, given Hegel's dominance, can we possibly squeeze round the bulky Hegel to recover a sense of philosophy that is about living and being, a style of 'yes' and not a style of 'no', and therefore not about negation in the conventional sense of the word?[31] He then proceeded to complicate the issue by agreeing with Hegel that negation *can* and should function as a positive force, when it is a double negation that leads to affirmation.

In 'The origin of negation and the human experience', lectures given in English at another American location, Haverford College, near Philadelphia, 1958, he also brought Hegel and Sartre together again as representatives of opposed extremes in the negation debate. In the 1950s, he also often omitted Hegel when he lectured on negation. By setting Hegel to one side, giving him his own *Aufhebung* treatment, Ricœur made himself some space in which to work and rework his interest in the Pre-Socratic philosophers repeatedly, and identified Heraclitus as the first thinker to identify the originary nature of negation, as in the 1958 series of negation lectures given in French in Paris.

There are therefore three clearly identifiable time-determined phases in Ricœur's philosophy of negation: Phase I is some of the Strasbourg time of c. 1952–56, Phase II is the Paris Sorbonne time of c. 1956–60 and Phase III is part of the Paris Sorbonne/Nanterre time of c. 1960–68. During phases I and II, he focused mainly on ancient Greeks as a response to Hegel and Sartre. Between phases II and III, he made a linguistic turn that caused significant disruption to the order in which he planned and delivered his material: he introduced structuralism into his thinking about negation and the disturbance to the lecture notes is localized and focused upon what he called Part II of his lectures; on language and discourse. The Part II folders are distinctive because they contain the widest time span of notes: here he assembled material from the early 50s to the late 60s. I believe this indicates clearly the change of thinking that led him to seek to insert the negative impulse deep within language – metaphor, parable, narrative and dialectic for example, a metaphor tells us what something resembles by explaining what it does *not* resemble, thereby facilitating new thought. This was part of a change of current that was energizing his linguistic turn elsewhere at the same time, in *Symbolism of Evil* and *Freud and Philosophy*, the turn towards hermeneutics.

The negation papers comprise one small part of the archives and their identity, depth and limits have yet to be fully established. In due course, Ricœur abandoned his quest for a philosophy of negation, yet once you notice the presence of the negative, it becomes more and more significant in his long-term project. It becomes transformed within linguistic tropes so as to be unrecognizable when compared with Hegel or existentialist *fear*, and yet he offers ways of dealing with fear, anxiety and ignorance. I will develop the proposal that this work by Ricœur shows us how different his approach is to that of much philosophy, which seems to fear failure: although modern and post modern philosophy seems to wallow in negative thought, its inability – or refusal – to face and attempt resolution of the negative is clear to me. In this journey, I will define the negative in several ways, derived from Ricœur and others. At all times his project remained an existential one, an attempt to answer the question; 'what sort of being is the self?' His answer was already partially formulated, that consciousness is a task not a given; we must work hard at working out who we are, and one way for him, was through teaching. One of the problems he worked and reworked during the repeated teaching of these negation lectures was the role of language in the negative: is the labour of the negative the work of language and if so, can this be diverted into productive work and action as well as leading only to the nothingness of death and Hegel's Absolute Spirit? We will begin with his work on the negative in the Pre-Socratics, especially Parmenides and Heraclitus, about whom he lectured repeatedly, but upon whom he has no voice in modern philosophy as he published none of these lectures in any form.

CHAPTER THREE

Heraclitus, Parmenides and Plato: Before the logic of negation

It is impossible for anyone to suppose that the same thing is and is not, as some imagine that Heraclitus said.[1]

This is one version of Aristotle's laws of contradiction, so influential in developing a model of negation. In his lecture in the Negation series entitled *Unthinkable nothingness: Parmenides or interminable exorcism*, Ricœur invites us to examine a commonly held modern view of the ancient Greeks and particularly the pre-Socratics as providing the hesitant beginnings of ideas that only modern philosophers are capable of developing – and then invert this view.[2] He sought to encourage a perception of the ancient Greeks as radical in the sense of being at the origin of ideas, and applied this challenge specifically to their view of negation. He also saw in the pre-Socratics and Plato the beginnings of the antilogies – the dichotomies, the contradictory binaries that were fixed into three laws of contradiction by Aristotle and have come to characterize much of Western thought and philosophy.

Here, Ricœur argues that neither Hegel nor Heidegger does justice to Heraclitus and Parmenides: he argues that Hegel exaggerates the difference between them and Heidegger minimizes it, thereby challenging their legacy.[3] Many philosophers have read and interpreted ancient Greek thought by focusing on two Pre-Socratics in particular; Heraclitus (c. 525–475 BCE) and Parmenides (515 or 540–450 BCE) and often taking them together as complementary opposites. Plato (427–327 BCE) initiated this by pairing them up in *Theaetetus* and polarizing them, describing

Heraclitus as theorizing discord (war is the father of all; everything is made and destroyed by discord) and Parmenides as theorizing unity (one is all and all is one).[4] Ricœur will show Heraclitus as caught in a pendulum swing between opposites in nature and the need for conflict, and he will show Parmenides as caught in having to use the negative to deny the existence of the negative – thereby also precluding movement and progress. There is a complex story to be told – not in detail here – about the many ways in which they have both been understood, as a pair or individually. Many voices clamour to make themselves heard on these Pre-Socratics, seeking to support or contradict one another through the centuries: Aristotle, Plato, Schleiermacher, Goethe, Hegel, Nietzsche and Heidegger (both influenced in different ways by their nostalgia for the Greeks), Gadamer (who was influenced by hearing Heidegger lecture on the Pre-Socratics in 1924), Simone Weil (who was fascinated by Heraclitus' poem) Lenin, Kierkegaard, Hyppolite, Beckett, Deleuze, Cassin, Badiou and Songe-Moller and so it continues.[5] Heraclitus and Parmenides form part of the context of understanding what Ricœur is doing, and we need to sample the original texts as well as take a brief look at some of the many interpretations of Heraclitus and Parmenides. Here, we will consider Heraclitus as a model of existence which includes the negative as 'both-and', Parmenides as 'oneness' that seeks to exclude the negative and Plato as postulating a negative as 'otherness'.

Ricœur left no trace, no echo at all in the copious published literature on these Pre-Socratic philosophers: his conversation on the pre-Socratics was with his students, some of whom researched this area. In his published *oeuvre*, he comments on them briefly and occasionally, as for example in *Time and Narrative*, with a discussion of *arkhe*, the search for the doorway that also functions like a rule, a principle, an ancient infinite condition of possibilities and the violent excitement of non-human time in the ancient god myths.

The Ricœur lectures are intrinsically interesting and are also interesting in comparison with some of the philosophers mentioned above. The lectures devoted to Heraclitus and Parmenides in the negation series are all focused on the questions he set himself about negation: what is it? Are there many forms of negation and are they compatible with one another? How is it possible to develop a philosophy of negation? How many ways are there of saying no? Clearly, for us, this is also part of a much bigger question; why was Ricœur so interested in the negative? Perhaps there are strong situational reasons: he was teaching philosophy, as a young husband and father, in a war-torn Europe that was full of doubt, fear and suspicion about what had happened in the World War II. Those around him, such as Jean Paul Sartre, were developing ideas about freedom as a necessary curse, the negative as an inevitably existentialist double bind that will often end badly and yet also the need to negate recent history. Much more recently, in 2013, Cannadine has argued that the dualistic tendencies of historical argument must be challenged. In early twentieth century France Hegel's work was becoming influential in intellectual circles, through the influence of Kojève's lectures at the Sorbonne (1933–37), which Queneau subsequently collated and published in 1947 and the translation into French by Hyppolite of Hegel's *Phenomenology of Spirit* (1939), followed by Hyppolite's *Genesis and structure of Hegel's phenomenology of spirit*, and in 1946, Hyppolite's *Logic and Existence*. From 1953 onwards, Deleuze was engaging with the limitations of the negative and developing his model of difference. Sartre's *Being and Nothingness* was first published in 1943 and contained major discussions about the negative. Alternative models to Sartre's were being built too: by 1967, Derrida had published *Of Grammatology*, in which he develops his idea of *différance*, an attempt to rework negative impulses, and by 1968, Deleuze had published *Difference and Repetition*. If we add to this the responses towards and away from Hegel (yet usually without being able to escape Hegel) of Lacan, Foucault and Derrida among others, it seems clear that all these trends require some response, however brief that may be in this book, in order that we can understand the negative forces swirling around in post-war Europe.

I suggest therefore that in order to approach these lectures by Ricœur, we must first attempt to contextualize them. Hitherto such contextualization has been impossible, given that none knew of the existence of these lectures, except the students who attended them 40 or 50 years ago. We need to start at the beginning of Ricœur's focus of attention by briefly considering the original ancient Greek poems of Heraclitus and Parmenides before, in subsequent chapters, setting them into context – the context of other literature and the context of Ricœur's *oeuvre*.[6]

Ricœur's work on Heraclitus and Parmenides forms part of a much longer project about his interest in negation; as an initial framework, we can agree from his published books that he was strongly influenced by Hegel, for whom, in a modern, idealist and often confusing way, the negative was an integral part of thought. In *Freud and Philosophy* (1965/1970), Book 3, Chapter 3, Ricœur contrasts what he calls the archaeology of Freud and the teleology of Hegel. By this time he was distancing himself gradually from Hegel, but his work was Hegelian in many ways before he started these several lecture series. I described in the previous chapter how Ricœur wrote in 1950 in his first major text, *Freedom and Nature*, about the essential contradictions at the core of human being, contradictions to do with contrary urges and aspirations and leading to negation, denial, a sense of loss and lack. However, we also already know from *Freedom and Nature* that Ricœur hoped to find in the negative movement a sort of Hegelian liberation that leads us to transcend the negative by first accepting it, then refusing it and challenging it (a double negative that seems to follow the Hegelian model in this early work – this will change in Ricœur's subsequent disillusion with Hegel). This is a vision of the negative that has affirmation at its heart, which challenges the better known dualist models such as the established church's good and evil. Affirmation within the negative is also clear in one of the few published works in which he addresses negation in detail (the last essay of *History and Truth*, of which more when we discuss Sartre), yet he does not declare his interest in Heraclitus and Parmenides in these early texts, so we need to consider these lectures and their chronology with care to investigate their relationship with his major known works.

These pre-Socratic thinkers predate Aristotle with his laws of identity, non-contradiction and of the excluded middle, and Ricœur wondered whether Heraclitus and Parmenides held the secret of how humans thought negatively – before Aristotle formalized the negative. Aristotle's law of non-contradiction decreed that contradictory statements cannot both be true at the same time and in the same sense. Aristotle's law of the excluded middle decreed that a proposition is either true, or its opposite is true or the original proposition is false. There is no middle state of partial truth. This led Kant to argue that there are two forms of the negative; real and logical, of which Kant presented the real as more useful. Aristotle's laws led Hegel in his turn to argue that such apparent contradictions are possible, indeed necessary for thinking dialectically, as a temporary state of affairs before synthesis and overcoming. We will see Ricœur leaping forward to Kant and Hegel and back again while studying Aristotle, before he is finally satisfied. Ricœur's collation of his negation lectures in the 1970s places Kant as the final, fifth section of his never completed oeuvre on negation. Most significant is his aim to analyse the negative in modern philosophy (i.e. for him that meant Hegel and after) through using a range of methods, including deploying what he had learnt from those pre-logical approaches of the Pre-Socratics in order to consider, as we will in later chapters, the negative in Kierkegaard, Nietzsche and Sartre.

In Heraclitus' and Parmenides' poems, form and content are very closely related: in the case of Heraclitus the aphorisms are complete in themselves and therefore take on a crystalline, free standing power that simultaneously demands and defies interpretation and disruption. Many of Heraclitus' fragments contain difference, contradiction, and yet they have an internal balance that seems unshakeable and held in a chiastic symmetry that seems to defy deconstruction yet, perhaps for that reason, tantalizingly are in need of being shaken up, such as Heraclitus' scorn about humans as lazy thinkers:

> Men are deceived in the recognition of what is obvious like Homer who was wisest of all the Greeks. For he was deceived by boys killing lice, who said: 'what we see and catch we leave behind; what we neither see nor catch we carry away.'[7]

Parmenides' poem on the other hand, presents contradictions in a different way by juxtaposing a section that rejects ordinary opinion in favour of pure knowledge with a section devoted to opinions. The former section is famous, the latter section, on opinion as the misguided and inaccurate beliefs of uneducated people, is often set aside by scholars, presumably because it contradicts Parmenides' famous section on *te on*, The One. Since

Plato, and at least partly as a result of Plato's own interpretation of them, Heraclitus and Parmenides have often been set up to exemplify an antilogy, with Heraclitus as a dualist or pluralist who incorporates the negative into his world view and Parmenides as a monist who rejects the negative. This perhaps simplistic interpretation forms a strong part of the response to subsequent interpretations of their ideas. Indeed, it may provide one reason for scholars dismissing Parmenides' discussion of the weakness of Opinion – Parmenides' rejection of popular ignorance – as that would make him seem similar to Heraclitus. By analysing Ricœur's lectures, we will see how he challenges and then rejects this antithesis as forced.[8] This tussle also forms part of Ricœur's debate with Hegel's ideas, as we will see in the Hegel chapter.

Heraclitus' poem

Heraclitus is often represented as writing about change, friction, conflict; he provides images to illustrate his thought, such as the picture of lemonade swirling in a beaker, arguing that lemonade only works as a drink because it is agitated to combine the lemon with the water. Everything is fluid, both literally and metaphorically – we cannot step into the same river twice, because the water rushes on and is never the same at one place:

> One cannot step twice into the same river, nor can one grasp any mortal substance in a stable condition, but it scatters again and again gathers; it forms and dissolves, and approaches and departs.[9]

This changing flow is a necessary part of the river's identity and development; the river is moving by definition; if we dam it, it is no longer a river. Thus, the water in a river is never the same. Everything has an opposite or contrast within itself that oscillates and everything also moves both away from and towards the source of change. Thus, this apparent fluidity and chaos is actually a sign of order in the cosmos. *Logos* is the orderly move of change, it is a kind of law, but it is not material, it simply is. The senses are untrustworthy but essential for giving us fleeting impressions of the real world. Heraclitus also tells us that the individual soul can learn a certain amount by being responsive to the logos within it, but is only really useful when responsive to the partial understanding we can have of the whole *logos* in the world; only a few can aspire to this, most men believe their own opinions.[10] As for the rest of men, they remain unaware of what they do after they wake up just as they forget what they were doing while asleep. Men do not understand how what is being separated must come together with itself; there is a 'back-stretched connexion like that of the bow or the lyre' that most fail to understand. Heraclitus perceives the necessity of friction and conflict, which includes agitating our glass of lemonade to achieve the mixture, or even the necessity of discord among people, which he even suggests is not only necessary but also just:

> Heraclitus: One must know that war is shared and Conflict is Justice, and that all things come to pass in accordance with conflict.[11]

In fact, however, Heraclitus can seem similar to Parmenides, as he, like Parmenides, asserted that *Logos* is unity, a rational oneness that guides everything including fire, water, earth and air. Here, we need to establish an understanding of Parmenides' poem in its own terms, because Plato's polarizing interpretation of Heraclitus and Parmenides is still influential. The centuries- old decision by many writers to *oppose* Parmenides and Heraclitus to each other may demonstrate a constant truth about the topic of negation; that we are determined to seek opposites even if it means distorting the facts.

Parmenides' poem

We must differentiate between Parmenides' original fragmentary poem and Plato's dialogue about Parmenides, and I will look at the poem first and then to Plato. Parmenides' poem is in three parts; the prologue (*proem*), the way of truth and the way of opinion; the puzzle is why he wrote the third part about opinion; it contradicts the second part, which asserts that truth can be found and is not a matter of opinion. Is this a presentation of reason versus sense perception? Aristotle thinks Parmenides' way of opinion is Parmenides reconciling himself with the real world of sense data. Sense perception and knowledge are related. In the *proem*, Parmenides relates how he was driven to the gates of truth by maidens representing the senses: one of the girls represents the sense of hearing – the axle of the carriage makes music for her. The maidens push their veils back from their heads, in an image perhaps of sensual abandonment and lack of caution, or of stepping outside of social convention. They persuade Dike, Justice, to let them out of the city (urban complexity and the law are left behind?) and they sweep young Parmenides in their horse-drawn carriage through the gateway (*arkhe*) and out of the city: *arkhe* – meaning principle or origin *and* threshold or portal – *arkhe* is thus both a limiting and a fresh possibility for new life, later to be picked up by Ricœur with the limit and creation within a metaphor. This is the nature of the negative that I believe Ricœur is looking for.

In the poem, Parmenides then chooses the goddess Alethiea's patronage, in order to learn how to let thought reveal itself to him by freeing him of all distractions, so that he can think clearly. He renounces both the maidens and the senses that they represent with their respective sensory and sensual conduits to understanding. It seems to me that this image encapsulates much of what Western philosophy has been struggling with ever since Parmenides. The intellect, not the senses, is made into the criterion for understanding, and the intellect decides that what it can *think* about does exist; what it cannot think, does not exist. Parmenides asserts that the mind cannot conceive Not-being, and therefore Not-being does not exist – so that suggests that non-Being is not a problem. Being is the only possible phenomenon, and being is all that there is and everything that there is; it does not come into being, it does not change or pass away. This seems to present a view that is masculine and that risks negating a possible balance between senses and intellect; the idea that something can only be what it is and not something else.[12]

Plato's dialogue Parmenides

Much later, from the time when Aristotle was a young scholar with Plato, we also have Plato's dialogue called *Parmenides*. This is a middle-to-late dialogue by Plato in which Cephalus (implausibly) tells *us* what Antiphon told *him* that Pythadorus described to *him* that Parmenides and Zeno had said: at third hand and 50 years previously! Socrates is depicted as young and inexperienced, unable to argue well against Parmenides. Whereas Parmenides in his own poem argues that we cannot speak about what is not, Plato in his dialogue *Parmenides* puts into Parmenides' mouth the words of the argument that we *can* speak about what is not, that therefore makes it seem that Parmenides is thinking Platonically. Plato's Parmenides asserts that neither *what is* nor *what is not* can be demonstrated and yet, in looking at language he notes that if we want to look at *what is*, we must account for *what is not*. Thus, it seems that Plato is deliberately putting words in his fictional Parmenides' mouth so that he can contradict the tenets which Parmenides established in his own poetry. In this dialogue, Zeno argues in support of Parmenides, yet presumably Plato accepts that we realize none of the conversation took place: Parmenides is shown by Plato as thinking and arguing as a Platonist, which we know from his *own* poem that he was not. Plato suggests that it is a valuable exercise in truth to accept that we *can* speak about that which does not exist. Plato's Parmenides became the forerunner of medieval 'negative theology' and many, including Leibniz, recommended the Neo-Platonist interpretation, as did Hegel who insisted that half his own dialectic logic is in Plato's Parmenides.

Interpreting Heraclitus and Parmenides

The views of the many commentators on Heraclitus and Parmenides often serve their own personal approach, and in addition to that complexity, there have always been difficulties in authenticating and translating the *texts* themselves from Heraclitus to Aristotle. Marcovich and Wheelwright, for example, disagree about Diels-Kranz's inclusion or rejection of certain passages from Parmenides.[13]

In addition, there have always been difficulties in interpreting the *arguments* of both poets: they appear to be opaque, contradictory and sophistical or even – particularly in the case of Parmenides, who seems to contradict himself frequently in one long, disorientating and not very funny joke. These two, Heraclitus and Parmenides, are grappled with by many interpreters, who often attack each other's interpretations and Parmenides in particular has attracted a following for centuries; Plotinus, for example, tries to explain Parmenides' 'One' by describing all forms as emanating from the One who is 'beyond being', the Godhead as unknowable and that is one reason why Plato's Parmenides came to be seen as the forerunner of medieval 'negative theology'.[14]

If we are to deal seriously with Ricœur's claim that the Pre-Socratics will help us understand the negative better, then we must of course consider Hegel, who is one, or even the, master of the negative, and who also had an interest in the Pre-Socratics. Ricœur's interest also presumably is influenced by Hegel in this matter. Kojève's interpretation of Hegel had a profound influence on twentieth-century French thinking about the negative and language in Hegel, and this must be woven into our understanding of negation.

Ricœur's contemporaries in the Anglophone world often rejected any such idealistic interpretation and took a strongly logical analytic approach to mastering the two Pre-Socratics; they often focused on Plato's interpretation of Parmenides and to some of them the second part of the Parmenides even seems like a sequence of ridiculous antinomies and contradictions. Taylor (1934) argues that Plato's dialogue 'Parmenides' is a parody, a joke played on us by Plato.[15] Cornford (1939) refutes this and argues that the apparent contradiction of the one and the others being both same and different shows no understanding of the ambiguity created by Plato: for Plato, the One is only negatively expressed in Parmenides' Hypothesis 1, whereas in Hypothesis 2, the one is a whole, and represents unity.[16] Modern logical thinkers, for example, Tenneman and Apelt, when analysing Parmenides' poem, assert that the whole text is 'consciously fallacious' and yet Cornford believed that he could show how the 'alleged sophisms almost entirely disappear'. Ricœur read Taylor, Cornford, Ross and others and referred to them in his lectures. He took a different line: whereas each of them sought to make rational sense of work that they believe to be strange and therefore to need explaining in their own terms, he sought to understand the works more from the authors' point of view as revealed by careful, sensitive reading that perhaps resembles Keats' 'negative capability', while at the same time acknowledging the impossibility of being fully open and aware of the other's mind.

Ricœur on Heraclitus and Parmenides

The individual, each one of us (not the One that is Parmenides' universe) is at odds with him or herself, discontented, and seeks, in vain, to be at ease

– there is a negative component to the human functioning that makes us unhappy and insecure, unwilling to commit ourselves to action in case we are wrong, and uncertain about how to find the happiness we desperately desire: this is what Ricœur wrote about in *Freedom and Nature* and he told his students that he wanted to understand whether there is a language, a discourse at the core of human being, a pre-logical language before Aristotle's laws, a *logos* that will express common truths and reconcile us better to the contradictions at the heart of our experiences:

> Let's re-read Parmenides's Poem from the perspective of a philosophy of negation. Perhaps it is not futile to seek the source of a reflection upon negation far back in the philosophy that, before Plato and Aristotle, brought to light the question of 'being' pure and simple.[17]

Ricœur wanted to analyse Hegel's interpretation of Parmenides and Heraclitus and sought a different approach from that of his predecessors, wanting to consider Hegel's unhappy consciousness and his use of the negative. Of his contemporaries, he wanted to examine Sartre with his bad faith. Ricœur used Heraclitus and Parmenides as a basis for initiating discussion about the sources of negation, which none of the others did. Could he use this to get inside Hegel's use of the negative? One Ricœur negation lecture from 1958 is called 'Heraclitus and originary contradiction',[18] and this topic of negation in the form of contradiction at the core of meaning is one to which he returns on several occasions in various different lecture series. Ricœur acknowledged that Heraclitus does not name negation, yet he argued that Heraclitus is the only Greek thinker to develop the originary character of contradiction as a prime form of negation, and we then had to wait two and a half thousand years for Hegel to complete the task; Ricœur explicitly rejected Kirk's interpretation that Heraclitus only saw that opposites are connected, an opinion which Ricœur thought 'trivialises Heraclitus a great deal'.[19] Ricœur argued that Heraclitus saw *'the coincidence, the coming together of opposites in the logos'* as the reality of life. For Ricœur, Heraclitus' approach did not show random connection but some deep ontological sense that explains the vital essence of all activity being conflict, whether it is communal or justice related.

Ricœur saw how Heraclitus' habit of juxtaposing opposites could become a dialectical progression, but believed that this is not possible because Heraclitus insists upon reversibility; discord is justice, justice is discord. This is a holistic style, yet also it seems segmented, chopped up into self-contained chunks, because it excludes any possibility of a dialectic progression that could provide the idea of order in negation. For Ricœur, this rigidity (also experienced when we read Parmenides) needed to be broken up by the Hegelian form of dialectics as this would have allowed the Pre-Socratics to use negation to get to negation and then affirmation as Hegel hoped to do. Heraclitus' form of negation never becomes a double negation, a negation of negation, as he wants to insist upon the interchangeability of opposites, even if we would argue that the path up is not quite the same as the path down. Later, we will see resemblances here to Deleuze's proposals about difference.

In conclusion, Heraclitus is valuable for drawing our attention to the necessity for conflict, friction and difference, yet for Ricœur he was of limited utility because of Heraclitus' inability (or refusal) to use dialectical forms. Differentiation that is not a mutually exclusive contradiction is the law of nature (*salt water* and *fresh water* both exist, both are necessary to the living world and yet are poisonous to those organisms that do not live in/on the one or the other), yet Heraclitus tends to use these natural examples to polarize our understanding because, Ricœur argued, he does not have Hegel's capacity for mediation and therefore cannot help us untangle modern philosophy. Heraclitus attempts to incorporate reason *and* empirical experiences in a pair of antinomies, attributing crucial importance to war for understanding life: for Heraclitus therefore, discord is integral to life and this may be the tragic necessity of the human spirit.[20] Like many commentators on Heraclitus, Ricœur cited Heraclitus' fragment 82:

One must realize that war is shared and Conflict is Justice, and that all things come to pass in accordance with conflict.[21]

Ricœur evoked here the image of the geological fault line that he uses in *Symbolism of Evil* to describe these difficulties and he saw in Heraclitus the beginnings of apophatic thought:

There is a fault line between the intelligence which is common to all in the sense of being available to all, yet which becomes distorted by most people who think they know it all, and the actual living reality of mortals' lives.[22]

Again, according to Ricœur, we cannot understand Heraclitus through Hegel, because Hegel interprets Heraclitus as Aristotle did, that is, as embodying the great challenge to the principle of identity, oneness.[23] Ricœur invited us to see Heraclitus as offering a poignant world view of terrible yet inevitable and often also perfectly balanced contradictions, reflected in the meaning of language as well as the ultimate rule-giving facility of language. He proposed that clarity and logical non-contradiction are not the same, and nor is logic necessary to clarity.

Yet how can we be clear when we don't know what this root of language is, *logos* before logic, where the principle of identity can be vanquished or mastered (depending on your interpretation) and where contradiction can be the soul of presence, where our human unhappiness can be resolved and where, for Ricœur, we can accept contradiction as inevitable and live beyond it?[24] I will argue that we see this acceptance of paradox incorporated later into Ricœur's dialectic and his work on metaphor. Heraclitus, before Hegel, is making logos *be*, demonstrating that the essence of life, logos, is both sameness and difference – the heart of all dialectic. We see this, for example, in Heraclitus:

> the road to the top and to the bottom is one and the same'; and 'whether dead or alive, it's the same being . . . because with change, this is all that and vice versa'.[25]

For Ricœur, all these utterances have something cosmic, anthropological, and theological about them, with apparently irresolvable contradictions that remain at a binary level – the road is the same road, up or down, with no apparent possibility of taking a different path.

Contradiction is a form of limiting, so how can we tolerate being *limited*, admitting *finitude*, which is a form of determination: determining requires making choices and that requires rejection of other options. Ricœur hoped to demonstrate that all negation has positive roots and that this positivity is at risk if negation is threatened by being stuck in binaries (Heraclitus) or by being denied existence (Parmenides). Ricœur also wanted to understand the 'nascent apophasis' that he detects in Heraclitus' *originary contradiction*. *Logos* as living fire . . . we see the beginning of Ricœur's engagement with language as the vehicle of thought and the price we pay for this of having to be responsible for meaning.[26] Heraclitus has an apophatic tone, not through transcendence or silence, but through showing us the separateness of thought from the mind.

Parmenides and being

Being for Parmenides is absolute and self-identical and constant; there can be no plurality, no difference, and no opposites: there is no room for doubt. This seems very different from Heraclitus, who seems at ease with difference. Yet Ricœur demonstrates three ways in which Parmenides' negative slips into being and exists in a way that cannot be suppressed or ignored, in spite of Parmenides' avowed intentions. First:

> Nothingness [is] implied in the very act that denies its possibility[27]

Paradoxically, Parmenides can only assert the positive nature of being by negating assertively all the signs of being: being does *not* become born, does *not* die, is *not* multiple and is *not* divisible. For Parmenides, not-being cannot be, because we cannot imagine non-being. Negation imposes itself on our thought as a result of Parmenides asserting its opposite (this is, however, not yet a double negative). Ricœur cites Parmenides' Fragment VIII – 'what is, is whole, single limbed, steadfast and complete';[28] yet if we are to imagine 'being identical with oneself', we must be able to imagine being non-identical with oneself, with which, of course, we have been preoccupied for centuries as the core existential problem of human nature. What Ricœur is arguing here, however, is that there is, if you like, a shadow of the negative present in all that Parmenides offers us, and like a shadow, it makes the identity of the real credible.

Secondly, Parmenides' idea of Being excludes all kinds of change and plurality and difference because they all imply Non-Being: when something changes, it is not what it was before. This argument bears a family resemblance to Aristotle's law of contradiction, in its ontological form, 'It is impossible for the same attribute at once to belong and not to belong to the same thing and in the same relation'.[29] Parmenides was much older than Aristotle, so we can assume that Aristotle's logic emerges out of Parmenides' own formulation, which was then codified by Aristotle, with its twin rule, the law of the excluded middle. Yet of course there are significant differences in intent, as Parmenides is denying the need to acknowledge an opposite. We will look at Aristotle's laws in the context of negation in subsequent chapters.

Thirdly, the negative asserts itself triumphantly through language, in section three of Parmenides' poem, which focuses on the fallible opinions of mortals, and such assertively proud negativity seems to contradict the cool rationalism of the young Parmenides as he was received by the Goddess Alethiea. The opinion section of Parmenides' poem is often thought to be describing the fallibility of ordinary human thought, weak and inaccurate by contrast with the clear, logical and rational thought that Parmenides became capable of with his coolly cerebral mentor Alethiea. In the Opinion section, we are faced with two alternatives as Ricœur phrases it;

> 'to be or not to be, or, to be *and* not to be . . . unthinkable nothingness is the absurd witness to relative negation, which is comprehended by humans in terms of birth and death . . . the idea of nothingness is never forgotten, because Opinion – the crude ordinary view of life – detects it and names it – birth death . . .'[30]

Ricœur believed that this renders impossible any assertion of absolute nothingness.[31] He wondered whether we should accept Hegel's interpretation and see Heraclitus as the dialectical partner, the negative side, to Parmenides' positive dialectic.[32] This is seductive, as we do not then need to reject either Heraclitus or Parmenides. Yet Ricœur felt that we may risk losing both, as Hegel's treatment of them makes Heraclitus, especially, seem naïve and primitive, and this would then deprive us of the opportunity to really appreciate Heraclitus: Heraclitus' aphorisms are brilliant and deserve to be enjoyed, even though they preclude dialectical movement because the negations are resolved within the aphoristic structure, contained in a closed system.

Ricœur argued that in taking Heraclitus and Parmenides as two Hegelian moments we reduce them to a very primitive level and suggested that this is why we need Heidegger.[33] When Heidegger helps us to see Heraclitus and Parmenides as contemporaries, this may be in order to not have them distanced from us by their dialectical inadequacy. Yet Ricœur also then argued that we may see in Heidegger perhaps the opposite difficulty to that presented by Hegel's polarizing interpretation of Heraclitus and Parmenides.[34] Ricœur wondered whether maybe Heidegger digs himself into his own rut when he, strangely yet unmistakeably, presents Heraclitus and Parmenides as being the same as each other. Ricœur argued that if *legein* means the 'gathering together pause', then there is nothing dialectical to resolve, being is simply that which unites by being the same; Heidegger executed a sleight of hand, nominating *logos* as *lesende lege*, and effecting a merger between Heraclitus and Parmenides so that they become indistinguishable from each other. Therefore in this sense no dialectic is possible between Heraclitus and Parmenides. Heraclitus becomes the philosopher of presence, not of war. The problem of the same and the other is engulfed, and the identical nature of the same and the other cannot be entertained, thus with Heidegger's interpretation, Ricœur believes we lose: 'nature loves to hide' and:

> one cannot step twice into the same river, nor can one grasp any mortal substance in a stable condition, but it scatters and again gathers; it forms and dissolves, and approaches and departs[35]

– there we see how the problem of difference and similarity with oneself are identified in the *logos*. The tension and counter tension of Heraclitus' bow and lyre disappear completely in Heidegger; we lose the idea that this contrary tension is the very soul of presence, of being oneself. Ricœur believed this suppression of the negative moment to be especially clear in Heidegger's interpretation of Heraclitus and Parmenides, where language and thing are inextricably related; there is for him no space for negation in language.[36] Using a Hegelian form to frame his musings, Ricœur then wondered whether we could therefore, in due course, find a third way of interpreting Heraclitus; neither Heidegger's way that Ricœur found to be without dialectical presence with Heraclitus and Parmenides seeming to be identical nor the relapse into the logical system of Hegel which is related to Hegel polarizing Heraclitus and Parmenides.[37]

Parmenides presents Being as one, a unity, not divisible. Yet this creates a major difficulty because in order to assert this, he must mention not-ness, and deny the possibility of non-being. Parmenides has to discuss the impossible phenomenon of non-being in order to deny it; and Ricœur's argument is that by paying it some negative attention, Parmenides arguably gives it existence, at least at the level of ideas. Thus in order to assert the positivity of 'it is' and try to maintain originary affirmation, Parmenides is forced to confirm existence by arguing that '*it is not this, it is not that*'. This gives Parmenides an apophatic tone, that is, a suggestion that we will not understand because it is all too complex, as we will see later with Plotinus. Heraclitus also has an apophatic tone, not through transcendence or silence but through showing us the separateness of thought from humans[38]; humans see *opposition* and *contrariness* but they don't see that they are the same, because nature loves to hide herself and needs to be discovered. Ricœur demonstrates the coincidence of contraries in *logos*.[39] So we can say that there is a fundamental paradox: the *logos* is hidden by nature, which means it is both the identity of transcendence (the divine outside the material world) and the immanence within the word itself (the divine inside, the material world within the word).[40]

What did Ricœur see in Heraclitus and Parmenides that many do not? He saw the stirrings of dialectic in Heraclitus and he saw the beginnings of finitude in Parmenides, both strands that had been taken up by Hegel; a finitude that we must accept and also refute, a negative movement that can lead to affirmation and positive action because it is unconstrained by the logical dialectics that come centuries later. However, we need the structure and the movement provided by dialectic, so there is an insoluble problem. How can we bring together the power of dialectic and the acceptance of finitude? At this stage, he hoped the dilemma could be at least partially resolved by Heraclitus and Parmenides together, yet later he would abandon the idea.

Ricœur on Plato and negation

In Louvain 1955, Ricœur delivered on consecutive days three lectures entitled, consecutively and in a very Hegelian tone: *Finitude, négativité, affirmation*. At this time, he was still working at the University of Strasbourg. In the three lectures, he amplifies the incipient Hegelian ideas from *Freedom and Nature* and asks whether our personhood is defined by our power to say no, or by our power to deal with negation with a double negative and say 'yes?' In other words, by accepting the negativity of my own finitude (I am not autonomous) and then denying it (I am not going to accept being not autonomous, even though it is true – this is quite a Kantian view of the human dilemma), I can then do a double negative and develop the positive approach that will allow me to affirm my capacity to make a difference even though I know that I am not autonomous. This sounds like Ricœur shadow boxing with Althusser or Lacan, which indeed he did do a little, although he chose to avoid them.[41] There is similar material in these lectures and in his chapter for the second edition of *History and Truth*, one of the few published pieces he wrote on negation. Both the lectures and the essay were probably written around the same time, the mid-1950s. In that essay, he uses the quotation from *The Sophist* that finishes off the three Louvain lectures, and which he initially placed in the middle lecture and then moved to the end of the final one.[42]

In exasperation the visitor, the sophist, asks:

> But for heavens' sake, are we going to be convinced that it's true that change, life, soul and understanding are not present in that which wholly is, and that it neither lives nor thinks, but stays changeless, solemn, and holy, without any intelligence?'.

Plato's Sophist then uses this to assert that both *that which changes* and *change itself* have to be accepted as existing.[43] This is a direct challenge to Parmenides. In Ricœur's lecture entitled *Unthinkable nothingness: Parmenides or interminable exorcism*, dating from the mid-to-late 1950s, Ricœur analyses Plato's middle period dialogue *Parmenides*: we identify the aged Parmenides with the unity of the self with itself, and with rejection of disunity, plurality, multiplicity.[44] If at this point we consult Parmenides' own words in his fragments of poetry, we note how he must use negative terms in order to assert the completeness of the One[45]:

> The other – that is not and that needs must not be
> That I point out to you to be a path wholly unlearnable
> For you could not know what is not (for that is not feasible)
> Nor could you point it out[46]

Thus, he denies the existence of that which he uses and relies upon in order to communicate his intention to assert oneness. Ricœur also notices how different Plato's tone is in *The Sophist*: in this late dialogue Plato actually has the visitor confess to parricide, to murder of the old father Parmenides, by destroying Parmenides' arguments for unity and asserting the existence of non-being. The old man's monist approach is, however, difficult to sweep aside, and Plato admits that both being and non-being are equally tricky.[47] What Plato seems to me to be concerned to achieve in the Sophist is to demonstrate that negation does not have to be a contrary: if I say this thing is not big, I am not necessarily asserting that it is small, but that it is different from something large.[48]

The Sophist argues for linguistic analysis, inspiration for structuralism; the need to define meaning, finite combination of elements in a system, but in *The Sophist* Plato is looking at false statements, not false beliefs. In his brief English lecture entitled 'The Origin of negation and the human experience', Ricœur emphasized the way in which Plato can be applied to real existential matters, the way in which negation proceeds from otherness for Plato[49]:

Hyppolite sums up a view similar to that of Ricœur:

> In the sense that philosophy does not give negation a satisfactory status, Hegel must be praised. Yet Hegel did not resolve the problem as well as Plato, who made negation into difference, otherness, whereas Hegel pushes it as far as contradiction.[50]

Camouflaged traps

Ricœur concluded, again and again, that the 'One is' of Parmenides cannot work – reducing everything to one fundamental concept will fail. For Parmenides all is one, but in order to do things in Parmenides' way, much (denied) negation is necessary to demonstrate what the one that is all is not. This is not a viable approach, if there exists, as Parmenides asserts, no such thing as the negative. Nor can we define being only through negation, by arguing from what it *is not*, which Parmenides may have thought possible: if we oppose *Being* to everything it *is not*, we get either no attributes (Being is like nothing else we know) or all attributes (Being is everything we know). Neither method allows us to discover what is distinctive about Being in itself and again we seem to be stuck in a dualism. We need to work out how to describe and understand the interrelations between things that are different from one another rather than negating difference. Ricœur took this from Heraclitus and Heraclitus plays an important role in Ricœur's lectures of the 1950s, yet by the late 1960s, Heraclitus has passed down river and is mentioned much less.

Ricœur taught his students that understanding Heraclitus is a task that we will never resolve; we can never grasp how it is that Aristotle noticed in Heraclitus what he thought to be a great challenge to identity, which Hegel then adopted from Aristotle. Aristotle reacted against the unrealized potential for dialectic in Heraclitus. Moreover, how can we understand what this root of language is, that demonstrates how contradiction can be the soul of presence? But we haven't got the language to talk about this root of discourse that would actually be the coming together of being as presence: these thinkers pre-date Aristotle's law of contradiction and the law of the excluded middle, as well as pre-dating Aristotle's proposal that the characteristics of the predicate should be distinguished from those of its subject. Ricœur read widely in the critical literature on the Pre-Socratics; he was attracted to the interpretative work on the Pre-Socratics by Reinhardt and by Axelos, he is wary of Beaufret because of the latter's Heideggerean tendencies, and rejected the rather positivistic interpretations of Parmenides by Burnet who he felt 'stutter with scientific effort' and Kirk, who (Ricœur believes) translates Heraclitus superlatively, yet trivializes Heraclitus' ideas. Since, for Ricœur, Heraclitus epitomizes the separation and reuniting of anthropology, cosmology and theology, we have to meet Heraclitus on his own ground. Heraclitus' vision seems rather realistic; a pre-logical earth full of geological fault lines that explain the necessity of conflict and change.

I believe Ricœur was undertaking something very different from his many illustrious predecessors and contemporaries who interpreted Heraclitus and Parmenides. For Ricœur, this was not an attempt to provide a rational account of the pre-logical verbal acrobatics of the poems of Heraclitus and Parmenides, as we see in Taylor, Cornford and others. As Marcuse puts it, in his chapter on 'The triumph of positive thinking' from *One-Dimensional Man*, the challenge from the analytic philosophy camp can sound rather like this:

> You may speak poetry – that is all right. We love poetry. But we want to understand your poetry, and we can do so only if we can interpret your symbols, metaphors and images in terms of ordinary language.[51]

Ricœur developed an immense respect for ordinary language philosophy, but he saw these ancient poems as, after all, poetic works and imagery has power as imagery. His approach was also not, in the end, a Hegelian approach, which as we shall see, risks removing the frightening and creative energy from the negative within us all by absorbing it, containing it within a dialectical form in which all is as it should be. Nor was it a longing look backwards to a great time that must be recreated, as we see in Heidegger and as we hear echoing in Mircea Eliade who critiqued the 'myth of eternal return'.[52] What Ricœur gave us is more a conviction that *logos*, presence, our grasp of the human condition can be better understood by questioning how we hold contraries together and how we try to pass beyond them, moving beyond contradiction with fresh action, action that takes its energy from contradiction, from the negative.

What is this root of language that predates logic, where the principle of identity/sameness can be vanquished and where, consequently, contradiction can be the soul of presence?[53] I know I have the potential energy within me to do evil, so I can use that energy to impel me to do good. He sought to understand whether the dichotomies that form an integral part of our thinking *now* could have been *thought* before we humans developed our use of language with the vital role that language plays in thought. He hoped to find some response within the fragmentary writings of the Pre-Socratics because they studied this area in a direct manner, using sophistical techniques to explore the possibilities of unity, disunity and not-knowing. He was also interested in the many scholars who have studied the Pre-Socratics and thereby contributed to philosophical debates and because these debates through the centuries must be seriously critiqued. So, he was conducting a conversation with his predecessors and with our Western philosophical heritage as well as with the Pre-Socratics.[54]

He believed that he would fail to resolve these issues and that this failure is a defensible philosophical position:

> It is better to leave this problem as a task, rather than making a mediocre amalgam of Hegel and Heidegger.[55]

His conversation with Hegel is of course constant: both in spite and because of Hegel's quasi-logical patterning of negation through dialectics, the questions still remain; is the negation implied in Hegelian 'mediation' and 'transcendentalism' an ultimate negation, or is it only the reverse side of some higher affirmation?[56] There are several different types of negation in Hegel's *Science of Logic* with *nothing* and *contradiction* (classical terms) referring to modes of negativity that are in the sphere of *being and essence*, and on the other hand, concepts like affirmation, double negation and freedom referring to the form of negativity that controls the ideas dealt with in Hegel's *Doctrine of the concept*, so that freedom is the highest mode of nothing. Yet Ricœur did not analyse Hegel in detail in these negation lectures. In the act of attempting to understand ourselves and our world, we may have to accept that unity (if it exists) has at its very core the differences depicted relentlessly by Heraclitus. Yet Ricœur seemed to abandon Heraclitus, who has dropped from view by the end of Ricœur's long run of lectures on negation. I conjecture that Ricœur has already shown us why he will abandon Heraclitus, without saying it in so many words: despite his magnificent imagery of conflict, tension and the ying and yang of the natural world, Heraclitus was caught like a child on a seesaw in need of Hegel to come along and lift him off and take him to a new place – the paternal, ever powerful Spirit of Hegel that was fatally flawed, but that did give us dialectic with a strong negative.

When this debate about *being* was first developed by the Pre-Socratics, it was conducted at a time when the idea of oneness, universal unity, was related to the *gods* and to mathematics, physics and the natural world. Now, in the twenty-first century, it is conducted at a time when the *individual* has replaced the gods as the measure of time, movement and control. Kant warned us that reason can create antinomies: these opposites place us in a dilemma, unable to make decisions that should be based on more than reason, and unable to resolve the antinomies positively, thus entering negation, denial, lack, loss and desire. Still, Ricœur will conclude after 15 years of analysis that the different functions of negation are unconnected to one another, except for the power of affirmation that gives birth to each of them over and over again. This happens because all affirmation is a form of determination, whereby we have to decide in favour of one idea, one interpretation, one approach, person, home, profession over one or many others; thus we deny those others in favour of one. This denial is a negation and also a source of energy, a determination to accept some things while also denying others.

In the interim, while we decide what to do, and in a quotation I have used before and will use again, Ricœur asks a question which 2-year-old children will affirm:

> Am I defined in the most fundamental way by my power to say no? Am I negativity? Is my being the nothing of the formed being?[57]

The final challenge is the attempt to go beyond Kant and Hegel and understand the negative mode in modern philosophy in the context of philosophy's tendency to polarize between philosophies of limits (identity as unity) and philosophies of mediation (identities as difference).[58]

Ricœur concludes that human thought will never finish exorcizing the idea of nothingness, because we cannot measure it and measuring is a defining trait of matter: 'Opinion' (the section of Parmenides' poem that discusses ordinary people's ignorant lack of understanding) notices nothingness and, paradoxically, names it constantly in order to deny its existence. Plato proposes that the essence of the world is beyond the world in his Forms, the essences that transcend reality and that are another sort of nothingness.

Aristotle proposes that the world of matter is energized by some power, potency that is also a kind of non-being, a sort of nothingness because we cannot measure it, and Plotinus resolves the problem of nothingness ontologically and by using metaphorical structures. We cannot know God, this is the ultimate nothingness to which we must surrender, and yet for Ricœur something new opens with this ontological closure because Plotinus offers the possibility to consider nothingness in its positive aspects as well as in its negative ones: the apophatic approach is life-giving because of God. This provides both an *idea* and a *method* and they will need to be both kept together for theological purposes and also separated from each other, for Ricœur's purposes.

The idea is that *nothingness* can be rich and wonderful by making it possible for us to accept our disunity with God (and Plotinus believed that this would eventually lead to unity). The method is *metaphorical*. This provides a possible solution to the challenge Ricœur had set himself – to make his ideas accessible to those with no theological sense, even with no apparent spiritual identity using linguistic structures.[59] He wrote theologically, of course, and from a profound personal faith, yet for existential debate that can be compared with Hegel and Sartre, he needed to move the argument about the richness of negation into a more 'secular' frame, so that some of the existential problems described in *Freedom and Nature* could be addressed. This also suggests a rapprochement with Hegelian dialectic, as there are similarities between Hegel's dialectic and the rhetorical use of metaphor that Ricœur sees in Plotinus. Now we will consider Hegel, because he is the major interlocutor for Ricœur, at least at the early part of the negation discussion, and Hegel attempted to provide a new understanding of negation, different from Aristotle's law that excluded a middle term: in a way Hegel took the bucket off the white rhubarb, forced and hidden in the dark, and made us aware of that leafy, rich middle stem that Aristotle denied and that is reflected every day in what we do.

CHAPTER FOUR

Hegel's dialectical dominance

Hegel was the first philosopher to give negation such high status as an inextricable component of everything that is real and true. For Ricœur this negation transformed our understanding of what came before Hegel and became overbearing in many philosophies that came after Hegel. Therefore as we saw in the previous chapter, Ricœur tried to study ancient philosophy *without* Hegel and as we shall see in this chapter, he examined later philosophies, Kierkegaard and especially Sartre, *by means of* Hegel's negative in order to understand Hegel's influence. He also studied Kant as if Kant had known Hegel.

Hegel's *Phenomenology of Spirit* and his work on history are extensively discussed by Ricœur. The relative importance to Ricœur of *The Science of Logic*[1] and *The Encyclopaedia Logic*[2] (much shorter and clearer than the *Science of Logic*) is debatable since I can find less explicit evidence that Ricœur worked much on either of the Logics. Yet there is evidence that he knew the Encyclopaedia Logic well: his review of Hyppolite's book on Hegel's Logic, a short unpublished paper called *Hegel et la negation*, the first lecture in a series he shared with Levinas, *Négation et Realité* c. 1968.[3] Hegel altered the way we think about negation and helped us to see the negative as initiating something vital, rather than leading to nothing, as Parmenides had argued.

> In terms of form, the logical domain has three sides: (a) the *abstract* side or that of the *understanding*, (b) the *dialectical* or *negatively rational* side, (c) the speculative or *positively rational* side. These three sides do not constitute three parts of logic, but are *moments of every properly logical content* [*Momente jedes Logisch-Reellen*], that is to say, of every concept or everything true in general. § 79[4]

In 1956 Ricœur believed that philosophies, since Hegel, 'have made negation the proper activity of reflection' and that in this regard Hegel's thought represented a break with what came before him and transformed all that came after him. In this essay Ricœur posed the question that he then attempted to answer with his negation lectures: Does being have priority over the nothingness within the very core of man, that is, this being which manifests itself by a singular power of negation? He argued that when I decide how to act I negate all other choices, and when I act I must negate my desire in order to avoid treating the other person as a mere object. This is a double negative: negation of choice and of desire and it becomes a positive, an action that is worthwhile: negation can thereby be flipped over into an affirmative Kantian position of valuing the other. However, by choosing and thereby negating all other possibilities, I will also negate the beliefs of others and therefore the apparent flip from double negative to positive, which works in logic, does not resolve Ricœur's desire to assert the affirmative within the negative. His negation lectures constitute his attempt to resolve this problem through Hegel, his interlocutor in much of the early negation work, even when he is not mentioned. Hegel's hegemonic arguments could not provide a solution: it was Ricœur's linguistic turn in the late 1960s that provided the answer in the form of language as act.

Hegel developed a model of dialectic that went beyond that of Kant by devising a productive opposition. Through an interdependent development, the two elements in opposition produce a new, third element. Desire to know or to have is negated, opposed and the third element provides an ever more encompassing view of reality, which, after a long succession of mediations, eventually becomes absolute knowledge. In his 1975 essay 'Le Lieu de la Dialectique',[5] Ricœur recommended that if we want to understand this we have to set aside Kant's essay 'Negative Magnitudes' because that only contains two oppositions. However, Ricœur warned us that we would then be faced with Hegel and with the impossibility of accepting Hegel's absolute knowledge. If, as Ricœur believed, our hands are full of the broken shards of Hegel's system, this throws doubt on whether we are free to use dialectic if its end result necessarily is absolute knowledge, a possibility that has already disintegrated and that yet preoccupies us.

Here, Ricœur found Kierkegaard thought-provoking, as I will demonstrate. Ricœur hoped, as with Kierkegaard, to use philosophies influenced by Hegel (but not Hegel's philosophy) in order to go beyond Kant's dualism and facilitate actions that emerge from the tension between free will and determination, willing and suffering. Kierkegaard proved too extreme to retain, but had heuristic value. Much of Ricœur's negation material, while setting Hegel to one side, is both a homage to and an attempt to get past Hegel while admitting the impossibility of doing so. Ricœur was determined to develop a non-consoling philosophical source of redemption and attestation; a way of refinding ourselves anew every day in order to try and live better for others. He hoped to do this by challenging Hegel and reinterpreting Kant in a philosophy of limits that, through its limitations, opens up new possibilities and leaves space for hope.

Hegel created a dialectic that incorporates various stages of the Spirit's world historical odyssey into the exquisite wholeness of an absolutely all-encompassing system: indeed the negative is an essential component, *the* essential impulse for his holistic vision of the world's life. Hegel's world system is implausible, yet difficult to refute because, if we read him, we are compelled to engage both with his powerful, invasive form of conviction argument and the content of the argument that is welded forcibly to its form. Feuerbach, Kierkegaard and Marx were repelled by Hegel's capacity to distort, omit, ignore and foreclose. Such a closed system is likely to evoke reaction: indeed Feuerbach challenged Hegel's idealism and rejected concepts such as 'pure being' and nothingness. Kierkegaard chose to emphasize the impenetrability of Hegel's ideas by refocusing the discussion on the individual and on existence, rather than on the system. Marx challenged Hegel's beliefs about the ultimately just state and Hegel's alleged identification of it with the Prussian state of his time. Perhaps all this criticism and rejection played a role in keeping Hegel almost ignored in France until the second third of the twentieth century, when Alexandre Kojève, following Koyré, brought Hegel to modern France and focused upon Hegel's phenomenology with strong emphasis on the master-slave dialectic and Marxism. Kojève delivered his famous lectures, 1933–39 at the *École des Hautes Etudes* in Paris, based upon his optimistic vision of European humans as post-historical and living beyond the confines of world wars and economic problems. Kojève saw Hegel's phenomenology through five forms of negativity: desire for recognition, struggle for recognition, work, speech and finally death; death and freedom are two aspects of the same thing.[6] Perhaps it is not surprising that in the 1960s many of those intellectuals who had attended Kojève's lectures in great excitement turned against Hegel in disappointment; they were not free of the horrors of two world wars.[7] Yet Hegel seemed to be in the air they breathed, so in France in the 1950s and 60s many French intellectuals clamped on a gas mask, in order to breathe Marx's version of Hegel.

Once exposed to Hegel, something that was unavoidable in twentieth-century intellectual Paris, one would feel perhaps permanently blessed (Kojève, Hyppolite), contaminated (Canguilhem, Althusser), lucky to escape (Deleuze) or inoculated, vaccinated in a sense of inevitability (Derrida, Ricœur, Sartre) depending on your viewpoint. Far fewer of these thinkers seem to have cared about the religious Hegelians; Protestant Lutherans like Gabler, Hennings and Leo. We can perhaps say that this is because, historically, from the time of Hegel up until our own day, the naturalization of dialectic was more appealing, for most, than the philosophy of religion. Sartre and Derrida each sought to dismantle Hegel's thought: they both used a rather extreme device by choosing to contrast him with self-confessed bad boy Jean Genet, which may indicate how difficult it can be to get Hegel out of your hair. Deleuze also developed his theory of difference and repetition which was framed as a revolt against Hegel. These major thinkers were very strongly influenced by Hegel, as was Heidegger, although the form this influence took, and the way they each tried to escape Hegel, was very different.

If we want to understand what the negative means to French thought in the mid-twentieth century, Hegel's work cannot be ignored. Hegel seems to have wanted to identify, address and overcome negation, while at the same time, clearly, 'needing' negation. He proposed a model of history that would see us attaining the absolute happiness of the end of history, through moving ineluctably towards improvement. Yet after a twentieth century of wars, we still have in place the poverty, class divisions, racism and wars in our twenty-first-century world.[8] Hegel's work is often very difficult to read and his legacy is rich and complex: there are Marxists on the one hand, religious faculties on the other, and on either count he has made far less impact in Britain than in continental Europe, although Francis Fukuyama made a big splash across the Atlantic by heralding the end of history through the end of alternatives to liberal democracy.[9]

Ricœur admired Hegel's attempt to explain and resolve negativity in his philosophy of history, even though he found Hegel to be profoundly disappointing in his predictions. What is compelling in this moment is that Ricœur also saw an overwhelmingly obstreperous and dominant dialectic between Hegel's *Phenomenology* and his *Logic*, which Ricœur commented on while writing a little about the *Logic*.[10]

Ricœur on Hegel-partly via Kierkegaard

Given Hegel's importance in itself, and also the influence he exerted on Ricœur, I want to pick up some of the points from Chapter 1- existential doubt arising from the need to make choices. I will consider some of what, for me, are the highlights of Ricœur's conversations with Hegel on the negative; how Ricœur interpreted Hegel. Initially, there is a significant flavour of the negative in *Freedom and Nature*,[11] 1950, in *Fallible Man*[12] 1960 and in *History and Truth* 1965. Ricœur lingers upon nothingness, contradiction, affirmation, double negation and freedom in *Freedom and Nature* 1950. It is clear that these seem to reflect the Hegelian forms of negation as seen in the *Phenomenology of Spirit*, yet with little overt reference to Hegel. The build-up of the negative is especially noticeable in the final chapters of each of these three early texts by Ricœur which shows us that he had an issue to resolve but circled around it, pinpointing more and more sharply in each book and gradually preparing, as he often did, a challenge for the next book. However, we never get the major text on the negative that one could expect, given that Ricœur wrote 26 major texts that chart his development from phenomenology to hermeneutics and back again, via an intense relationship with the ideas of Hegel and his growing conviction that he himself was, in the end, a post-Hegelian Kantian.

In his 1955 review of Hyppolite's *Logic and Existence*, Ricœur describes Hyppolite as an apologist for Hegel, one who is honest but puts the reader in a dilemma: either to be disappointed by the extreme power of knowledge in Hegel; or, if agreeing to take the plunge into absolute knowledge, s/he must accept that we have all always been Hegelian for ever.[13] Negation is the most extreme example of Hegel's attempt to discredit Kant's recognition of the limit condition, Kant's insistence upon seeing the limits of understanding, yet as we will see in the Kant chapter, the Kant of the *Critique of Pure Reason* draws the negative deep into our critical thought processes, deep into the *noumenon*, that which we can never know. Ricœur comments on Hyppolite's attempt to present a different Hegel from the humanistic and Master-Slave Hegel of Kojève.

Hyppolite, a committed Hegelian (whose 1939–42 translation into French of *Phenomenology of Spirit* Ricœur uses for *Freud and Philosophy* (1965/70),[14] shows 'brilliantly' according to Ricœur, how negation and nothingness cannot be seen (although Bergson thought they were) as false problems. Ricœur applauds Hyppolite's rejection of Kant:

> Negation resurfaces as the principle for differentiating between objects, between organisms, between individuals, and also, in a more spectacular manner, as the inversion of the creative impulse, from which comes all materiality, all understanding and the geometry thereof; nor can we insist upon using contradiction as a sign of error, in the way logical thought does empirically, or as an *aporia* within rational thought reason as in the *Critique of Pure Reason* in the paralogisms and the antinomies.[15]

So, here we see that Hegelian negation was neither a mistake (as Bergson thought) nor a problem (as Deleuze came to believe). Rather Ricœur saw it as a means of differentiating between phenomena in order to develop new thought about such phenomena. Here, Ricœur showed us that Hegel offers liberation from Aristotelian binary logic by proposing a different sort of negative, that is, one that refuses to see the negative as a form of error and Hegel insists upon using it to create thought in his novel use of dialectic. Ricœur also believed that Hegel created some manoeuvrability by refuting Kant's use of paralogisms and antinomies to demonstrate negation as a problem within rational thought. In the late 1960s, Ricœur returned to this area and saw the strength and utility of Kant's model of limitation, whereby a philosophy of negation becomes a philosophy of limits. He changed his mind from this 1955 paper to argue in his negation lectures that Kant inserts the negative deep inside his model of human perception and thought. To argue this, Ricœur analysed Kant's early essay 'Attempt to Introduce the concept of Negative Magnitudes into Philosophy' (1763) and then applied Kant's 'positive' form of the negative to Kant's *First Critique*, which I demonstrate in Chapter 5.

At times Ricœur chose to set Hegel aside: many of the negation lectures make little direct reference to Hegel, and yet it seems to me that Hegel was in fact Ricœur's chief interlocutor. Ricœur's analysis of Heraclitus and Parmenides, for example, is taking a broadly Hegelian position, as I suggested in Chapter 3. Given that Hegel is little mentioned in the negation lectures, most of this chapter will deal, selectively, with Ricœur's published work on Hegel. At times he seemed to ignore Hegel, at times he was in tune with him ('Retour à Hegel' 1955) and increasingly he critiqued him ('Hegel Aujourd'hui' 1974 and 'Le Lieu de la Dialectique'/The place of dialectic? 1975) or even accepted the need to reject him ('Should we renounce Hegel?').[16] Hegel appears in Ricœur's last works *Memory, History, Forgetting*[17] and *The Course of Recognition*,[18] and in the latter it is the young Hegel's Jena drafts, about which Ricœur lectured in USA in 1958, as I discuss in Chapter 2.

Evil and Kierkegaard's challenge to Hegel

Ricœur developed into what he described as a post-Hegelian Kantian, a term that he took from Eric Weil.[19] One way of attempting to deal with Hegel was to read him via Kant and vice versa, which Ricœur did. Ricœur welcomed Hegel's challenge to Kant's ethics of duty; and held that Hegel saw the Kantian concept of duty as a theoretical construct, a thought about formal morality that is only one part of a search for personal and societal freedom.[20] On the other hand, Ricœur in due course imagined Kant making a riposte to Hegel about a philosophy of limits that is ultimately more useful for humans than Hegel's philosophy of the will or spirit. Hegel's *Philosophy of Spirit* although magnificent, is nevertheless the Hegelian will that Hegel sought for himself; *his* freedom and *his* system of enormous proportions, not ours. For Ricœur, Kant's transcendental philosophy is ultimately more reliable, because more sober and accurate, than Hegel's dialectic. Hegel's dialectic is based on an ideal system. So in mid-career, Ricœur was reading both Kant and Hegel as if Kant had known Hegel's work, as he explains in his essay 'Freedom in the Light of Hope' in *Conflict of Interpretations* (1969/74). The Kantian philosophy, for Ricœur, prevents us from believing we can ever reach Hegel's absolute knowledge: rather, what we have in Kant is a practical philosophy that stresses the human capacities for action.

For Ricœur, one of the most intractable problems posed by the negative in Hegel is the idea of evil as a necessity that has to be folded into the historical mix. Evil seems to be somehow accounted for by Hegel because it can be reduced in a historical manner that shows it to be necessary: according to Hegel, evil will happen and we will move forward. Yet Ricœur saw evil as a real problem that cannot be resolved in this determinist way. He was fascinated by the difficulty we have in describing or analysing evil, and the way we approach it indirectly, for example, by symbol and metaphor, as we find in *The Symbolism of Evil* (1960/67). Later, in his Kantian essay, 'Freedom in the Light of Hope', Ricœur believed that Hegel's monumental attempt to integrate evil into philosophical thinking should not and could not be sufficient:

> The Hegel I reject is the philosopher of retrospection, the one who not only accompanies the dialectic of the Spirit but reabsorbs all rationality in the already happened meaning[21]

Kierkegaard presented a real challenge to Hegel by distorting his dialectic and also by suspending the sinfulness of evil acts if done for faith. On both counts Ricœur was impressed but not in agreement, and I show here the journey of identification that Ricœur undertook from the late 1950s to the early 1960s in order to categorize Kierkegaard to his satisfaction. In one of his two published encounters with Kierkegaard – 'Kierkegaard and Evil' – Ricœur asked how we can celebrate Kierkegaard without falling victim to his sweeping ridicule for the human race. Ricœur saw evil as the key that links Hegel and Kierkegaard – according to them, once understood it is no longer evil.

In 1963, Ricœur challenged the idea of Kierkegaard as one of the three or four fathers of a philosophy of negation, with Hegel and Nietzsche (Marx, the fourth father, being only a sort of father of negation, because negation becomes for Marx a rather formulaic opposition between classes). In fact he was challenging his own ideas: back in 1957 in his Husserl essay 'Existential Phenomenology', Ricœur proposed Kierkegaard as one of the 'fathers' of existential phenomenology, alongside Nietzsche. With his anti-system stance, Kierkegaard established the categories by which the individual replaces the system: with the passing second of experience instead of the eternity of logic, the individual instead of the whole, paradox instead of mediation and existence instead of the System.[22] As discussed in Chapter 2, in 1958 in the set of eight unpublished lectures at the Union Theological Seminary entitled 'Anthropology and Religion in the philosophy of existence', Ricœur experimented with the idea of Hegel, Kierkegaard, Marx and Nietzsche, as the 'fathers' of negation with four 'sons': Jaspers, Marcel, Heidegger and Sartre.[23] We see here that for Ricœur there are familial connections between existentialism and negation: the triumph of the individual over the whole and the banishment of time and history by the intense feelings of the moment. The individual negates both the rest of the world and the history of the world. By 1963, in two essays published in French, Ricœur had abandoned the idea of establishing this genealogy of existentialist fathers and sons, asserting that Jaspers, Marcel, Heidegger and Sartre cannot really be seen as cousins related in existentialism, with Kierkegaard as the father figure, because they are so different from each other.[24]

Ricœur's revision of his own ideas takes place in his analysis of Kierkegaard's books *The concept of anxiety*[25] and *The sickness unto death*[26] (also called *The treatise on despair*). We also need to refer back to *Fear and trembling*[27]. Both Kierkegaard books are based upon two negative feelings; dread/anxiety and despair – it is never made clear what the fear is about and these negative feelings also then need to be compared. If evil is that which is most opposed to the system of living, then it is transgression of laws, wrongdoing etc., but Kierkegaard is doing something different, he is exploring evil within each of these two moods, and so each of these two books gives a different version of evil; dread is anxiety, an idea of sin as 'event or upheaval', an exploration of the possibility of evil, whereas despair is a state of being fully immersed in sin, evil. Giving up on action and effort to be good in a Kantian sense is a source of potential evil for Ricœur, whereas for Kierkegaard, it may be necessary to do precisely that.

Kierkegaard's *Fear and trembling*, once read, is difficult to forget; if sacrificing one's own son would be a sin in moral law, in faith terms it would be an act of obedience. This contradiction between ethics and faith leads to an understanding of sin and despair; for Isaac to commit such an unethical act in the interests of his faith would lead to despair, and Kierkegaard demonstrates this structurally by elaborating the sense of lack that he sees in sin, to the structure of lack in his unresolved two-term dialectic. Kierkegaard refuses the resolution of the Hegelian dialectical form, instead insisting upon either too much finitude or too little, too much possibility or too little, too much desire to be at one with oneself or too much desire *not* to be at one with oneself. Ricœur sees this as an extraordinary dialectical framework that is based, very incongruously, upon 'a hyper intellectualism linked to a fundamental irrationalism'.[28] For Kierkegaard, we are able to submit to the insistence of despair if we lose our capacity to relate ourselves to ourselves, the result of failing to relate to another. This is much worse than dread, which is the *idea* of such possibilities. Sickness, despair is much worse, it would be abandonment, dereliction by God of us, and by us of ourselves and others. Such dereliction means that we would see ourselves as if we were only another, no longer ourselves relating to another and this has implications for despair. In early existentialism, *Either/or*[29] is the torment. Psychology sees it as a fall, then as a lack, that is, nothing.

Encapsulated in despair we find the final form of sin as Kierkegaard sees it within the Christian faith establishment, as a position, not as a negation.[30] Kierkegaard saw philosophy, and most especially Hegelian philosophy, as a despicable attempt to deal with, to manage sin:

> 'To comprehend evil philosophically is to reduce it to a pure negation: weakness as a lack of force, sensuality as a lack of spirituality, ignorance as a lack of knowledge, finitude as a lack of totality.'[31]

If Hegel found the negation of negation at the core of comprehension, then Kierkegaard opposes that strenuously:

> 'If to comprehend is to overcome, that is, to pass beyond negation, then sin is one negation among others and repentance one medium among others.'[32]

If managed by Hegel, this process makes negation and the negation of negation into purely logical processes, whereas for Kierkegaard, sin is not to be understood, negated or made logical, but *believed*. Sin is a position of ignorance; this is a paradox that must be accepted and cannot be understood. This is not negative theology that Kierkegaard has in mind, nor Kant's abolition of knowledge in favour of belief, but Socratic ignorance. With his suspicion of the ethical as teleological, Kierkegaard wants to argue that God is beyond being and understanding. We must believe and not understand and the connection between sin and God arises because sin is only possible because of God. For Ricœur, evil is the key between Hegel and Kierkegaard – evil understood is no longer evil. Kierkegaard protested against Hegel's technique of making evil manageable through absorbing it into the negative impulse, but Ricœur wonders what Kierkegaard was really protesting about and why. Kierkegaard, with the personal mythology arising from his difficult life, his outrageous writings and his many pseudonymous alter egos, seemed like an outsider, yet also seemed to Ricœur to belong within philosophy and theology. It is the despair that Kierkegaard evokes that concerned Ricœur.

Hegel on Kant

Another aspect of Ricœur's problem with Hegel lies in the latter's interpretation of Kant and areas around the negative. Hegel often misunderstood Kant, although he agreed with Kant that pure reason produces antinomies if it lets itself be ruled by our faulty understanding of the world around us. Dialectic produces antinomies and is itself an artificial movement. For Kant, these antinomies are not resolvable. But Hegel went further, accusing Kant of not understanding that *everything* we think about is full of antinomies (not only the four antinomies with which Kant deals in the *Critique of Pure Reason*) and that for all antinomies resolution is attainable. If we have to understand what something is not in order to understand what it is, then the *is not* would often be the ideal form, the *is* would be the reality and so a dialectical process leads us to accept the discrepancy between our dreams and the reality of life. Of course, this is a strong mechanism for living, yet Ricœur saw the possibility to exaggerate it, as he believed Hegel did, becoming stuck in the ethic of the imperative – that this dialectic is the way things always are. This is very different from Kant's dialectical logic, which Hegel sees as falsely attempting to give understanding of the transcendent noumena, things in themselves as they really are, rather than as they appear. Hegel accuses Kant of overemphasizing the role of the 'divisive understanding' and of not grasping reason's full potential. Hegel misunderstands Kant and, rejecting Kant's vision as fragmented, Hegel is concerned to demonstrate a holistic view, reality as totality. Kant's other form of logic, the analytic logic of understanding, provides a sense of guidance for understanding natural phenomena. In Hegel's opinion, Kant's analytical logic is only good for science and everyday life, but not for philosophy. Yet Ricœur asserted the inexhaustible richness of Kant's philosophy of limits as a way of seeing the potential to imagine beyond our limitations; we will see in the Kant chapter that Ricœur also saw the disadvantages of such limitations, yet in 'Freedom in the Light of Hope' he insisted upon its power to let us find hope, which is a very different emphasis from the Hegelian one of seeking to justify past events.[33]

So for Hegel – and Ricœur – Kant excited us with conjuring up limits that we can push against, yet also disappointed us in not being able to go beyond dualistic thought. The relationship of dialectic with duality is also complex and Ricœur explored it by using Hegel in many situations: one of the more celebrated contexts is in *Freud and Philosophy*, where Ricœur sees Hegel as capable of drawing us away from Freud's negative view of the subconscious and towards a rebuilding of the fragmented consciousness. Possibly, the most important part of Hegel for Ricœur is Hegel's development of a form of dialectic that gives the negative an equal footing with the positive and uses negation to go beyond Kant and facilitate a third state. For Hegel, the third state will become part of another iteration of negative: positive, and a new third state and so on. Ricœur described this third state in the last book published while he was alive (*The Course of Recognition*) as 'states of peace', a desirable form of equilibrium and contentment, yet during decades of studying Hegel, Ricœur also saw the need for ragged, tense or uneven third states. He made much use of dialectic structures in demonstrating his failure to resolve tensions as a result of analysing different philosophical debates. Some problems are more productive when left unsolved, open-ended, to be worked on further – and some problems can never be solved, yet require our constant attention. One such is our relation to the negative, and our related pursuit of happiness.

Hegel used the power of ideas to develop an idealist philosophy with negation at its core. In so doing, Hegel took a very different path from his predecessors, creating a completely different approach to the negative, different from Aristotle, different from Kant. Hegel used his negation for abolishing the difference between practical and theoretical reason, by contrasting them and moving them both on to a new combination of real and theoretical. Hegel's 'labour of the negative' showed us that thought and reality are the same as each other to the extent that we *think* reality; yet they are also not the same as each other, because we can only understand the world by seeing how it is different from us. This involves labouring to understand difference, contrariety and polarity and using positive and negative poles to develop dialectic. It should also become clear that Hegel, called 'idealist', was also determined to deal with reality as well. Thus, Ricœur became wary of using the 'idealism' label for Hegel without refining it, as he knew it would be easy to then criticize Hegel in the light of Marx: idealism versus materialism, as Ricœur commented in his 1975 paper on dialectic, and in his unpublished paper '*Hegel et la Négation*'.[34]

It seemed as if Hegel could become an insurmountable barrier to new thought either through the slavish acceptance of Hegel as the master or through critiquing the master Hegel so much that one finds oneself rejecting him. In order to think through Hegel to get beyond him, in Ricœur's style, an approach requires critiquing him but not to such an extent that one cuts oneself loose from him. In addition to being integral to French thought, Hegel was of interest to Ricœur for using the negative: positive impulse to create reason as a dynamic force. He tried to go far beyond Kant, by refuting Kant's doubts about our capacity to be morally or perceptually accurate and reasonable in our understanding of the world. By integrating the negative impulse fully into the idea that humans can think, Hegel exercised his belief that we have to accept the need to think about not-ness. Yet, Ricœur adds, we also need Kant for inviting us to challenge our fallibility through using reason. Such rational thinking will be inadequate yet invaluable for limiting our imaginings. We can see how important the negative was for creating energy (Hegel) and criticality (Kant).

Hegel's negation and the unhappy consciousness

In Hegel's most famous text, *The Phenomenology of Spirit*,[35] there are at least three major forms of negative. Negation functions to control the otherness that it faces: it domesticates or subdues. Another sort of negative (as in '*the truth of self-certainty*') shows how consciousness negates its subjects by consuming or assimilating them. Thirdly, *Lordship and Bondage* presents a model of the negative as domination and subjugation and even annihilation. In the third form, it is clear how the positive and negative, master and slave, find each other; not unidirectionally of course, as the dominance of the master requires the acknowledgement of the slave and vice versa and there are subtle shifts of power. I believe that this can be immensely problematic for a non-Hegelian: how does the negative seek out its alterity? Ricœur selected carefully the partners for each dialectical dance. We see in his work on Hegel and Freud how the Hegelian dialectic made it possible to compare and contrast two thinkers as long as they shared enough similarities to be in some way in parity, and yet were also very different in ways that related to their similarities; in this case he creates a tension between the archaeology of Freud's infant and the teleology of Hegel's world history. Creation of such similarities and tensions can be seen to be rather like the tenor and the vehicle of a metaphor as developed by I A Richards in 1936, and even more so in to Plotinus' metaphorical structures.

Ricœur not only accepted the influence of Hegel, but also believed that he could never free himself from Hegelian thought. This is proved by the fact that Ricœur kept reading and discussing Hegel even after he had admitted that we have to 'mourn' Hegel because we do not think *like* Hegel anymore, but rather *after Hegel*.[36] Negating Hegel would exclude much that is rich and useful, such as the habit humans have of contrasting the real with the ideal – we often do think like Hegel! Seeking an alternative to shaking oneself free of Hegel was therefore clearly a preoccupation for Ricœur as well as for many of his contemporaries. For Ricœur, Hegel was the beginning of the problem of the negative in modern philosophy, with – for Ricœur in the 1950s – Sartre at the opposite end of the spectrum. Spinoza had offered a similar idea about the inherence of negation in all actions, by asserting that 'all determination is negation' – that is, we can modify this in a pragmatist manner to suggest that every time we make a positive decision, we negate many other possibilities. Yet the problem Hegel posed by emphasizing the negative so much was perceived in early twentieth-century France to be pervasive, as Butler demonstrates in *Subjects of Desire*.[37] Also, Hegel may offer the trigger for positive change in the way we see the world: Ricœur comments at the end of his only published text on the negative that those who followed Hegel (presumably Kierkegaard, Nietzsche, Sartre, among others, yet perhaps not Heidegger) have all forced us to wean ourselves off the Thing, the essence, the form of experience, and move actively towards a philosophy of action, agency rather than formalism. This was, for Ricœur 'living affirmation, the power of existing and of making exist'.[38] Perhaps here Ricœur is taking up his own challenge to see whether we really can replace Parmenides' One with the Many: diversity, non-identity, difference.

For Hegel, discussing, say, for example, salt water and fresh water as examples of Heraclitus' world view, we have to start by describing *this* as different from *that*, an approach based on agreeing that this *is not* that. This necessitates subsequent analysis of what *this* really is, followed by some way of synthesizing key features of the phenomenon in order to develop a clearer sense of how it fits into the world as a whole. We may use this phrase 'the world as a whole', very loosely in daily language, yet it sums up Hegel's most treasured goal, the desire to explain the world as a unified whole, at one with itself, in which the 'with itself' seems to be Hegel at one with himself, a goal related in that sense to Parmenides' vision of the one unity. The 'oneness' is deeply problematic, because of the leap necessary from this subject (one person) and this object (one thing) to the whole world. The most dominant way in which he argues for this holism is through idealism; his philosophy is about ideas, and he asserts that we have the cognitive power to incorporate each item holistically into a world view by the sheer power of thought.

Hegel achieves this cognitive control of ideas by insisting that three dialectical steps must be followed and also incorporated into the finished vision. The three steps are as follows, and are broadly similar in both the *Science of Logic* and the *Encyclopaedia Logic*. First, there is sense perception of an object as a distinct object that is not other objects. This is a phenomenological device; when I notice something it is because it is different from all that surrounds it, like a friend's face in a crowd. That face I see is different from the faces of the strangers in the crowd, it is one I recognize. Second, I take a critical approach to sense perception that becomes a self-conscious subjective interpretation of that object: is that face really the face of my friend, whom I alone identify in my own unique way, *or not*? Third, I can then enjoy the self-knowledge in which my understandings of both object (the friend) and subject (me) are no longer separable and comprise the Absolute, the Whole, the joy of being reunited with my friend and feeling, briefly, invincible and at one with the world.

Ricœur developed this idea of friendship as the attestation of love in many ways, the most detailed way being in his book *Oneself As Another* (1990/92), and this is based upon the belief that we only come to know ourselves through our understanding of the other person and also by seeing ourselves reflected in the other person too. How much more hopeful this is than Hegelian models, in which mood is controlled by Hegel.

The unhappy consciousness

The example that I give of seeing the other person, my friend in the crowd is perhaps too Sartrean for Hegel (and too optimistic for Sartre). Hegel's examples are rare and often complex, often attempting to relate higher human functioning to basic events in the natural world, as in the long sequence he develops about light and dark, virtue and evil.[39] Nor is my 'friend example' straightforward, as for me my friend *represents* a friendly, familiar idea, as well as *being my friend*, not like Hegel's Absolute, which is an *idea*; the Absolute is where the Idea of humanity and the universe 'thinks itself', that is, *thinks* reality as a whole. This is also very different from Sartre's look, in which I cease to exist under the gaze of the other; I become object under the gaze of the other, I become object, objectified, no longer subject of my own life.

Hegel has, however, used some unforgettable examples: he made a significant and unique contribution to debate about the negative by populating his idealism with a few manifestations of negation that have become highly influential. One such is 'the unhappy consciousness' – I am ill at ease with myself because I define myself according to what is currently called a deficit model: I measure myself against what I do not have, the person I am not and the losses I have sustained. This consumer culture that is an unhappy consciousness machine has huge influence over my ability to buy happiness, to buy drugs for happiness and to shop for normality. If I am deficient in the sense of not behaving in an acceptable way – like a very lively child – I can easily be moulded to be more biddable, which requires assessing me by my deficiencies, not by my strengths, as this case study demonstrates.

THE UNHAPPY CONSCIOUSNESS AND ADHD

Hegel's unhappy consciousness has modern resonances and relevancies: having worked as an educational psychologist I find unhappy consciousness to be, perhaps surprisingly, the norm in much 'special needs' work; we are encouraged to define a child (or an adult) by their deficits, by what they cannot do or by what they do that we deem abnormal. Labels proliferate and conditions such as Attention Deficit Hyperactivity Disorder (ADHD) are created to serve the new observable conditions and espoused states that multiply. At an existentialist philosophical level, Sartre takes this image and fashions it into 'bad faith', extending a deficit model into passivity justified or rationalized by situational problems that

(*continued*)

give us the excuse to avoid taking positive action. But we do not expect, nor should we, to see such a negative image at the heart of the caring profession of teachers and psychologists. Thomas Szasz, an American psychiatrist, asserted that what we call mental illness is in fact explainable in terms of social adjustment, and the coming together of medical and pharmaceutical interests. While I accept that some mental illnesses exist, there is a good match between Szasz's ideas and labels like ADHD, created in my view, to provide a market for drugs. Moreover, if we have drugs to pacify the naughty child, we do not need to address the root causes for the misbehaviour which often lie with the rest of us, as we were there before the child was and we set the situations up – it is as if the child is taking drugs on our behalf.

The Global Consensus on ADHD/HKD of 2004 demonstrates how language is used to enhance the status of the 'condition', naming ADHD a common neurobehavioral disorder which can be considered a syndrome because it has neurobiological aspects and benefits from administration of drugs like Ritalin. Yet we know that methylphenidate, commonly sold as Ritalin, has the same effects on supposedly 'normal' humans: improving ability to concentrate, potentially reducing the need for sleep, facilitating long periods of alertness and acting as an appetite suppressant. Moreover, the DSM IV descriptions of symptoms are worryingly vague; they list, typically: 'often does not seem to listen when spoken to directly' and 'is often easily distracted'. The reasons for doubting the diagnostic narrative are the vagueness of the criteria and their infinite relativity; and also the nature of the criteria, which suggest to me a normative pressure to control, and a return to the child deficit model that was briefly replaced in the 1970s and 80s by emphasis on context, surroundings, nurture rather than nature and goodness of fit between the children's needs and their environment. We could, therefore, also see this situation as resembling Nietzsche's depiction of the weak depriving the strong of their energy: adults depriving strong children of their energy. Ecclestone and Hayes analyse this well as the 'diminished self' in their groundbreaking 2009 book *The Dangerous Rise of Therapeutic Education*.

Ricœur developed a stinging critique of this way of using pseudo-diagnostic language in this way to create a new reality that distorts and does harm, in his work on ideology and utopia,[40] where he demonstrates how it is impossible to discuss distorting terminology when one is in the grip of an ideology; ideology will not talk, ideology makes neither space nor time to do so as that could compromise the lies it tells us. It would indeed be very difficult to persuade the many good people who are using diagnostic labels for good reasons, that they should reconsider the practice, and indeed they might retort that such labels are liberating for the sufferer and their family, thus avoiding worse labels . . . but this again evokes the need to discuss what normality is.

The servants in the snow

Another influential Hegelian image is that of the 'master-slave', worn smooth through overuse and perhaps overplayed by Kojève in his famous Paris lectures of the 1930s. Still, it offers an apt summary of one of the most recurrent features of human relationships; the possibility of using power in a relationship in order to deny another person the full recognition they seek and thereby unintentionally deny oneself one's full potential too.

In *The Servants and The Snow*, 1970, Iris Murdoch, Anglo-Irish philosopher, Hegel scholar and author, wrote a wonderful play about Anglo-Irish relationships that embody a clear and evocative example of master-slave dialectic: the Catholic servants are bound to their 'noble' English masters in ways that extend beyond conventional servants' duties to *droits de seigneur* that create sexual complications and even dominance of servant over ruling class. The master and the servant *think* their dominance – subjugation such that it is real, even when there is an opportunity for individuals to break away. In a subtle stage direction: Murdoch indicates that Patrice (slave) and General Klein (Master) must be played by the same actor. Wei H. Kao writes persuasively about this complex symbiotic relationship that will have no end until bigger social forces intervene, as Hegel proposed.[41]

Hegel saw each of us as one particulate that is a tiny part of the universe as it appears in thought by *thinking* it. Our daily humdrum activity builds the energy for the ideas of idealist thought: and then of course we die, but our living thinking existence has contributed in a small way to the Absolute that is the world. Hegel inserted the negative deep into the folds of our skin, enjoining us to incorporate negation into our being instead of rejecting it. It was Ricœur's desire to achieve this full incorporation of negation into our world, by demonstrating that the affirmative is at the core of negation, which in turn is at the core of being, yet Hegel's method proved too all encompassing; Ricœur came to feel that if the negative is to be useful it needs to be an abrasive irritant and as such cannot be fully assimilated into the body and mind of a society as Hegel wished.

Giving Hegel his own Aufhebung treatment

What about *Aufhebung*? This is a very interesting word that contains its own dialectical tension internally: it means three things: lifting up, keeping and also putting an end to (not necessarily by destruction but by taking something out of circulation, setting to one side). The term *Aufhebung* is an essential component to our understanding of Hegel's negatives and yet I contest that it is deeply ambiguous. Hegel plays obfuscatory and multivalent games with the reader, and this reminds us of the lack of clarity around the use of the term negative, that started Ricœur on this exploration in the first place. We see reactions to Hegel in Derrida who developed his own version of *Aufhebung*, with his neologism *différance*, and his proposed French equivalent for *Aufhebung*: *la relève*. Ricœur used the term himself, as a verb, in *Hegel Aujourd'hui* and comments on this as 'Derrida's very apt translation' and gives his own gloss on it: 'Hegelian *Aufhebung* [sublation, transformation that partially cancels, a reinterpretation to a higher level]'.[42] *La relève* relates also to current debates among scholars of religion looking at Paul's Epistle. Given its Greek origins in *katageigne* (to act right up to the limit, perhaps to effect a change in the state of another), should *la relève* be understood as active, *relief* as substitution (a rising up), or as passive (being promoted), *relief* as a rising up or a form of promotion? This is the idea of action by one upon another but we have no information about the one who undertakes action: perhaps this is appropriate, given that I am coming to think that the idea of a middle voice is possible, neither active nor passive, neither acting nor suffering, but somewhere in the middle.[43]

The difficulty in defining *Aufhebung*, which plays such an important part in Hegel's philosophy, may be one of the root problems with Hegel. It may also be that the term is so ambiguous that it does not fulfil Ricœur's requirement of language – that it speak its meaning and thereby assert its agency: he wanted to retain some mystery in hermeneutical processes, yet I argue that a term this important should not bamboozle us completely. Where is the agency of *Aufhebung*, who is its keeper and what does it do as a term:

> I believe it is possible to show that in every contestation of the real, which is the way in which a value surges forth into the world, an affirmation of being is included. This can be shown by an analysis of the valorising attitudes, such as indignation, protestation, recrimination, and revolt, which, on the surface, are the most annihilating.[44]

The quotation above comes from Ricœur's only published writing that is explicitly about negation (the essay 'Negativity and Primary Affirmation' (1956) at the end of the second edition of *History and Truth* (not published in English until 1965). Primary affirmation is the decision to believe one can act well, despite the difficult decisions, the need to exclude the choices not made and our finitude. So this essay belongs to the phase that I have labelled, broadly, the first phase of his negation work and it is a strong indictment of Sartre's version of existentialism. This essay also functions as a commentary on Hegel and Husserl, *as if* Hegel had read Husserl – by this Ricœur meant that the implications for negation are hidden by Husserl in his *Logical Investigations*[45] until we read Husserl through Hegel. In *From Text To Action*,[46] Ricœur also returns to Husserl, hoping Weber will give Husserl strength to resist Hegel, which I discuss in the final chapter. From the early 1950s, Ricœur had been hammering out some tentative answers to these questions in his lecture series on negation; sometimes he discussed Hegel, sometimes he omitted Hegel completely. From 1956 to 1958, which marks the move from Strasbourg to the Sorbonne, he sought the roots of negation before Hegel and set Hegel to one side in terms of the content of his lectures. Hegel is mentioned occasionally:

> Here we are at the very heart of Aristotelian philosophy; everything is really founded upon essence as the first meaning of *to on*: This argument is exactly that which the first three chapters of Hegel's *Phenomenology of Spirit* wishes to refute: . . . for Hegel, meaning is never self-identical, it is discordant with itself and this is how discourse is possible.[47]

This comment shows how important Hegel is, but another solution for Ricœur in attempting to understand Hegel is to set him to one side because he is so dominant (give Hegel his own *aufheben* treatment!). Ricœur did this in the 1958 series of negation lectures given in French in Paris, from which this quotation is taken. This lecture series contains three that were probably typed out by students, and Hegel is mentioned therein 4 times in 140 pages. I suggest that Hegel is ever present yet often set to one side to give Ricœur space to explore the history of the negative *before* Hegel. Setting Hegel to one side gave Ricœur space to work and rework his interest in the Pre-Socratic philosophers repeatedly, and he identified Heraclitus as the first thinker to identify the originary nature of negation. Ricœur suggested, however, that Heraclitus is stuck in a closed pattern of opposites and needs Hegel's dialectic to free him. In terms of the history of philosophy, Ricœur referred, tangentially, to the problems of modern philosophy, exemplified, he suggested, in the way both Hegel and Heidegger misrepresent the relationship between perceived opposites as manifest in Heraclitus and Parmenides; Hegel exaggerating differences and Heidegger playing them down.[48] This Hegelian approach to the negative is indeed different from Kant but actually has resonances in Kant's early essay on 'Negative Magnitudes', which we will discuss in detail in Chapter 5.[49]

Also and rather differently, in 1958, writing in English for an American audience, Ricœur lectured on 'Anthropology and Religion in the philosophy of existence'.[50] On this occasion, he places Hegel at the heart of a series of lectures about the negative in modern continental philosophy, that is, since Hegel. He takes up again the post-Hegelian legacy of Marx, Kierkegaard and Nietzsche. He sets the scene historically, in a very Hegelian manner, offering his American audience a historical run through Hegel's development. Ricœur experiments with negation and nothingness, replacing one with the other sometimes. For example, he translates the first five pages or so of this USA series from his paper entitled *Hegel et la Négation*, which he translates as *Hegel and Nothingness*. Here, Ricœur is clearly experimenting with nothingness as an existential form, rather like Sartre used it for despair, *and* an awareness of Plotinus' use of nothingness as a rich albeit complex model for understanding through not understanding – in Plotinus' case God. When he does this replacement juggling, negation for nothingness and vice versa, presumably he is experimenting with what he thinks the negative means, and whether it can be nothingness at times; if so, what sort of nothingness and whether Plotinus' nothingness and use of metaphor can function in non-spiritual situations.

Adapting Hegel's dialectic

We saw earlier how Hegel's dialectic can free us from the fixed reversibility of Heraclitus' model which emphasizes natural phenomena such as night and day. With Hegel however, there is a different difficulty; the negation of negation keeps the problem bound to binary logical structures, denying the possibility of originary representational thought like Heraclitus', which developed before Aristotle's logic and before idealism. Yet Heraclitus, in Ricœur's opinion, did not follow through these possibilities. We may critique Hegel's assertion (as Schopenhauer did) that negation of negation is positive and is real movement: we should also see it as tied to a formula related to formal logic which may constitute false, artificial movement superimposed upon our own two-legged, two-armed movements around our body in the middle.

In 1950, with *Freedom and Nature*, Ricœur was responding to Hegel, but rather obliquely and indirectly. A few years later, he was actively engaged in grappling with Hegel's thought, particularly in thinking about Sartre as well. He moved consciously between being Hegelian and being not-Hegelian.

As a feature of his lectures on negation, Ricœur compared Hegel and Heidegger in their treatment of Heraclitus and Parmenides, and asks how we can achieve a third way and avoid the excesses of each; Hegel overemphasizing the differences between Heraclitus and Parmenides and Heidegger underemphasizing them. Ricœur felt he had not got the tools to forge such an amalgam and therefore it would be better to keep this as an ongoing task than to make a mediocre amalgam of Hegel and Heidegger.[51]

Ricœur starts with conflict; yet contradiction is not of interest as such – if contradiction is part of ideas as well as of reality itself, then we can understand how opposed pairs need each other because to describe one means to describe the other as they are inextricably linked epistemologically: for example, Inner/Outer. Being opposed in thought does not mean they are necessarily otherwise in conflict, which Kant will address in his distinction between real and logical negation. They need to be similar and also different, commensurable. Ricœur detects or creates a conflict by juxtaposing two thinkers whose ideas are discordant; for example, Freud and Hegel. However, he only uses this approach when the thinkers concerned have enough common ground to facilitate conversation in the first place. This seems very Hegelian. He then gently and insistently dismembers the arguments, showing their similarities and differences from each other as well as, most importantly, their internal contradictions. This raises the issue of how he chooses his dialectical pairs, because he does not select thinkers whose ideas are incommensurable, and where there therefore would be no real conflict, simply a stand-off.

We can conclude that Ricœur was not attracted to Hegel's narrative in which it seems irrelevant that we may get both more than and less than we want or deserve, because we die anyway and thereby contribute to the greater good of the Spirit that represents mankind. Ricœur insists upon primary affirmation, the value of the individual's existence, rather than the Spirit. Indeed we want more than what seems to us like the chance fling of destiny, even if we don't know what we want; partly because we cannot formulate quite clearly enough who we want to be and also because these desires are therefore, by definition, unattainable because unknown. It is sad to be so insignificant. We also are embroiled in the world of unintended consequences; for Hegel, they are part of the rich pattern of necessary horrors and wonders, because all is moving towards the realization of the Good. For Ricœur, it is necessary to hope for more: we can attest to our own attempts to achieve more. Yet paradoxically, Ricœur saw that Hegel has helped us to move from *form* to *act*:

> No doubt, the virtue of the philosophies of negativity since Hegel is to have put us back on the road towards a philosophy of being which cuts away from the thing and essence.

This includes being; which negation makes difficult, as Plato knew – with his assertion that being and non-being embarrass us equally, and therefore:

> Under the pressure of the negative we must re-achieve a notion of being which is *act* rather than *form*, living affirmation, the power of existing and of making exist[52]

However, Ricœur published this in 1956 and was to continue to lecture on negation for more than 10 years before he let it drop, so there was clearly still a problem, and this may be partly reflected in continental philosophy which, itself, is faced with a paradox – because of its recent history (Kojève and others), it could not avoid working within Hegel's idealist, rationalist legacy in the middle third of the twentieth century and yet in the light of two world wars and more horrors afterwards, many intellectuals believed that rationality cannot resolve the problems that remained. This was a problem for Ricœur as well, for two major reasons: he could not see how reason was a major factor in understanding the twentieth century because of the irrational wars and conflicts that gouged into the body of Europe; and he was religious, which meant that belief always provided a separate, if often complementary and also contradictory pathway to understanding. His faith-based approach to these issues marked him out from the fashionable and squabbling Paris philosophy pack although many of them shared the same distress at the failure of the Enlightenment, and the desire to impede instrumental reason (in the form of genocide and death as industrial production). Ricœur's faith poses an interesting challenge for looking at his handling of Hegel's idealism: if the major difference between Hegel and Ricœur is the refusal of Hegel's logic as a solution to human problems, then what happens to Hegel's dialectic in Ricœur's hands? Ricœur wrote in a very reasonable, measured and balanced way, yet he knew that Hegel's Absolute Knowledge could not provide the solutions.

Because no major philosopher has given so much space to negation, Hegel bestows an advantage upon himself and creates a category that he dominates because he gives negation a major role and renders it inextricable from his Absolute Knowledge. However, it does not seem to me that Hegel necessarily solved the issue better than Plato: Plato reduces negation to differentiation, to otherness, whereas for Hyppolite, Hegelian dialectic pushes this otherness further apart, into contradiction, an oppositional and potentially violent solution. The absolute Hegelian self is not itself until and unless it exists in a negative form that negates itself and, in opposing itself, becomes itself absolutely. The same is true of the philosophy of Hegel itself; it is so complex that it cannot be dismembered and analysed, it must be allowed to proceed to negate itself, and only thereby will it become the full Hegelian philosophy. Does it mean that meaning 'understands' non-meaning, the anti-logos? Ricœur thinks this is only possible while pushing to its logical conclusion the anthropological reduction initiated with the transcendental in Kant. For Ricœur, it would be hard to achieve unity or comprehension while working within the frame of a Hegelian philosophy that seems to understand everything, even non-meaning. Meanwhile, these post-Hegelians Marx, Kierkegaard and Nietzsche necessitate a remaking of Hegel, but Ricœur believes it is only possible to do this with what came after Hegel, and after those whom he influenced profoundly, which may signal a return to the phenomenology of younger Ricœur, to Husserl. Hegel's pervasive use of *Aufhebung* – lifting up, setting aside even rendering null and void by suspending the use or consideration of an item – allows Hegel to absorb and control time within his concept of the eternal present in absolute thought.[53] However, for most of us, post-Hegelians by default, this is impossible, which means that ultimately all oppositions are reduced beyond repair and collapsed into one another, so no sense of time remains. Hegelianism itself brooks no dismantling, no deconstruction and no rebuilding, we have to clamber over it to achieve something else, using – language as an act, metaphor and parable as transformative and finally again and always going back to Kant. I propose we find a partial resolution of the problem of Hegel and the negative in Ricœur's linguistic turn.

CHAPTER FIVE

Kant: Negation in a philosophy of limits

He becomes childish, and since in his year-long contemplation of the doorkeeper he has come to know even the fleas in his fur collar, he begs the fleas as well to help him and to change the doorkeeper's mind.[1]

. . . the limit oscillates between a purely negative sense (restriction of the pretension of sensibility of extending beyond the phenomenon) and a positive sense (what understanding would see if it were intuitive). . . Restriction and opening up of a horizon in a not objectifying sense. The whole of the Kantian philosophy of negation is in suspense in this oscillation.[2]

This second quotation is one of the conclusions that Ricœur draws about Kant's relation to the negative in the last of his unpublished five lectures called *Kant et la Négation*.[3] I will come back to the fleas later, which, like Homer's tale of boys and lice, remind us both of our humanity and our limitations. These five lectures come from the time when Ricœur lectured on Kant extensively, in the 1960s and 70s, in the United States as well as France. In these five unpublished lectures, he focused on Kant's early essay 'Attempt to introduce the concept of 'Negative Magnitudes' into Philosophy'[4] (1763)[5] and related this early Kant to the later *Critique of Pure Reason* (1781).[6] These five Ricœur lectures show Ricœur's use of Kant's early negation work to develop his own early work on negation and clarify what had happened to ideas about the negative in western philosophy since the ancient Greek debates about monist and dualist thought and the one and the many. I will demonstrate how the five lectures make explicit for the first time how very useful negation is in Ricœur's own 'philosophy of limits' that he developed from Kant: Ricœur charted Kant's development of the category of negation from the 'Negative Magnitudes' essay to *The Critique of Pure Reason*.

In Ricœur's five lectures, the negative is presented as a limit idea in Kant, which is of two kinds according to Ricœur; one that can possibly guide our thinking, (the noumenal as a guide to our limitations) and one that stops dead, the schema of negation that diminishes to nothingness. Ricœur enjoyed the affirmative aspect of Kant's view of negation, but he also challenged Kant's negative, with Hegel's help.[7] Ricœur found that it would only make the Kantian negative truly powerful if we complemented Kant with Hegel in our view of negation, even if doing so would distort Kant's argument – yet Ricœur believed this to be worth the risk. The negative in Kant's 'Negative Magnitudes' essay has a vital and active role to play in setting up a dialogue for Ricœur: the sections on the antinomies in the *Critique of Pure Reason* provide some of the material for Ricœur to develop his post-Hegelian Kantianism, using the negative impulse. These lectures by Ricœur on Kant's early work give more depth to our understanding of early/mid Ricœur, the negative and his relationship with the negative of Kant and Hegel.

The history of Kant's 'Negative Magnitudes': patterns in the dust and static socks

The origins of Kant's positive approach to the negative are important, as they give a sense of how he transformed the negative, yet remained caught within a binary model; this binary model undergoes some transformations, from the division of negation into two different types in the 1763 essay (logical contradiction and what he calls real opposition), to the broader, more general oppositions that appear in the *Critique of Pure Reason*, such as the phenomenal and the noumenal, sensibility and understanding, or the antinomies. These origins are to be found in his rejection of Aristotle and of Leibniz' negative imagery and they also have their roots in scientific experiments: electricity discoveries were causing great excitement during Kant's working lifetime and seem to have influenced his philosophical thinking about positive and negative, and about negative as the equal partner of the positive, not its inferior. Symmer (1759) took his socks off and put them on again to demonstrate static electricity, arguing through the demonstrable repulsion and attraction of his socks that positive and negative in magnetic forces of electricity are both 'positive' forces: there is no privation or lack, but the responses to each other of equal forces. Repulsive socks or not, in this Symmer is echoing Newton, as Kant did, and contradicting Franklin, for whom the negative was a weak force. Lichtenberg experimented with dust to show energy forces in both negative and positive electrical currents. Kant was able to use these examples to illustrate his ideas about negative and positive being equal, balanced or co-operative and this approach influenced Kant's views on good and evil also. Walford, in his translation of Kant's early essays,[8] tells us that Kant argued in favour of Leibniz's view that evil is the mere absence of good, in *Optimism* (1759) and yet in 'Negative Magnitudes' (1764) he asserts that evil is, in fact, like pain, a real phenomenon and in order to understand it we require the negative to adopt an active meaning. Extrapolating from ideas, and using examples from the real world, Kant argues that whenever we find a positive force, there we will also find its negative counterpart. So, natural phenomena are paired, and the negative aspect is as important and 'positive' as that of the positive. Kant gives examples such as the ship under sail that is not responding to wind, because there is a water current working against the wind. Kant's model of the strong negative is a good way of trying to break the hegemony of Aristotle's law of the excluded middle, but Ricœur concluded that the way the current cancels out the wind leaves us with a homeostatic model with zero, (which is what Kant wanted to argue) and this cannot help Ricœur's concern with nothingness: is it zero, is it nothing, is it a vacuum or a way to God? There is even more at stake, as Kant insisted upon the ultimate incomprehensibility of causality in order to show that such positive–negative relationships exist but are beyond our understanding; for example, between the ideal and the real, between concept and being, and this will be a major focus later in his first Critique where he uses the *noumenon* as a vehicle, a carrier, a vector of the negative that is a way of explaining our conceptual limits. For now we need to work through Kant's model: so a negative magnitude is in fact a positive force and is only 'negative' by virtue of opposition to another force:

> Negative magnitudes are not negations of magnitudes, as the similarity of the expressions has suggested, but something truly positive in itself, albeit something opposed to the positive magnitude. And thus negative attraction is not rest, as Crusius supposed, but genuine repulsion.[9]

While some of Kant's examples seem to be more to do with his response to Kästner (for whom the negative was less than nothing) and his interaction with Leibniz than with his personal philosophical development, it must have been very useful, almost liberating, to have the positivity aspect of thought emphasized by physical examples, and Newton's work influenced Kant in the *Critique of Pure Reason*, by emphasizing the laws of physicality that bind us to the physical, phenomenal world; Kant was attracted to the idea that with a real power like electricity, negative is better thought of as another positive, that is another creative force, and only negative (limiting) when in relation to an opposing magnitude; this can be seen in the mathematical procedure of subtracting. Instead of thinking along the lines of a vacuum as negative (privation) and compressed air as positive (excess), Kant proposes that positive and negative impulses in physics and particularly electricity are of equal value and importance and that in this dualism, one should not be seen as the lack of the other. Kant did not refer to Symmer (nor did he seek to challenge Benjamin Franklin, although he was presumably aware of his work), but he did refer to Aepinus, who in the same year as Symmer (1759), wrote about electricity in a similar way to Symmer and impressed Kant into extrapolating to other natural occurrences:

> It seems that a rise in temperature cannot occur in one region of the atmosphere without producing the effect, so to speak, of a negative pole in some other region, that is to say, coldness.[10]

We shall see how this homoeostatic conjecturing will fatally weaken Kant's model, in Ricœur's opinion, yet it played a significant role in Kant's pre-critical phase and remained with him in fact, and he developed an additional model of negation as limit.[11]

In this early flurry of writing activity, 'Negative Magnitudes' shows us Kant dealing with an issue that was of major importance at that time; the relative potency of mathematical and philosophical knowledge, a contest of faculties that mathematics was generally thought to win. He later championed the rights of philosophy to count as a rigorous science alongside mathematics, even though he drew a sharp distinction between the two, philosophy proceeding from concepts, and mathematics creating concepts. We could argue that these electrical patterns are simply metaphors to help Kant to deal with epistemological issues, and this may be so, yet we can also consider that they simply trapped him further in dualist thinking. Kant was attempting to show that mathematicians and philosophers think similarly:

> The motive force of a body in one direction and an equal tendency of the same body in the opposite direction do not contradict each other; as predicates, they are simultaneously possible in one body.[12]

Unlike French scholars, English-speaking readers have only had access to a good and consistent modern translation of these early Kant essays, which include 'Negative Magnitudes', since 1992. In the first of five lectures, Ricœur praised Kempf for his introduction to the French translation and for the translation itself of 'Negative Magnitudes'.[13] In the Ricœur archives, there are the first five lectures of a course on Kant and negation, which Ricœur placed in folder 5 of his five-part folder collection on *La Négation*, possibly with a view to ending his negation work on a Kantian note, with Kant as part of the solution to the enigma of negation. These seem to date from his time at Nanterre (late 1960s and early 1970s). Indeed, while planning his lectures on negation and subjectivity in 1969–70, to teach with Mme Granier,[14] Ricœur considers that a final section should rightfully be called *Towards an ontology of finitude; Kant and the notion of limit.*[15]

In his own work, Ricœur discusses negation most specifically in three courses: first in his course of lectures from 1957 to 1963 (Strasbourg and then Sorbonne) called *Le Fini; La Négation dans la Philosophie Moderne*, then in his course of 1959 called *La Négation*, a variation of which with much more emphasis on language he gave in 1968 at Nanterre, for which the archive holds a copy of one student's notes (Guy Basset) and also in this lecture course on *Kant et la négation*, the focus of this chapter. This latter is the first and possibly the last occasion on which he works through his understanding of Kant and the negative explicitly. We will see later that Kant cannot provide a full long-term answer for Ricœur, although his work provides lifelong guidance for him.

It is worth summarizing some of Ricœur's main early published work on Kant, but this may not make it quite clear why Ricœur became interested in 'Negative Magnitudes', as the negation work remained unpublished and 'off piste'. I hope to show later in this chapter that Ricœur was able to chart a progression from Kant's 'Negative Magnitudes' to the First *Critique* in which Kant, having rather flaunted his sparklingly positive model of the negative, progressively conceals it in his first *Critique* in places where it becomes very hard to find. Gradually, by these seemingly obscure means the negative comes to fulfil a valuable heuristic function of indicating limits to our thought, while nevertheless not being able to free itself of binary movement.

Early published Ricœur on Kant

In *Freedom and Nature*,[16] 1950, Ricœur's first major text, he hoped to show how defeat by dualism gives way to a victory over dualism: he locates what he believes is a double movement within Plato, Descartes and Kant – there is little of Hegel or Kant at this stage. The unity of the voluntary and the involuntary is seen as a limiting idea, a way of thinking about the limits to our desires that are set by our bodies, our beliefs and our potential for thought. In *Freedom and Nature*, this is demonstrated in the relationship between willing and desiring. This nascent dualism begins to emerge as soon as I see my body as the 'pole of resistance' at which point it becomes 'construed as an objective being'. Thus develops a dualism that progressively resists co-operation with the mind in a way that permits cause and effect of the sort we expect: I desire, I attempt to achieve, I succeed or I fail. Thus is introduced into the self a 'specific negativity'.[17] Necessity is affective and therefore also wounding: 'I am not at home in my own nature'. Ricœur shows us his 'concrete dialectic', in which 'the voluntary life is a debate with the body' and he calls on Kant to help turn what can become a distressing split between mind and body into a 'motivated, incarnate, contingent freedom'[18] by some limiting regulative ideas for unifying 'any field of inquiry whatever'. In *Freedom and Nature*, Ricœur did not yet connect the negative to Kant's handling of desire, he simply explores available solutions to many problems related to emotion, desire and reason, from Janet and James and

Sartre's discussion of them in his book *Sketch for a theory of the Emotions* and Hegel's understanding of 'negative labour' in which Hegel recognized an escape from consciousness.[19] We see here the early preoccupation with Hegel's dialectic and the place of negation within it, which at that time Ricœur saw in terms of desire, habit and emotion:

> Human beings aspire to this quality of habit and emotion which makes the body both retention and, if it were possible, spontaneous expansion of freedom itself. This ultimate synthesis is the unattainable limit, the mythical terminus of the voluntary and the involuntary from which the negative cannot be eliminated[20]

In *Fallible Man*, (1960/65),[21] his second major text, he identifies this desire that separates the mind and body as *lack*, a negative impulse: desire wants change and change has long been an area of contention, denied by Parmenides and celebrated by Heraclitus. This is an intensely Kantian text, in which Ricœur shows how Man is suspended between a pole of infinitude (desire) and a pole of finitude (actuality) and the negative is still seen as aversive, with only a Kierkegaardian suggestion of evil as 'an upheaval, a leap, a positing'.[22] Ricœur used the geological image of a fissure, a fault line, an image that is contained within the French word 'la faille': this fissure represents error and is the rift, the gulf between who we would like to be and who we are, the actions we would like to carry out and the ones we actually achieve and our inability to think beyond our own personal point of view and perceptual responses. In *Fallible Man*, Ricœur warns us that he has taken liberties with Kant's view of respect as relating to the law, by 'putting respect and person in a direct relation of intentionality' and hoping thereby to show that he sees a resemblance between Kant's view of respect and of the transcendental idealism.[23] Transcendental idealism, seen in the imagination, is Kant's belief that perceptions are based upon subjective decisions by us and so do not present the real objects in themselves. Similarly to the way in which understanding and receptivity (poles apart) come together in the transcendental imagination, so do the person as fallible and as ethical come together in the concept of respect. Here is an early phenomenological experimentation by Ricœur with Kant's treatment of fallibility, describing the impossibility of eliminating the negative from the attempt to unite the voluntary and the involuntary in one's own body, through the laws exercised by the mind.[24] Ricœur will later decide to go beyond Kant with Hegel's version of dialectic, in order to demonstrate Kant's potential.

In *Symbolism of Evil* (1960/1967), his third major text, Ricœur had to accept that phenomenology will not explain sin and guilt because of what he saw later as phenomenology's unwillingness to deal with the negative. He was also still struggling to find a way out of the Sartrean influenced existentialist discourse that, to him, seemed to make human guilt seem finite and beyond forgiveness and to make finitude, in its turn, inextricably bound up with the sadness and despair of guilt. This form of negative reflection was one of the motivating impulses that led him to start his lecturing on negation in the 1950s, and we can see from 1957 how he is already beginning to wriggle out from under the weight of Hegel:

> The 'sense of the negative' of which Hegel took possession on behalf of philosophy (and to which . . . Husserl lost the key), re-emerges in contemporary philosophy with Sartre. This dialectical sense is enriched along the way with the Kierkegaardian and Marxian themes of anxiety and conflict.[25]

In *Symbolism of Evil*,[26] he wanted to investigate how these themes are related to the metaphors of evil and demonstrated how difficult evil is to explain except by symbolism (the fall, the stain, the deviation from the path) and yet also clearly positive, in a Kierkegaardian way, as already explored tentatively in *Fallible Man*. As we saw, Kant recommends this approach in 'Negative Magnitudes', which Ricœur knew as a student, but he did not activate his knowledge until later. Ricœur was beginning to explore the possibility of turning the negative in us into a positive: so he was still caught within dualisms and polarities. Later, in *Freud and Philosophy*[27] and in *The Conflict of Interpretations*,[28] Ricœur saw the existential implications of Kant and reached back past Freud and Nietzsche to find the origins of our discontent and a possible solution being described by Kant, as does Monique David-Ménard in her praise of Kant's 'positive' negative as liberating; we have our worries about the nature of the individual human and our difficulties in recognizing and overcoming our suspicions of how we respond to the world, to ourselves and others, and she sees this as often negative in an unrelentingly depressing manner in psychoanalysis. She wishes to consider that we have desires, urges and fantasies that should not always be seen as pathological – she thereby recruits Kant to a use of negation that he would not have found attractive.

We have an understanding of our desired perfection that also indicates our fallibility. We are painfully aware of this mismatch between ideal and real: we can imagine that state of perfect harmony with the self and long for it.[29] I believe that one of Kant's great gifts to us is how to understand this possibility, indeed the inevitability of error in our attempts to understand the world, ourselves and others – perceptual, epistemological and moral – and this is crucial to the way Kant developed his understanding of negation and used it in different and evolving ways to theorize about our mistakes and to help us to be clearer in our heads about our state of mind, the way we live and, above all, the way we decide how to behave and manage our desire to understand. Yet then we will need to ask ourselves whether perceptual, epistemological and moral issues will suffice for living: do they include love, personality and family? Kant saw the human as included within moral structures such as laws, so his ethical, legalistic approach will not suffice in the end – laws cannot resolve all these problems. Love and justice in impossible tension will be the only solution for Ricœur. He will argue that the law tends to be blind, and therefore there are occasions in which only by disrespecting the law can we actually care for people.[30] Yet in 'Negative Magnitudes' Kant provided a refreshing challenge to old, mainly Aristotelian thinking on negation as contradiction.

Ricœur's lectures on *Kant et la négation:* 'Negative Magnitudes' and the *Critique of Pure Reason*

There are five extant unpublished lectures by Ricœur on this early Kant essay on 'Negative Magnitudes' – Ricœur probably delivered these lectures at Nanterre in the late 1960s to early 1970s, judging by handwriting and paper.

Ricœur devoted most of the five lectures to discussing Kant's *Critique of Pure Reason*, developing an argument that finds no real continuity in the idea of the negative from 'Negative Magnitudes' to the first Critique, while at the same time acknowledging the importance of the earlier paper because it freed Kant to an extent from old models of negating negation. First, Ricœur set the scene as an attempt to mediate between and possibly combine a philosophy of limits and a philosophy of mediation, and suggested that it might be possible to combine Kant's philosophy of limits with Hegel's dialectic.[31] He cited Kant: 'limitation is nothing other than reality combined with negation'.[32] However when he considered the early stage of Kant's relationship with the negative in 'Negative Magnitudes', Ricœur noticed a problem for a transcendental logic such as Kant's: when Kant wished to get rid of logic, at the same time, without meaning to, he also rendered the concept of reality vulnerable to challenge, because the historical and philosophical reality he was aware of was inextricably linked to Aristotelian logic and is weakened when logic is challenged:

We do not know what real means, when real is dissociated from Logic[33]

In Lecture Two ('The category of negation in the Critique'), Ricœur observed the change of status for negation from being centre stage in Kant's early essay 'Attempt to introduce the concept of Negative Magnitudes into Philosophy' (1763) to its occluded status in Kant's first critique, *Critique of Pure Reason* (1781). Ricœur showed the regression of Kant's negative from being one of two, vitally hinged with the positive (in 'Negative Magnitudes') to being one among four and then merely one category among 12 in *The Critique of Pure Reason*. This new status gives negation in fact a more potent position and will allow Kant to insert negation deeper into his model of our thought processes:

> The regression of negation in the constitution of phenomenal reality is the counterpart of the shift of negation towards a much more fundamental function, that of the limit: this function will no longer be the function of a category, but will rather determine the signification itself of phenomenality in all its generality.[34]

Ricœur showed how Kant appreciated the possibilities of the triadic sequence that he developed in preparation for this deeper insertion of the negative into our thinking ('affirmative, negating, infinite' and then 'reality, negation and limitation') but did not develop it into a Hegelian-type dialectical form:

> Kant realised its intellectual fecundity but without reaching the conclusion that would incline him towards Hegel's Logic, that negation is not a particular category but rather the constitution of every triad.[35]

So, Kant has discovered that the negative is the condition of thought and common to all three of his triads. Negation is caught in the middle: it follows affirmation and reality and precedes the infinite and, alternatively, the limiting, so Kant saw the value of three categories in interrelationship with one another. However, he did not use the triad formation to follow a Hegelian dialectic but undertook a different movement instead. This movement is an inner movement, one that draws the limits of our knowledge from the inside: negation shows us what we cannot know, the limitrophal nature of being near to understanding, nourished by it but never fully of it.

In this philosophy of limits, Kant is actually using two forms of negation; Ricœur abandons the binary one of Kant's 'Negative Magnitudes', and enjoys the negation embedded in both the idea and the process of the *noumenon*. Thus, Ricœur showed how with this noumenal negation Kant is able to *promote* negation through this apparent demotion of negation by incorporating it into the very substance of human thought. Kant's antinomies are a model of the negative, and Ricœur will show how he goes even further by drawing the negative deep into the structure of how we think, with the *noumenon* which is the act both of not knowing and also being aware of it. The apparent demotion of negation was an illusion! This is part of what Ricœur was looking for in his 1958 lectures on negation as we saw in Chapter 2 – a sense in which the negative is at the very core of our being. Yet we will see that, in my opinion, this will not quite be good enough for Ricœur and may be related to the first, binary idea of negation; negation as schema, a measurable state that can become nothing, as described in the section 'Anticipations of Perception' in the *Critique of Pure Reason,* where

Ricœur felt that all advantages gained by the approach to the negative in Kant's essay 'Negative Magnitudes' had been lost. This happens because Kant's model of the negative constructs a positive–negative balance in which the polarities are on a continuum from empty to full and when they cancel each other out as they should we are left with zero:

> Time's characteristic of being empty or filled does not allow a real opposition to appear, but only inexistence . . . that inexistence is not a negation as opposition of forces, it is rather a negation of disappearing[36]

In Lecture Three, Ricœur looks at Kant's assertion that space is the condition of the possibility of experience and can only be understood from a human perspective, not in any accurate sense. Kant deduces both the reduction of empiricism (we cannot believe what we see) and of the conceptual (we cannot think clearly about concepts): after this double negation, all that is left is the intuitive. Thus, being is negated in the space-time continuum precisely because we imagine space and time and therefore we cannot inhabit our own imaginings or space and time – except in our dreams, where according to Freud there is no time, no causality, no negative, but that is another story, that Ricœur followed with Freud.

In Lecture Four of this *Kant and negation* series, Ricœur discussed how we find what seems to be a different sort of negation in the second edition of Transcendental Analytic in the Critique of Pure Reason, and one that has become more elaborate since the first edition. Kant differentiates between two senses of the noumenal (that which can be thought, but not really known and understood). In the negative sense, it is an object that is not, and cannot be, grasped by the only intuition that we can have, that is, sensible intuition. In this sense, the concept of the noumenal is useful, because it points to those objects the knowledge of which we must accept is not within our grasp. A positive sense would be to take it to be an object that could be intuited by some sort of intellectual intuition; but because such intuition is not at our disposal, such active, positive sense is merely illusory; Kant will dedicate the whole 'Transcendental Dialectic' to dissolving the illusions that reason necessarily creates, but that must be unmasked, if we are to think in a sound manner. This second form of negative of a transcendental sort is the work of speculative thought; the 'limitation of the pretensions of the sensibility' is no longer merely a negative limit, but becomes also a beneficial constraint. To imagine something that does not exist is a creative and therefore positive impulse that enables us to develop new thought, as long as we *understand* that we are imagining things that do not exist. Perhaps we cannot really conceptualize this, but we must accept, if we think like Kant, that the noumenal is a positive feature precisely *because* it is a negative restriction.

Limit, illusion, antinomy

In the fifth lecture of the *Kant and Negation* series, called *Limit, illusion, antinomy*,[37] Ricœur asserted that Kant had incorporated negation into his model of reason and had given negation three forms: *paralogism* within rational psychology, *antinomy* within rational cosmology and the 'ontic realisation of the transcendental *ideal* in the case of rational theology'. Having lectured to students using several different negation narratives in the 1950s and early 60s about a philosophy of negation that contained very little reference to Kant, Ricœur was now discussing a philosophy of Kantian limits, in which he believed that Kantian negation is operating more to provide evidence than to stand in judgement.[38, 39] This new model requires the antithetical contradiction of reason, which must be overcome. Kant is clear that negation has a task to undertake in demonstrating the fictions of reason (paralogism, antinomy and ideal).

Ricœur believed that negation is developing into the guardian of the critical function as a doubled negative at the heart of the *Critique of Pure Reason*: with regard to the empirical, we cannot believe what we see and with regard to the conceptual, we are prevented by the antinomies of time and space from thinking accurately. So, if we use this understanding of the role of the negative, it can help us to think more clearly, negation acting as a guardian that sets limits to our thought while not stopping us from speculating about possibilities. Ricœur saw this more clearly in the Transcendental Analytic (where Kant gives intellectual definitions of objects) than in the Transcendental Aesthetic, which is more pre-phenomenal, in that it defines the conditions of possibility of every phenomenon, that is, their positing in time and space. He focused upon this in the fifth lecture when he asked where this negative impulse is actually to be found; it may be in the critical question itself that asks what we are looking at, perceiving or seeking to understand:

> We have seen in the Analytic that the limit oscillates between a purely negative sense (restriction of the pretension of sensibility of extending beyond the phenomenon) and a positive sense (what understanding would see if it were intuitive) . . . Restriction and opening up of a horizon in a not objectifying sense. The whole of the Kantian philosophy of negation is in suspense in this oscillation.[40]

The final section of Lecture 5 has a faintly Heideggerean tone; Ricœur tells us (without referencing a specific text) the problems that he saw with Heidegger's interpretation of Kant. Ricœur's understanding of Kant contrasts with Heidegger's understanding of Kant, as Heidegger proposed that space and time in themselves constitute some sort of ontological disclosure of Being. They would be the only way in which a finite being can have a transcendent relation, a relation to objects. But if one follows Heidegger's ontological reading, Ricœur believed it would completely subvert Kant's intentions in writing the *Critique of Pure Reason*, because it would entail a radical ontology of finitude that overemphasizes the role of the Aesthetic over and against all the other sections of the first *Critique*. As Ricœur puts it:

> This amounts to decapitating the Analogy, Dialectic and folding all the Critique into the Aesthetic.[41]

Connections between Negative Magnitudes and First Critique

Ricœur saw discontinuity between the negation of 'Negative Magnitudes' and that of *Critique of Pure Reason*. The Italian Kant scholar Marco Giovanelli sees it differently in his study *Reality and Negation*.[42] He sees continuity between the notion of real opposition from Kant's 'Negative Magnitude' essay of 1763 and the category of negation in the *Critique of Pure Reason*. In both, for Giovanelli, there is a quantitative dimension: he sees negation as the 'quantity of quality' and he has decided to read 'Negative Magnitudes' as if through the 'Anticipations of Perception' of the *Critique of Pure Reason*. Ricœur took a different view; he saw a break in Kant's thinking between 'Negative Magnitudes' and the *Critique of Pure Reason*, and did not see negation as quantitative. He believed that real opposition as a form of the negative loses itself as soon as it is seen in quantitative terms, because it becomes nothing, zero, and 0.

What we gained in the positive approach towards negation in 'Negative Magnitudes' is (according to Ricœur) lost in *The Critique of Pure Reason* because Kant still thinks in terms of the measurement he used in 'Negative Magnitudes' (more or less and zero), and thus we lose the possibility of real opposition between phenomena, and end up with the possibility of nothing again, inexistence. This seemed clear to Ricœur in the section 'Anticipations of Perception' of the *Critique of Pure Reason* where Kant argues that intensive and extensive perceptions are sensation that is felt but immeasurable (intensive quality) and sensation that can be calibrated (extensive quantity), respectively. Ricœur saw the Kantian development of negation as being a 'philosophy of limits' shown in sketch form in Kant's assertion that we can never see nothingness in the world and that the principle of perception that Kant puts forward will guard us against false inferences.[43] This guarding against false inferences takes the form of accepting the Kantian model in its proposition that it is possible to have intensive sensation (felt but immeasurable), like my desire for a Weetabix in the middle of the night, and extensive sensation (calibrated quantity), like my ability to measure how much milk will make the Weetabix crisply delicious rather than hopelessly soggy, or the latter depending on my mood. Although Kant does not comment on the nature of that principle, he is referring to the critique of reason as the power that will make it possible for us to differentiate between truth and illusion. I do not need that Weetabix but I desire it.

Kant, desire and negation within a philosophy of limits

Kant's philosophy is based on a strict discipline. He draws sharp distinctions between our faculties, such as sensibility, understanding and reason. He argues forcefully for the impossibility of synthetic *a priori* judgements in philosophy and tries to show how reason must be limited if we are to be set free from the chains of illusion. Critical philosophy, even though it wanted to have a practical import, was nonetheless very much an epistemological procedure, and it was happy to remain that way. Yet for later thinkers this inability was not accepted so stoically; the characters in Sartre's novels produce a poignancy to this existential struggle that is very much more than an epistemological issue: formulaic and didactically motivated they may be, yet they speak for us perhaps when they fail to be able to enjoy a situation or an emotion, and are painfully aware of that failure, yet unable to conceptualize where their ignorance lies. Ricœur identified in *Fallible Man* the desire we have to *know*, to use reason, to perceive what we wish to and to exercise some strange sort of ownership over what we perceive by the power of our will. The ground on which we stand has shifted – away from Kant's desire to help us solve the great intellectual problems to Sartre's desire to help us to find a reason for living, so we are grieving for a different loss from Kant's loss – but this is crucially important too. Sartre describes and fears unbounded freedom, unlimited space in which to moan and feel lost; form and content become confused and jumbled up; desire and disgust become interchangeable and indistinguishable one for the other and affirmation of self becomes untenable under the feared gaze of the other. Ricœur describes how 'existential negation is a negation of this affirmation'.[44] Iris Murdoch's character Jake at the end of her 1954 novel *Under the Net*, which is a direct response to Sartre's novel *Nausea*, is excited by the profusion of life and his desire to *know more* buoys him up, whereas this possibility has the opposite effect on Roquentin, Sartre's anti-hero in *Nausea*.[45]

Kant's version of the existential revolves around a person who would see negation as just one category among 12; however, negation is also depicted as being the condition of possibility of a synthesizing movement: *a priori* synthetic thought allows us to use negation to decide what something is not, yet Roquentin felt overwhelmed by this possibility – maybe Kant had not accounted for this existentialist fear and Kierkegaardian despair, induced by total freedom, the conviction that there are no limits, which was Sartre's challenge to us. Yet, as we saw above, Ricœur detected a gradual movement in Kant towards a sense of limits, incorporating negation within the very substance of phenomenal life and thus edging Western thought unintentionally towards negation as existential anxiety.

Negation was becoming more than a simple category; even though it is a category, it becomes the most important of them all, to the extent that it is this category that draws the boundaries to the whole philosophical system, to what we can know and, ultimately, to reality. Roquentin needed to read Kant's first Critique. We need a limit to our desire for knowledge; this epistemological search requires containment as we will otherwise believe wrongly that reason can grasp any object whatsoever and maybe even Totality, as in Hegel. We will still use negation to see what things are *not*, in order to see what they *are*, but as negation becomes a guardian of the critical function, we will also use Kant's ideas to formulate the questions that will allow us to search better for meaning.[46]

It is possible that negation was a more important part of all this for Ricœur than it was for Kant, as we see in the following word switch: in these five lectures Ricœur usually keeps closely to Kant's original wording in Kempf's French translation of 'Negative Magnitudes' but Ricœur replaces 'Transcendental critique' with 'negation' and writes in his fifth lecture that the permanence of such mistakes as those perceptual and cognitive errors that Kant describes are a demonstration of why negation is 'permanent and not circumstantial'.[47] This comes from the Transcendental Dialectic where Kant differentiates between logical illusion and transcendental illusion; the former arising when we misuse logical rules and structures, the latter arising when we are deceived by natural illusions that are impossible to detect, such as the illusion Kant evokes, that we believe the ocean at the horizon is higher than the ocean nearby. Here, Kant shows therefore how:

> Transcendental illusion . . . does not cease even after it has been detected and its invalidity clearly revealed by transcendental criticism.[48]

The *noumenon* as limit vector

When in the second edition of the *Critique of Pure Reason* Kant explains that there is a positive and a negative side to critique, in fact he means that it is the same characteristic of critique that is both positive and negative, and it is positive *because* of its negative characteristics. These 'negative characteristics' should be seen as a counterbalance to the positive, not as a force to be rejected. The negative aspect is the limit imposed by boundaries laid down to restrict the free play of our reason; here, Kant is also sketching out the device that he developed later of identifying two apparently opposing phenomena, demonstrating that they seem to be incompatible and then creating some sort of connection between the two by suggesting deeper structures that facilitate agreement while also making understanding impossible. He clarifies this in *Critique of Pure Reason* where he shows how the negative is an integral part of everything, by arguing for the existence of a transcendental substratum to all our reasoning:

> which contains as it were the entire storehouse of material from which all possible predicates of things can be taken. . . All true negations are then nothing but limits, which they could not be called unless they were grounded in the infinite, the All.[49]

In the Transcendental Analytic, Kant argued that the *noumenon*, the idea of a possible concept, functions as a limit. The *noumenon* is where the negative has burrowed its way inside, to be a temperer of our faulty search for knowledge:

> If by a *noumenon* we understand a thing in so far as it is *not* an object of our sensible intuition, because we abstract from the manner of our intuition of it, then this is a *noumenon* in the negative sense. But if we understand by that an object of a *non-sensible* intuition, then we assume a special kind of intuition, namely intellectual intuition, which, however, is not our own, and the possibility of which we *cannot* understand, and this would be the *noumenon* in a positive sense.[50]

Kant uses negative terms in language, both syntactical, like 'not' and nominal, like 'illusion'. Negation thereby represents illusion and antinomy and I suggest that precisely because Kant designates them as 'negative' phenomena, he can argue that negation becomes necessary and productive for a philosophy of limits, yet he gives few examples, except the fact that the horizon of the ocean seems higher than the water on the beach. I note that the negative is still there, but Kant has moved it from the subject ('not an object') to the predicate ('object of a non-sensible intuition') and the predicate becomes indissolubly bound with the action of our desire to know. So here the verb (in this case a verbal noun – 'non-sensible intuition') retains some of the potency that Ricœur ascribed to the verb in *Fallible Man*,[51] where phenomenology breaks down, incapable of allowing me to say what it is that I see, partly because Husserl's phenomenology finds the negative unbearable (saying what I don't see in order to describe what I do see). It is unbearable because use of the negative moves us towards categories (this is an ocelot not a lion) and even hierarchies of things (this is a species not a genus) as with Aristotle, and Husserl wants to focus on the essence of the thing, not its comparators. Unlike in Aristotle, where the predicate is the source of a need to progressively cancel out the features of a subject that are not core to it, until the bare object is left, Kant on the other hand celebrated the predicate as a sort of free radical – but only because he could limit it with the negative law in the *noumenon*, sign of our ultimate inability to know anything properly!

Kant makes it very clear that we will remain neighbours to knowledge at best, limitrophal, we will never attain true unity with whatever it is that matters, by which he means accurate understanding of the natural world and the idea of God and the discrepancy between the two: primary affirmation must teeter on the edge of determining who we are and knowing that we can never be quite sure. Thus, we – the subject, the agent – will never be in perfect alignment with our own predicate even though we can use language to describe ourselves: I am never going to attain true 'standpointless' thinking, philosophy pure and without an absolute. It is difficult to find Kant satisfying, now that we have Freud, Marx and Nietzsche with the unconscious mind that we cannot know properly and that enables a false consciousness to determine our concealment, sublimation or repression of our desires – as well as some fulfilment of desire. Indeed later Ricœur found them indispensable, yet also, in a different way from Kant, inadequate. Kant does not qualify to be a master of suspicion because he ascribes our errors in perception and understanding to self-deception of a sort that relates to powers of reasoning that require humility about their own limitations, rather than self-deception that relates to sex, money or power, like these three musketeers of doubt and the unconscious mind.

To return to Kant, Ricœur pointed out that for Kant the *noumenon*, by showing us the conjectural nature of our perception and the possibility of using concepts and categories to identify an object in reality, has two sides. . . . *Noumenon*, confusingly, has an ostensibly positive, yet actually useless side, which gives us the impression that we can identify objects and use concepts and categories – this seems a positive approach but is in fact useless as it allows us to pursue thoughts based on antinomies, false assumptions that we do not recognize as false.[52] Kant analysed antinomies as being dogmatic polarities that we use as a basis for reasoning, without understanding that they cannot be resolved by any other method than critical philosophy. In the antinomy about space and time, Kant asserts that we believe them to be properties of real objects and that this is both unproven and unprovable. If we can become aware that our thought processes are in fact severely limited, not only in preventing us from such thoughts, but also in preventing us from understanding that we do not understand, then we can suggest to ourselves that we are deploying noumenal thought.

The path of doubt is indicated by the *noumenon* as a limit, and the *noumenon* is the path, the vector of this way of thinking in and through doubt as limit. That is all that we have as possible pursuit of truth and it is imperfect, yet Kant is here making huge demands upon the power of our imagination, which he does not try to redress until the third critique, by which time his preoccupations are more aesthetic than moral. Kant announces the following:

> Now in this way our understanding acquires a negative expansion, i.e., it is not limited by sensibility, but rather limits itself by calling things in themselves (not considered as appearances) *noumena*.[53]

Yet in spite of all this doubt about perception and categorization and ordering of our world, Kant robustly refutes Descartes' fundamental doubt that we can believe in anything in the world around us and his failure to resolve the bad use of the will that he saw coming from human weakness, default in being and in understanding. Ricœur elaborated this unresolved difficulty with Descartes at the end of *Fallible Man* – we have noted that discussion of negation is an issue to which Ricœur sought resolution, as it forms part of the concluding sections of these three texts: *Freedom and Nature*, *Fallible Man* and *History and Truth*.[54] Kant, in a challenge to Descartes, asserts the impossibility of understanding anything inside our own heads if we do not have the outside world as stimulus and material.[55]

Ricœur was seeking a way to break the blockade of the negative idea of nothingness in order to release the power of affirmation, a more optimistic version of Spinoza's effort to exist, as he discusses it in *Fallible Man*.[56]

This Kantian negation work emerges in Ricœur's *Fallible Man*, where he elaborates further upon this sadness and the flaw in my personality that makes it impossible that I can live fully according to my desires and values. He describes Spinoza's sadness and Kant's third category of quality (limitation) as both demonstrating the limiting and finitude of human life. However, we see in *Fallible Man* that Ricœur had not yet made the transformation that he made in the *Kant and Negation* lectures in which he analysed the rich fecundity of Kant's negative in the first *Critique*. Kant used the negative to demonstrate that we are under illusion at the heart of a dynamic contradiction of thesis by antithesis and vice versa. This sounds very Hegelian, and indeed Ricœur started the five lectures by conjuring up the possibility of combining Kant's philosophy of limits and Hegel's dialectical being.[57] So, Ricœur was using this Hegelian structure to analyse Kant's limits and postulate a different philosophy from Hegel's Absolute Knowledge. Here, Ricœur argues for limits to knowledge – limits that give us the perceptual strength to realize our desire to understand more than we can, more than empirical evidence as in *phenomena* alone, to try and understand the things as they really are, the *noumena*, and all the time accepting illusion:

> Illusion springs from the antinomy itself, that is, from the pretention to exclude contradiction to the advantage of the thesis or the antithesis.[58]

In the first edition of the first *Critique*, Kant proposes that 'the concept of the *noumenon* is merely a boundary concept, in order to limit the pretension of sensibility, and therefore only of negative use'.[59] In the second edition, he has changed his mind, to seeing positive merits in this negative feature of the *noumenon* as a boundary concept, and I repeat the quote as it is important:

> If by a *noumenon* we understand a thing insofar as it is not an object of our sensible intuition, because we abstract from the manner of our intuition of it, then this is a *noumenon* in the negative sense. But if we understand by that an object of a non-sensible intuition, then we assume a special kind of intuition, namely intellectual intuition, which, however, is not our own, and the possibility of which we cannot understand, and this would be the *noumenon* in a positive sense.[60]

This is a much more assertive statement about the power of noumenal thought to be negative and, in so being, to have positive potential, because in signalling our limits in a negative way, it clarifies our capacity to understand our limits and therefore potentially to address the limits to our knowledge to a certain extent.

Kant argues that intellectual intuition lies completely outside 'our faculty of cognition' and that we therefore cannot understand the pure form of anything as it would be given to us by the *noumenon*; yet this is what makes the negativity, that is, the impossibility of the *noumenon* into a positive feature, as it functions like a limiting device that shows us how restricted we are. Precisely by grasping this restriction we are set free to *try* and understand.

Ricœur saw the tension between freedom (will, desire and understanding) and nature (the world around us and our perception and understanding of it) as being insoluble. He saw Aristotle's attempt to resolve the problem as being dichotomous, Kant's as being antinomous and Hegel's as being dialectic.

For Ricœur, the only real solution to negation's victorious march is love; emotional, spiritual or physical or all three, love as a concept that is not integral to Kant's thinking except for love as respect, a form of love sublimated in duty. In Kantian terms, love and justice function as an antinomy – we know they are incompatible, yet they must work somehow if we are to survive as a species. This Ricœurian insistence upon love is of paramount importance for modern philosophy, particularly now when individual identity seems narcissistic and solitary in the world around us. Ricœur certainly found Kant both indispensable and also lacking in this regard, since Kant valued the human fundamentally as a subject, that is, a moral agent, belonging to a group, a 'practical and ethical totality of persons', and not, as we see ourselves now, as individuals with subconscious minds and friends and families. These are necessary yet not sufficient characteristics of a civilized person, who must also be understood to need to love, and whose love will create necessary disequilibrium. In his late essay 'Love and Justice', Ricœur points out the discrepancy between the power of love and the demands for morality.[61] This point is also made in a more succinct manner in *Figuring the Sacred*:

> Thanks to this kinship between the command 'love me!' and the song of praise, the commandment of love is revealed as being irreducible, in its ethical overtones, to the moral imperative, so legitimately equated by Kant to obligation, or duty, with reference to the recalcitrance of human inclinations.[62]

Kant seemed to want to free us from the illusion of desire for the One, for unity with the One, and one way he hoped to achieve this was by asserting the cognitive content of the negative impulse so that we have at least a binary opposition between positive and negative.

RESISTING NEGATIVE IMPLICATIONS OF KANT

I suggest that we can extrapolate from our failure to perceive accurately and our refusal to accept Kant's analysis can be seen in our often cavalier use of the terms negative and positive: we use the term negative especially loosely to reject a phenomenon that we do not understand, instead of accepting the limits to our perception and our understanding and being aware that we are often speculating when we use the term negative. Maybe this is one of the great failings of philosophy as well, the inability to deal with failure. We will see Ricœur using similar ideas in his dialectic, with perpetually open-ended issues and unsettling results. He accepted the need to fail to resolve issues satisfactorily and indeed sees this as a respectable philosophical position – yet it renders us intellectually humble and vulnerable to multiple stimuli and opinions. I will use Kafka to illustrate the danger of being overawed by Kant's interpretation of our lot, that is, that we will never fully understand. Kant does not tell us not to act, but Kafka shows that we could draw that conclusion in the face of a doorway, a possibility, an idea, an *arkhe* that appears closed to us. Such parables demonstrate the potency that Ricœur ascribed to narrative with its power to show us something so ridiculous that it could not happen like that.

Kafka and Kant before the law

In his parable-like short story 'Before the Law' (1919), Kafka tells of the man from the country who seeks the law and is not allowed to pass through the door by the doorkeeper.[63] In the style of a parable, the characters are types rather than real individuals, and the story is open to many interpretations, but, according to Ricœur's definition of a parable, it *requires* interpretation and has the potential to make us think more clearly. Such a story can fulfil the function of making us feel vulnerable, implying also our intellectual vulnerability because we do not really know what the story means. Derrida

(continued)

looks at 'Before the Law', in his eponymous essay, as manifesting the equivocal relation between signifier and signified and points out nicely the end of the story as mirrored closely in its content; the doorkeeper slams shut the door after revealing that the door had been there for that man only. I want to look at it existentially as a response to Ricœur's description of the world's ironic question: 'and you, what will you do?' Should we answer by taking Kant's conclusions as signal that we should not really try, because we cannot resolve the discrepancy between the way we understand things and the way they really are? Clearly, if I ask the fleas on the doorkeeper's coat for help, I am delusional, yet this is the state which is normal for humans, according to Kant, who is often seen as rather depressing in this respect. I would say that we must try. If the door is blocked, then we must try another way, but not leave it so long that we lose our sense of reality and perception and start asking the fleas for help. It would be worse to be told at the end of one's life that this was the door for me and me only and that it will now be shut, rather than to try and fail to achieve what I want to do. Ricœur himself did not write parables – as far as I know – but he analysed them, as in 'Biblical Hermeneutics', where he shows us the heuristics in the metaphorical structure of parables like the Prodigal Son (2 Cor: 5:17-21, The Wicked Husbandmen (Mark 12:1-12) and The Sower (Matt. 13:1-23). Nor did he write novels, like Murdoch, who used parables in her narratives. Ricœur needed other linguistic techniques for tempering Kant's indictment of our cognitive powers, and dialectic would prove invaluable.[64]

We can see here, from these five lectures on Kant and negation, how Ricœur made extensive use of Kant, partly for an attempted *deus ex machina* resolution of what he called, in *Fallible Man*, the 'victorious march of negation' from Hegel to Sartre. Although they are generally not heeded by academics and indexers alike, Ricœur set down many clear indications of his work on negation within his published work on Kant, which we can begin to see as being informed by his unpublished work.

There is clearly even, in Ricœur's mind, a need to use Hegel's dialectic in some fashion to temper Kant: in his 1975 paper 'Le lieu de la dialectique',[65] he pressed the point by arguing that Kant is locked inside insoluble dichotomies: the binary 'Negative Magnitudes' model lacks a third element. I want to go through the door to seek justice and I am forbidden to go through the door. I am trapped in this way by binary thinking that precludes any alternative, such as trying to find a different solution. He argued that Kant is trapped by dichotomies such as nature versus liberty, or theoretical reason versus practical reason and that these must be interpreted not by means of Hegel, but by a philosophy informed by Hegel. Who could do this I wonder – maybe Ricœur? He would insist on being supported by Hegel and Husserl, as well as Kant himself, as Ricœur was fastidious in remaining within the arguments of those he studied, in order to demonstrate internal inconsistencies. I believe that Aristotle, Kant and Hegel each and in combination provided Ricœur with magnificent yet flawed binary models for establishing a philosophy of the negative: the negation model most attractive to Ricœur is not theirs, it is Plotinus' model of nothingness as a powerful understanding of what I don't understand in order to love God. There is a Kantian antinomy here of course, but Kant was rather dry and rationalist. There is not a model like Plotinus in mainstream secular western philosophy – we can find it in the East but Ricœur did not look there. He had to develop his own structure for showing how close negation is to the essence of who we are, emotionally, spiritually and cognitively, and the only approach open to him was language itself.

In the next chapter, I will show how he wrote about integrating negative patterns into linguistic structures such as parable (like Kafka), metaphor, narrative and dialectic. He thereby offered us a model of action, of agency in living thought that avoids the 'bad' sort of nothingness; Sartrean fear, Kierkegaardian despair and Heideggerean death and yet he created a space that we can populate with our ideas and challenge our dichotomies, antinomies and dialectics in order to understand the world and ourselves as best we can through experiencing the unrelenting *noumenon* of not really knowing. Ricœur thereby offers an alternative to our dualistic, loose axiology whereby we attribute value to a phenomenon because we ascribe a negative to counterbalance it, like Aristotle's ascription to women of wet humors that make them weak and irrational compared with hot, dry men. This could even give us the humility to accept that we may be wrong, as Plato's Sophist argued, and have the courage to challenge our preconceptions about some of our favourite binaries.

CHAPTER SIX

Affirmative Negatives: Nietzsche, Sartre, Deleuze, Murdoch – and Plotinus

In the latter half of the twentieth century, there was a heady atmosphere of debate and discord among Parisian philosophers; yet Deleuze (1925–95) and Ricœur, almost exactly contemporary, did not feel drawn to each other; they were not-friends, they neither wrote nor lectured about each other although their paths must have crossed: both were lecturing at the Sorbonne in the late 1950s, Deleuze on Kant and Ricœur on negation among other topics. Despite this vacuum between them, François Dosse, in his biography of Deleuze and Guattari,[1] sees many similarities between Deleuze and Ricœur. Both Deleuze and Ricœur stood against philosophical tradition and accepted that it is impossible to resolve contradictions by totalization and synthesis. Both welcomed the non-philosophical and believed that problem-solving is the best way to think while also accepting that many problems can never be solved. Both preferred 'and' to 'but' and enjoyed tension between ideas and in-between places, as well as thinking about controversies that were in the public domain. Both attempted to reject Hegel, or rather, Ricœur accepted, perhaps more than Deleuze did, that it is probably impossible to do so. Both wrote extensively on Kant and were dissatisfied with Kant's formalism, yet Ricœur continued to use Kant. Both admired Bergson, although Ricœur less so, and it took Ricœur until his old age to use Bergson significantly in published work, namely in *Memory, History and Forgetting*. In addition, according to Dosse, both wanted to carry on living and distrusted death.

Nietzsche, Deleuze and Ricœur

In this chapter, I will look again at Sartre and the negative, this time through Iris Murdoch's writings and at Plotinus' significant influence upon Ricœur in his early writings. Metaphorical thinking was important for Plotinus and for Murdoch and became highly significant for Ricœur. First I wish to contextualize Deleuze's and Nietzsche's approach to the negative within Ricœur's thought. Deleuze rejected the idea of the negative as something that is simply bad and encourages fruitless dichotomies, and sought to replace it with an idea of difference that functions as a 'many-and' model. I propose that Ricœur, for his part, concluded that he could not meld the different models of negation into a philosophical model, and displaced the debate on the negative into language structures: dialectic, metaphor, parable, as well as the (short lived) hermeneutics of suspicion and a long lived model of attestation in which the negative is acknowledged as existing at the core of being. Both drew on Nietzsche in different ways. Nietzsche saw the negative as a subtraction, the slave taking the strength of the other. Nietzsche is an interesting hinge element of their non-encounter, not much explored by Ricœur, yet deeply admired by Deleuze.

There were other significant dissimilarities between Ricœur and Deleuze, which may help to explain their lack of contact with each other. Not only did they keep different company – Deleuze was close to Guattari and Foucault and saw himself as a man without religion, whereas he described Ricœur, accurately, as a Christian. In a broader sense, Dosse and Mongin wonder if Deleuze perhaps would see himself as expressing excess, whereas Ricœur saw himself as expressing debt.[2] For significant reasons that are of interest in the context of the negative, they differed on Nietzsche too, with Deleuze publishing much more on Nietzsche than Ricœur did. Ricœur, in his youth, saw Nietzsche as one of the fathers of negation, and although he retracted that, he also called Nietzsche (alongside Marx and Freud) a master or a teacher of suspicion. Deleuze led a very influential revival of Nietzsche and then moved away from Nietzsche's influence and Ricœur seemed to lose interest in Nietzsche after his book on Freud, although he returned to Nietzsche at various points.

Nietzsche was named briefly by Ricœur a father of negation, and for a short while he even posthumously had a son: Jean-Paul Sartre. Who is the mother of negation in this immaculate birth? Perhaps nihilism; poor child! In his essay 'Existential Phenomenology' (1957), Ricœur developed a similar picture to that in his 1958 lecture series at the Union Theological Seminary, called 'Anthropology and Religion in the philosophy of existence'.[3] He described the 'methodical disillusionment' that Nietzsche applies to discover the 'powerful and wily instinct for dissimulation at the centre of human existence', and although Ricœur was impressed with the genuine phenomenology that he saw in Nietzsche, he also saw how Nietzsche had in fact destroyed himself with the intensity and the pitiless analysis of 'the self by the self, a coming to awareness of the sense of the times and a recapitulation of Western history in its totality'.[4] Yet by the third volume of *Time and Narrative* (1985/88), Ricœur was writing more warmly of Nietzsche, arguing that he turned the idea of the historical present from negative to positive.[5] Sartre was never rehabilitated in this way, and remained an important irritant in Ricœur's exploration of the negative. First to Deleuze and Ricœur: Deleuze has a different relation, or rather non-relation with Ricœur from that of Sartre, as Ricœur did not write about Deleuze and the compliment was returned, yet Deleuze is a fascinating thinker, important in this debate because of his rejection of the negative. Deleuze also took on the challenge of attempting to decouple the negative from the positive, and draws not dissimilar conclusions from those of Ricœur about the vital importance of affirmation:

> The negative is the objective field of the false problem; the fetish in person . . . Practical struggle never proceeds by way of the negative but by way of difference and its power of affirmation.[6]

Deleuze's book *Difference and Repetition* (1968/1994)[7] is an important attempt to overturn classical and modern ideas of negation. For this reason, as well as Deleuze's importance and his impact on Nietzsche studies, it is valuable to consider his work, albeit only in part. I hope to show that there is a productive difference between Deleuze's idea of the negative as bad and counterproductive, related to Oedipality and hence very destructive and Ricœur's idea of the negative as potentially productive and arguably a core component in our identity as functioning humans. In many matters, although perhaps not negation, Ricœur and Deleuze shared many similar philosophical interests and worked in Paris at the same time, yet they kept themselves to different academic circles and had a sort of non-relationship (what Dosse calls a 'non-encounter' in his book on Gilles Deleuze and Felix Guattari[8]). There was very little and rather too late a reciprocity of sorts: in *Difference and Repetition*, Deleuze references Ricœur's broken cogito and belatedly in 2004 Ricœur paid tribute to Deleuze, by then dead for a decade, by saying in the *Cahiers L'Herne* that he was happy to be considered a lesser philosopher than Deleuze and Foucault. This sounds like a form of negation on the part of Ricœur.

In the late 1950s, Ricœur called Nietzsche one of the fathers of negation, with Hegel, Kierkegaard and Marx. I will show later how Ricœur seemed to lose interest in Nietzsche after writing his big book on Freud, until again finding him useful in *Time and Narrative*. Having said that, Ricœur commented in the 1980s that he felt the term masters of suspicion was inadequate, which merits another look back to Ricœur's work in the 1960s when he presented Nietzsche as a *maître du soupçon*; at that time, Ricœur paid tribute to Nietzsche by naming him as one of three *maîtres du soupçon*, Nietzsche, Marx and Freud, a term usually translated by 'masters of suspicion'. Of course, *maître* in French also means teacher – we would probably be better off calling them the teachers of suspicion, as they taught us to doubt ourselves.[9] As Ricœur explained, since Nietzsche, Freud and Marx it is impossible for us to think as we used to about power, sex and money, respectively. Each, in his own way, told us that we do not really understand the state that we call 'being ourselves, being conscious'; thus when we believe we are consciously thinking, we are deluded, this is a false consciousness that must be challenged, and that thereby challenges Cartesian dualism. They reopened the debate about Cartesian doubt by telling us that we do not really have any idea about how we find meaning, and all three sought to destroy false beliefs in order to initiate a new clarity and honesty. Whereas Descartes overcame our doubt about the accuracy of our consciousness by assuring us that we can be secure in our knowledge of things, Marx, Nietzsche and Freud told us that we cannot be sure about how we find meaning because we cannot trust our own conscious thoughts. So, according to Ricœur, Descartes reassures us, whereas Marx, Freud and Nietzsche deliberately make us nervous. Freud is the one who interested Ricœur most of the three, leading to Ricœur's book *Freud and philosophy* (1965/1970). Freud developed a theory of subconscious urges and mythical patterns that shows how far we may stray from Enlightenment ideals of rationality. Ricœur was not interested at this stage in Marx's theory of ideologies, alienation of labour and false consciousness. He was also less interested in Nietzsche's definition of genealogy as a kind of error whereby we distort our sources/history as we seek root meanings. Ricœur commented on the risk that we stereotype each of these three great thinkers within their own ideology, whereas in fact he saw them as seeking to extend the possibilities of consciousness, as long as we are prepared to tolerate uncertainty and disorientation.[10]

So, Ricœur saw how these three opened a new way of challenging our ideas, our beliefs and our understanding, by issuing a brutal challenge to our own personal thought processes. He found Nietzsche and Freud to be far closer to each other's thought than Nietzsche and Marx, or Marx and Freud. Their brilliance gave great opportunities to think anew and Ricœur took the opportunity he found in these matrices. However, he also felt that the triumvirate got rather carried away with their critique of religious belief, attacking not only corrupt religious practices (a useful challenge) but also by attacking faith itself (which for him was a different debate). Yet even here, their ideas provided him with great stimulus.

Nietzsche and Freud developed a radical new critique of religion, where society and culture play a pivotal role in reflecting guilt, fear and suppressed desires through religious frameworks. To challenge this we have to deploy suspicion, critical doubt and thinking that go beyond the British empiricists and the French positivists. Both Nietzsche and Freud (Nietzsche did it particularly well) killed off God the father figure; or rather Nietzsche showed us, with great relish, how we have done just that for ourselves even though we deny it. Ricœur welcomed the challenge to the parody of the Old Testament father figure who offers protection as long as he can also mete out punishment and demands obedience with no questions answered. Yet if this leads to a form of atheism, made possible by Nietzsche's proclaimed absence of guilt, then Ricœur found it wanting: he sought acceptance of guilt and the unmasking of false genealogies (as we see with Nietzsche and Foucault and Lyotard) and saw no reason why such criticality should automatically lead to atheism. Yet for Nietzsche religion *is* its social practice and he found its social practice to be hypocritical and false. In this, Ricœur believed that Nietzsche trapped himself into resenting the resentful: the concept of *ressentiment* first used by Kierkegaard and taken up by Nietzsche encapsulates the fears of the weak that they turn into prohibitions to restrict others, and is a term that has no real German equivalent for Nietzsche to use. Nietzsche criticized the weak ones who use religious power structures to create morals that conceal their weaknesses, yet Ricœur argues in *Critique and Conviction*, Chapter 4 on 'Politics and Totalitarianism', that Nietzsche became absorbed in the very *ressentiment* he attacks. Ricœur, as a committed Protestant, was fascinated to ask what sort of faith could be possible after Freud and Nietzsche and Marx have made such a strong and persuasive attack upon the ethics of organized religion.

Nietzsche was very much influenced by Schopenhauer, but in his first major text, *The Birth of Tragedy*, Nietzsche challenged what he saw as Schopenhauer's Buddhist-influenced negation of the will. There is an early trace of nihilist discussion in 1865–66 about Schopenhauer's Buddhism, and Nietzsche retained a connection between Buddhism and nihilism. Later, in *Ecce Homo*, Nietzsche saw aspects of *The Birth of Tragedy* that he wished to repudiate: 'it smells offensively Hegelian, and the cadaverous perfume of Schopenhauer sticks'.[11] Nietzsche's use of the term nihilism comes after he developed his ideas of the 'will to power' (1880) and the 'eternal return' a year later. In his correspondence with Russian thinkers at around that time, he used nihilism as coterminous with terms such as pessimism, decadence, radical critique. However, it was when Nietzsche started to explore the idea of the Superhuman in 1882 that he looked at nihilism in the context of superman who will overcome both Christians and nihilists. Nietzsche demanded very high standards of himself: in 'The wanderer and his shadow', he writes the aphorism *Positive and Negative* 249 '– This thinker needs nobody to refute him: for that he suffices himself'.[12] Ricœur argued in *Conflict of Interpretations* that nihilism has not achieved its endpoint of negating and destroying religion because it refutes rather than engages; it would be better to adopt atheism as a hinge between religion (organized faith) and faith (personal belief).

Deleuze on Nietzsche

In the 1960s, Deleuze led a significant revival of Nietzsche's thought in France, as charted by François Dosse.[13] In this Nietzsche resurgence Deleuze saw Nietzsche as embodying vitality, life affirmation, and being stridently anti-Hegelian and anti-dialectic. In 1962, Deleuze published his first book on Nietzsche, which was reviewed by Jean Wahl, who, as a sort of Hegelian himself, saw Nietzsche as not so far from Hegel. In 1965, Deleuze published his second text on Nietzsche, now to be found in his book *Pure Immanence* where he read Nietzsche as influenced by the pre-Socratics, seeing thinking and life as conjoined twins dynamically alive together.[14] In 1967, Deleuze and Foucault wrote an introduction to the French edition of Nietzsche's complete works. In 1972 at a conference at Cerisy la Salle, Deleuze presented a new view; he distanced himself from Foucault's masters of suspicion idea, which Ricœur had worked on a decade earlier and which included Nietzsche.[15] By now Deleuze saw Nietzsche as more radical and harder to assimilate into cultural frameworks than Freud(ianism) and Marx(ism), yet also as very witty and thereby also liberating.

THE CLASSROOM OF THE SLAVES

This case study from my past as a child psychologist suggests how Nietzsche's ideas can be used to interpret phenomena that seem harmless, even morally good and show them as otherwise: from the 1960s onwards, there was an exciting move in educational circles away from the deficit model (that the child is the source of its own ills) towards analysis of context in order to improve the learning environment (seeking goodness of fit between child and context). This was manifest in many educational programmes which often contained elements of behaviourism, positive reinforcement in particular, and social learning.

As the educational psychologist I was then (1980–94), I and my colleagues had, crudely speaking, two assumptions about pedagogy at our disposal; first that, according to Piaget, children of normal intelligence may learn from their mistakes and these mistakes can provide them and us with a window into their thought processes. The second assumption is that children with learning difficulties cannot learn from their mistakes, indeed making mistakes may have a negative effect on their capacity to learn, so it would be a good idea to reduce the likelihood of them making mistakes. Clearly, the very use of the term 'learning difficulties' begs many questions, yet notwithstanding that, many of us welcomed this educational approach, and use texts such as Ainscow and Tweddle's 1984 *Early Learning Skills Analysis* to plan structured behaviourist learning programmes;[16] we used it very enthusiastically for reducing the frustration of children with learning difficulties and we can see a version of it at its dramatic best in Weiss's play *Marat/Sade*, where adults with learning difficulties are successfully enabled to take dramatic roles in de Sade's play within a play; if mistakes serve no useful purpose, then errorless learning becomes the goal. Backward chaining became the rage, teaching a slow learner to master the steps of a process such as tying shoelaces by starting at the end of the process and gradually adding in more steps. Such approaches certainly helped teachers and carers to see the difficulties of such exercises as tying shoelaces, long since mastered and made automatic by the adults themselves.

Through the use of such approaches it was possible to make learning a more positive experience for children with learning difficulties.

Gradually, the idea of errorless learning became more attractive, no longer the territory of child psychologists and special school staff, and somehow made its way into the mainstream classroom, leeching its way into the water and the air of mainstream education – more and more highly structured learning was considered to be desirable and was intended to reduce negative effects of failure and increase enjoyment in learning: now we have children of normal ability learning like children with learning difficulties and the education system in Britain has created new generations of slow learners, incapable of independent thought and suffering greatly from the idea that they may have to learn something by using memory or willpower. Now the teacher must cut up the curriculum into bite-sized chunks and the child must be able to learn, to consume without choking on indigestible bits. It would now be unacceptable to argue that children should learn to fail and then make success out of that, and millions of British children are able to avoid learning a foreign language because it is 'too difficult'.[17] There are no worries, there is no thinking and we accept no negatives. Of course to an extent this is a caricature, but there is much truth in my position and I want to attempt an analysis of what is happening.

Why are we avoiding negatives? Why, even more to the point, have we created negative: positive poles that postulate happiness as free, unfettered and untroubled and the negative as the opposites of such a state? This may have to do with mature capitalism: Mustafa Mond in *Brave New World* instructed citizens that their duty is to consume and be happy; 'they get what they want and they never want what they can't get'. Maybe there is also a sense of bureaucratic control: slave teachers in harness to a pitiless system of education as bureaucracy, teachers being hounded to be totally in control of their pupils' learning, rather than the pupils taking shared responsibility, and the teacher is assessed on results. However, there may be deeper currents here that cannot be unearthed by looking at surface features of capitalism and bureaucracy; rather we need to apply philosophy to seek out the sources of these mechanisms.

Ricœur concluded that the negative must retain its potency and provide a vibrant counterpoise to the positive. He sought to demonstrate how contradiction can be the soul of presence, and to show what price we pay for that prize through our language. Ricœur's model of affirmation and attestation could perhaps offer me a more pragmatic, optimistic approach, and implore me to think positively, once I have identified the 'negative' features of the situation. More brutal arguments come from Nietzsche, with his imagery of the slave, the weak subtracting the energy that the other, the strong, possesses. This can certainly be seen in the deficit model, in which a child's potential is measured by what it cannot do rather than by what it can. The part of the slave then, oddly, seems to be played by the teacher, depriving the child of her/his potential raw energy to learn and make mistakes and benefit from them. Perhaps this slave teacher has been created in her/his turn by a system of performance-measuring bureaucrats, again weak and vicious in their need to emasculate the creative potential in many teachers. In this

(*continued*)

process by which the child learns the slave mentality of under functioning, is this a useful model for the negative? According to Deleuze – yes, this is exactly the way the negative works, as the nasty underbelly of the positive and it is to be rejected. But as a professional child psychologist, I failed to recognize it in time, thereby endorsing a form of education by my actions, which I did not understand fully to be so noxious and disempowering. Both Nietzsche and Deleuze would surely have railed against this, but I am not convinced that the alternative versions they offer would have helped: Nietzsche's idea of creativity is quite eccentric for the classroom and Deleuze's version of difference relies heavily on the negative as a bad force. Yet Deleuze has a lot to offer.

Difference and repetition

By 1965, in his last major text on Nietzsche, which has an ancient Greek flavouring, Gilles Deleuze is clear about his disapproval of negation.[18] In a very different approach from Ricœur's attempt to incorporate the negative impulse within our functioning, Deleuze ends up with a vision of the negative that would not appeal to Ricœur. For Deleuze, the negative is a harmful force. Limitation and opposition are the two components of negation as he sees it. Reactive forces are characterized by 'their opposition to what they are not, their tendency to limit the other: in them, negation comes first; through negation, they arrive at a semblance of affirmation'.[19] He asserts that history shows us how the reactive forces win, the power of No defeats the power of Yes, and reminds us of the three terms that Nietzsche uses to explain this phenomenon: the reactive forces and the will to negate pair up to create 'nihilism', which can also be called the triumph of the slaves. Three years later in 1968 Deleuze published *Difference and Repetition*, with his new approach to the negative.

Duns Scotus was a major influence on Deleuze, with his emphasis on the 'thisness' of things, the intensity and unity of the natural world. This combines with the anti-Platonist celebration of difference in Nietzsche, so that Deleuze can propose difference as the fecundity of life, and repetition as the repeating, as in nature, of similar yet different circumstances.[20]

One of Deleuze's major aims, certainly in the early phase of his work, up to and including *Difference and Repetition*, and before his long and intense friendship and collaboration with Guattari, was to override Hegel's dualist model of dialectics, which can be argued to have negation at its core, of course. One of the major problems that Deleuze experienced with Hegelian dialectic was its apparently infinite and possibly unattributable fecundity: does dialectic's energy come from a negative or a positive impulse? He would prefer to have emphasized the positive, which he defined as affirmative – yet here also we have definitions of possibly meaningless fecundity: what is affirmative and positive? He found Bergson invaluable in this undertaking, taking his tone also from Hyppolite, who contrasted Bergson with Hegel. As his philosophy of difference developed, Deleuze used Tarde and others too, all of whom saw nature in its infinitesimally separate, pullulating complexity as the definitive model for difference *and* as the most relevant context for arguing that difference is the key to understanding ourselves and our world.

What is difference? According to Deleuze, it is naturally and overwhelmingly positive, it is changing and it is non-dialectical. In fact these three characteristics will turn out to be complex: first, positivity is problematic to define if you exclude the negative, second, the idea of change is complicated by the way in which difference becomes a sort of substance, and finally, both Bergson and Deleuze made free use of dualisms, in order to argue their case. Yet for Deleuze the dualism cannot comprise negative and positive, as the negative is 'always derived and represented, never original or present'.[21] So, the dualism is comprised of two different features, difference and affirmation. Yet each must be defined as being not the other, so again we have a repetitive straining at definitions here about how to define negative – why must it be seen as 'bad'? What can we measure difference against? Is this merely a semantic nicety or is there a real problem with the negative? For Deleuze, difference is companionable rather than confrontational and affirmation must be the Nietzschean impulse that transforms negation from an adverse influence into a creative impulse – a rather Spinozist assertion of the vitalist, transformative power of human energy. This is all part of Deleuze's reworking of Nietzsche's idea of eternal return: instead of seeing it as the reoccurrence of mistakes and cyclical reception, he saw it as the victory of the strong over the weak, willing as creating strength.

Ricœur was much less interested in Nietzsche than Deleuze was, yet he made good use of Nietzsche in *Time and Narrative* in various ways. There is an affinity with Nietzsche in Ricœur's hostility to totalization and metanarratives, although Ricœur is wary of Nietzsche's genealogies, whereby the agents of power *inevitably* influence the representation of history. Ricœur puts more of a distance between himself and Nietzsche, by rejecting Nietzsche's recommendation of anarchy and disorder, with no attempt to create order. Ricœur sees this as a direct threat to the possibility of narrative creating order, sequence and even the impossibility of such order and sequence in a form of honesty that he does not see in Nietzsche.

Deleuze on difference and repetition

Ricœur and Deleuze continued to maintain near complete silence about each other. Whereas Ricœur was working towards an affirmative negative, Deleuze construed the negative as debilitating, yet he retained a binary model. I argue that this was necessary for him because he could not argue for the positive against the negative nor create 'difference' without a negative force being present. This need for a counterweight – the maligned negative –contradicts his model of difference as being a range of alternatives and not dualistic: Deleuze argues, on his own and Bergson's behalf, that 'Whatever is composite must be divided into two tendencies'.[22] Here, we see how difficult it can be for a modern continental philosopher like Deleuze to wriggle free of Hegel, even with Deleuze's desire to develop a unified and unifying philosophy.

Deleuze adopted a model that was both monist and dualist; monist in that there must be an understanding of a holistic vision of the universe, and dualist in that we need to accept binary thinking so that we can order and organize our thinking through contrasts. Maybe, this tempts him to seek a binding unity to bring everything together in the end, which sounds rather like the Rig Veda.

Difference and Repetition was first published 1968 in French; the same year when Ricœur's student Guy Basset took notes during Ricœur's course on negation at Nanterre, where Ricœur seeks to challenge the idea of difference as part of negation. These Guy Basset notes have not been verified for their accuracy – yet they will surely become part of the archival narrative, and in them Ricœur describes Hegel as the source of negation and modern philosophy as 'difference'.

Deleuze's model of difference and repetition was influenced by Bergson, who, following a monist approach, like Deleuze, of a unified universal concept, saw time – duration as he configured it – as crucial to understanding difference. This is how Deleuze summarized this aspect of Bergson:

'Duration is what differs from itself. Matter, on the other hand, is what does not differ from itself; it is what repeats itself'.[23]

But actually for Bergson, difference becomes a substance, with degrees of difference within itself, and is a form of coexistence, whereas matter is succession. Bergson introduces the idea of degree, degrees of differences that are in difference, not in nature.

Perhaps it helps to think of Deleuze's model of difference as being analogous to Mandelbrot's set, which is a mathematical model and is also found in nature. Such patterns as Mandelbrot's repeat perfectly, and can be used to understand those repetitions in nature that, albeit imperfectly, must repeat themselves to ensure growth and will do so again and again. These patterns in nature will repeat themselves and will also change according to feedback from the environment and therefore there will be both difference and repetition. Repetition can manifest itself in obsessive behaviour, repeating itself, or in a Kantian-style dichotomy that makes a left and a right or a more and a less: but it is more likely to be phenomena that repeat themselves in normal events and where the repetition is an integral aspect of the event and its changes, for example, I breathe, I love, I think and I must do so again and again. Repetition, by definition, cannot be curbed by limitation and opposition and therefore stands, along with difference, as the vibrating heart of human life. We cannot predict where changes will take place, but we know there will be changes and difference in repetition because they have to happen, in a Heraclitean sense.

How did Deleuze see difference? Did Deleuze seek to avoid both these solutions (retaining contradictory forces or rejecting one of them and retaining the other) with his terms of difference and repetition? Negation is difference, but difference seen from its underside, seen from below.[24] Seen the right way up, from top to bottom, difference is affirmation. Deleuze repeatedly asserted 'difference'(both–and) as a protest against what he saw as Hegel's all-encompassing idea of unity arising from difference that is mutually incompatible, and writing as form in flux, rather than a structuralist code. Deleuze sought to avoid the dialectical tension of Hegel and used Nietzsche as one voice to achieve that.[25] This is a rejection of the Hegelian dialectic because that dialectic rests upon contradiction rather than opposition. Except that we could argue that it is not quite like that; maybe Hegel was also presenting a 'both-and' model and saw contradiction that was an integral part of opposed phenomena, which is the unique and fascinating contribution he makes.

Phenomena that become caught in a Hegelian dialectic are characterized by differences as well as by similarities. The major problem with this model is the making of the choice to capture phenomena in a dialectical pairing; how do we know which things have both similarities and difference of this certain kind and what do we then do with them? Hegel asserted that the individual must be determined by negation; as we see in *Science of Logic*, something must be the negation of something else if it is to have any identity. Deleuze did not find this to be true, arguing that differentiation is never a negation, but it is a creation – difference is creative. Therefore, a critique of the negative is necessary and will be useless as long as it assumes as given 'the form of affirmation readymade in the proposition'. For a critique of the negative to be both radical and well grounded, it needs to 'carry out a genesis of affirmation and, simultaneously, the genesis of the appearance of negation'.[26] In other words, why accept Hegel's systematically heavy binary logic of positive, negative, synthesis?

Deleuze describes the negative as the shadow of the positive – very different from the early Kant who shows two positive forces opposing each other, by the nature of which one functions as the negative, as the opposite.[27] Interesting to see a similarity between what Deleuze argues in 1968 and what Ricœur had argued in 1950; that is, there is a risk in seeing difference as opposition, 'life sums up all that I have not chosen and all that I cannot change'.[28] Ricœur concluded that the inherently tragic essence of human life can be usefully served by a wary deployment of some version of dialectic. Deleuze, in contrast, tried to reject Hegel's dialectic, the concept of negative and the aspects of religiosity in Hegel as identified by Nietzsche. It seems to me that Deleuze protested too much about the negative, and created a sense of positivity that is as unclear and as dependent on the idea of negation as the idea of dialectic is.

Murdoch on Sartre

It is symptomatic of Ricœur's preoccupation in the late 1950s with Sartre and other modern continental thinkers whom he saw as architects of a void, that he should steep himself in their language:

> All the Sartrean expressions – wrenching away, detachment, disentanglement, nihilating retreat – testify with genius to this philosophy of transition . . . thus an expression such as 'to be one's own nothingness' is ultimately devoid of meaning.[29]

Indeed, Ricœur was to find language analysis of various kinds to be invaluable later in resolving the issue of the negative. Iris Murdoch (1919–99), strongly influenced by the continental tradition of philosophy, provides a view on Sartre and his use of language that complements that of Ricœur and arguably goes further with the keen eye of shared experience because Murdoch was, like Sartre, a philosopher, a novelist (of philosophical themes like Sartre, although she denied it), an essayist and a highly respected public figure.[30] She also shares much in common with Ricœur as she saw language as a moral medium and made much use of parable and metaphor in her novels.[31] In her excellent 1954 monograph on Sartre, the first in English, she captures the problematic nature of his thought and of his writing and shows how he uses Kant's antinomies to highlight the negative essence of life and yet also is caught by these antinomies himself. She looks at Sartre as a fellow philosopher and sees him using bleak, irretrievably negative forms of Kantian antinomies, and too dependent on Hegel for deconstructing Descartes. She believes that he longs for the metaphysical values that he abjures, deploying as he does socialist action as the only form of solution. She looks at him as a fellow novelist and finds him to be caught between the risk of ossification of language and its descent into the senseless. Yet her gaze is not intended to annihilate him in the way that he feared the gaze of the other would do: Murdoch found *Being and Nothingness* invigorating after World War II and also after being immersed in Oxford philosophy, that she found inadequate. Murdoch, with a long friendship with Raymond Queneau and a deep affection for the work of Gabriel Marcel, admired Sartre for his witnessing of the horrors of Europe at war, but found his version of negativity to be, at base, almost a romantic longing for individual dignity, without him being able to describe it clearly in his philosophy or his plays:

> Sartre's great negatives are not the negatives of cynicism, but of an obstinate and denuded belief, which clings to certain values at the expense of seeming to make them empty . . . what Sartre wishes to assert is precisely that the individual has absolute importance and is not to be swallowed up in a historical calculation.[32]

What Murdoch finds unacceptable in Sartre is the manipulation of our emotions and perceptions in a negative way: while assuring us that emotions are fixed entities, Sartre then often proceeds to 'fix' them for us, by telling us what to think, assuring us that something is only universally known because he says so: Murdoch cites his famous description of a seminal, cold viscous substance, which he tells us even babies find disgusting, yet for Murdoch this is more a projection of self-loathing than a useful value judgement.[33] In her novels, some of which I cite as examples of hope-giving texts at various places in this text, Murdoch herself presents parables and narratives from which we can learn how to hope, how to pay attention to others and how to live as well as how to think. Ricœur and Murdoch were both fascinated by the ambiguities of the parable of the Good Samaritan, seen in Ricœur's *Political and Social Essays* of 1974 and in Murdoch's An Accidental Man (2003). This makes her similar to Ricœur, both of whom wrote in order to help us live as well as think. Another similarity is the interest she took in Sartre as an artist, a writer, which Ricœur demonstrated in his lectures 1952–56 on Sartre's plays. She is a Platonist, proposing that love is the great motif and rationale and she cites Plotinus as a neo-Platonist, with little comment on his language.

Alain Badiou is, like Sartre, explicitly political in his use of the negative, and he believes that the essence of negation as destruction was the key idea of the twentieth century. He presents a negative that destroys what it disrupts and affirms that which it subtracts from by innovation: thus negation is newness, breaking new ground and as such the negative for Badiou is positive. For him, both destruction and subtraction are necessary for the negative to be affirmative and so, like Sartre, he would see civil unrest as necessary for giving meaning and participation to those in democracies. There is something Heraclitean about his approach, with more emphasis upon friction that we find in Plotinus, who had a mystical and very different goal.[34]

Plotinus' mystical path to metaphor

Plotinus, in a different way from Murdoch with her novels on the Good, creates mystical, repetitive language to inspire a love of God for a perhaps rather solitary experience of serving God, yet his language was useful for Ricœur.[35] For Plotinus, the apophatic way to God is characterized by negating knowledge of God in order to be full of humility and open to God, as Ricœur goes on to explain:

> . . . it would seem that Plotinus uses the same terminology in describing the soul captivated by fascination for its body and when he sums up the approach toward the One in the heroic precept; 'suppress everything else' [*Enneads* VI, 8, 21]. But the same words convey another meaning, since they are caught up in the movement of affirmation.[36]

As I mentioned in Chapter 2, Ricœur explored various ways of tackling Hegel, and one of them was through Plotinus' neo-Platonist analysis of the mystical negative of loving God: God who is nothing yet everything, and the human soul which seeks unity with God, yet is merely mortal, nothing of significance. Plotinus developed a tripartite structure that consisted of first, the One (God), second a differentiating of belief into the many and third, returning to the One through differentiation. This maps onto Hegel's tripartite structure because of the backwards and forwards movement between differences, yet it also differs from Hegel in an important way, namely Plotinus' less explicit, perhaps more supple use of the negative as a counteraction to the positive: in Plotinus there is more emphasis on the metaphorical, in the sense of positioning the negative *within* the phenomenon rather than juxtaposing two contradicting elements.

Perhaps we should consider what the characteristics of a metaphor are. The classical example often used is 'Achilles is a lion'. Although the lion is rather old now, this is considered to be effective as a metaphor because it brings two phenomena together that are clearly not the same as each other, and yet in their very difference they highlight similarities; I now consider Achilles to be a wonderfully brave, strong and dangerous man whom I would want on my side. He has the characteristics of a lion and yet remains a man. We see how, later in his writing, in, for example *Semeia* (1975), with his paper on *Biblical Hermeneutics*, Ricœur attributes to language in the form of metaphor and parable the power to employ, transgress and disrupt a given form, for religious, intellectual and ethical reasons. In seeking to widen out the rules for a philosophical hermeneutics that Kant set out in his essay 'Religion Within the Limits of Reason Alone', Ricœur suggests that the narratives and symbols of our actions, which must combat evil as well as pursue the search for personal freedom, can be valuable and reasonably successful in these two goals, as long as we understand that they are linguistic devices on the boundary line between reason and imagination. This is where metaphor is. And in *Rule of Metaphor*, Ricœur asked:

> should we not say that metaphor destroys an order in order to invent a new one; and that the category-mistake is nothing but the complement of a logic of discovery?[37]

The metaphor is immensely valuable for Ricœur. Ricœur showed in his analysis of Kant's 'Negative Magnitudes' in Chapter 5 that he understood Kant's use of the negative to be flawed because, in one of its two main iterations, it led back to a homeostatic sort of mutuality in nature that would balance out to nothing. However, he also saw the richness of how Kant placed the negative impulse at the very core of Kantian man's thought by presenting the *noumenon* as the limiting factor in our desire for knowledge – which is the opposite of what Aristotle does. Thus in developing his model of metaphor, Ricœur drew upon not only theological approaches, but also the major philosophers: Kierkegaard with his paradox, Hegel with his limitless control and, most important for metaphor, Kant with his philosophy of limits. Given that Kant understood language as empirical, literal and not symbolic or metaphorical, Ricœur then applies these limit ideas to a problem that Kant had not foreseen, namely the possibility of indirect language, and writes of the metaphor:

> We must preserve the philosophical awareness that this kind of language is indirect, figurative, that it draws its strength from its hermeneutical potential; therefore that it is not objective . . . . It [the limit] reminds us that the 'is like' implies an 'is not.' That is why I will not give up the Kantian vocabulary of the 'limit' imposed by reason on the claims to objective knowledge.[38]

This resonates with metaphor in Plotinus. Paul Henry, S. J., describes in his introduction to Kenna's translation of Plotinus's *Enneads*, how Plotinus uses three metaphysical metaphors and also an additional thought pattern that is not metaphorical.[39] The first metaphor is that of a journey upwards as being similar to finding God – whom one cannot find, the second is the internal and the external as being similar yet different and the third is the return to one's origins as being like the end of the first journey and finding God after all. There is a dialectical thought structure superimposed upon the use of these metaphors to give them unity; it is the dialectic of the antithetical many and the one.

Through these metaphors, Plotinus presents God as possessing both positive and negative features, such as being both attainable and unattainable, and the human as also possessing both positive and negative features. Hegel's approach is different – he may juxtapose positive: negative or ideal: real as separate components that are subsequently required to make some, as yet unclear accommodation. This is very important because it means Ricœur has found an alternative vehicle for the negative to the domineering one of Hegel or Sartre, at least within the frame of these negation lectures. Ricœur uses Plotinus' forms of the affirmative negative which, in a way, prefigure Hegel, and yet differ in creating a metaphorical rather than a dialectical movement. Ricœur demonstrates how Plotinus develops Plato's idea of essence – as the supreme expression of the One or God. Here, there is a metaphorical expression of will and essence, in which the soul (or the human spirit as *nous*) is both desire for unity (with self and with God) and proof of lack of unity and Ricœur shows also how this legitimizes the use of metaphor – saying what something is by saying what it is not: 'The metaphor here consists of postulating a duality and then suppressing it'.[40] This also gives metaphor the advantage over analogy, as metaphor intends us to *think* even though we *know* it is not true, that we *are* One and at the same time clearly not One. Achilles and the lion are as one, and yet clearly are not one. In analogy, something is *like* something else, there is no negative, and Ricœur found this frustrating in Aristotle. I suggest that in Ricœur's reworking of Plotinus, we see an early use by Ricœur of the metaphoric structure as emancipatory and genuinely able to help us think freshly. He describes a movement within Plotinus that resembles metaphor:

> a discourse that suggests something, by giving the energy to go beyond it, yet retains something of that which it has passed, to show what it is moving beyond.[41]

This offers a different model from that of Kojève, whose understanding of Hegel's language saw *arkhe* and *telos*, foundation and outcome, structure and meaning to be identical. Negativity and death are one and the same, but this would cause thinking to be stuck in a Heideggerean manner, which Ricœur seeks to avoid through Plotinus' supple, reflexive use of language. Ricœur believes that Plotinus goes beyond Plato and Aristotle into a rich and promising use of affirmative negation, which he hopes to develop into a model of negation that demonstrates its origin in human subjectivity, our personal ability to think about what we do not have. In one lecture on Plotinus, he states:

> I would now like to show how, and I indicated this in the introduction, this peak of ontological reflection upon negation is in fact the culmination of the Greek philosophy of negation which has made possible another style of philosophical reflection, a style according to which negation is born from subjectivity and movement is born from subjectivities.[42]

Subjectivity – the personal response to our world and, in Plotinus' case, to God, to whom we cannot respond, but we can try – this creates the movement, the agency of new becoming, and metaphor, in this case, is its vehicle, within which negation is an indispensable and inseparable component. Here is the nub of a major difference between Hegel and Ricœur: Ricœur wanted to demonstrate to us how we could use our own voice to harness our needs and deploy existing linguistic devices to think more clearly in the metaphorical patterning that we naturally use anyway. Hegel developed a new way of thinking that mirrors the existing human use of the dualistic negative followed by a synthesis, and the way he did it, with often powerful examples such as the master: slave binary, was very much in his own voice. However, this is the late 1950s and Ricœur was still testing out whether he could be clearer than Hegel:

> whether it is possible to inscribe the negation that I will develop as subjectivity into an ontological negation, and this will be the Hegelian problem.[43]

We could of course argue that most people can be clearer than Hegel, but that is perhaps not the point. In 1958, Ricœur explained in English to his

American audience that the starting point in Hegel's early writings is not philosophical, but cultural, religious and social: 'Hegel found in religious experience both the sense of negation and the sense of the whole dialectical structure'.[44] Yet in a comment similar to that made in his review of Hyppolite in 1955, he conjures up Hegel's later intransigence as a mature writer, and Hegel's demand that we imagine the *Logic* as thought without a thinker:

> we have to admit that we are already, that we have always already been in this space of intelligibility and that the question 'how?' is not only without answer but must also be challenged as being without meaning.[45]

I believe that the point for Ricœur was to avoid precisely this Hegelian use of language, to see how to transform a mystical use of language into accessible language that reflects our subjective selves, belongs to us to use well and is a moral medium, as Murdoch described it. Ultimately he achieves this, with regard to metaphor, in the *Rule of Metaphor*, and by this time Plotinus has disappeared from view. However, it is interesting that in one of his very last works, *Memory, History, Forgetting*, Ricœur footnotes Plotinus' *Enneads* and the use Plotinus makes of the epistrophe, which Ricœur describes as a search for knowledge and at the same time as an affective impulse.[46] The epistrophe is a rhetorical term for the repetition of words or phrases at the end of successive clauses. It is taken to mean the 'turning about', the 'wheeling round', and is associated with Neo-Platonism and the realization of the intellect of how far it is from God. However, Plotinus, as well as being mystical, was a monist, rejecting any form of dualism. Plotinus' epistrophal style, repeating words or phrases at the end of sections of language, and anaphora (repeating at the beginning) may have been conducive to meditation:

> Anything it [the Supreme] could contain must be either good to it or not good; but in the supremely and primally Good there can be nothing not good; nor can the Absolute Good be a container to the Good.[47]

The epistrophe also reminds me of Deleuze's repetition: the word is the same and yet not the same and it recurs repeatedly, a search for knowledge and an affective impulse.

Nietzsche used negative arguments as heuristic devices and polemics to make us think. He sought a creative disruption in order to try and spoil pre-existing systems of thought and he wished to undermine Kant. Sartre presented an unrelentingly negative vision of life, in the sense of hopeless-seeming scenarios, yet he hoped to thereby spur us into action. Deleuze hoped to escape binaries of negative positive, yet in his desire to devalue the negative, he incorporated it into his argument for difference such that it seems to be indispensable, in a way reminiscent of Parmenides. Iris Murdoch was sensitive to the ethics of language, critiquing Sartre not only for his negativism, but also for his linguistic excesses which she described as equally risky neurotic and didactic tendencies. She believed, like Ricœur, that language – and certain forms like metaphor – may function to bridge the gap between us and the world, and may also provide implied meanings that are new and may help us to act better. She also understood that a thinker may be dialectic and yet achieve different outcomes with dialectics: in 1952 in her essay 'The Existentialist Political Myth', she describes how Kant and Hegel were both dialectical thinkers, yet Kant deployed his dialectic in dualisms (the impossibility of us as thinkers uniting the phenomenal world with the true world). Hegel on the other hand deployed his dialectical model towards monism: for him there was the absolute world unity of the Transcendental Spirit.[48] Plotinus provided Ricœur with a way of using metaphorical language to create new and clinically productive ways of thinking: the affirmative-negative. Another way of achieving this was through dialectic.

Dialectic, less and then more so – but not a jack of all trades

Ricœur developed a dialectic over many years, a way of creating and exploring a gap that makes our ignorance demonstrable and partially operable, in looking at what we don't know, the meontological. This I see as a dialectical dualism that leads not to monism or dualism, but provisionalities, yet often still within a dualist framework. If we sample Ricœur's views at 10-year intervals, we can see how his dialectical dependency evolved from keeping dialectic at arm's length, to gradual then full adoption, yet always with concern about its capacity to affect content. In *History and Truth* (1955/1965), Ricœur offered a dispassionate and balanced view of dialectic as a tool, advocating its use as one of several approaches:

> . . . the idea of a *unique and exhaustive* dialectical understanding of the social dynamic must be exposed as false; dialectics is a method and a working hypothesis; it is excellent when it is limited by other possible systems of interpretation . . . , and when it is not in power.[49]

In his Kantian early work, *Fallible Man* (1960/1965), Ricœur confronted the contradictions that characterize the human condition, embodying them in polarities like mind-body dualism, the existence of good and evil, values and facts, the finite and the infinite, the real and the ideal, freewill and necessity, despair and hope. He made explicit the tension between such polarities and, at the most intense point of dispute, attempted a reconciliation that is dialectical in character. By dialectical he meant that his existence is shaped by these polarities and also that he must seek to resolve them by incorporating previous contradictions from each extreme into new ways of thinking. This could resemble Nagarjuna's third way and would not necessarily provide solutions that arrive somewhere in the middle between two opposites, but could guide us in incorporating features that are common to both extremes and making something new, viable and ethically robust; a third position.[50]

Ten years later in 1975, in 'Le Lieu de la dialectique',[51] Ricœur wrote of the necessity of using dialectical patterns for arguing – he saw this as proven by comparing Kant and Hegel, the former being stuck in insoluble dichotomies: it is necessary not only to create such dichotomies but also to meld them – for which historical task Hegel is not appropriate, because his dialectical patterning is too strong, but a philosophy influenced by Hegel must be necessary. A philosophy of action must lead to dialogue, which in turn must lead to dialectic.

In 1985, in a paper called 'Irrationality and the plurality of philosophical systems', Ricœur gave a description of how to tackle philosophy by using a method that appears to be a subtle form of dialectic because it involves tensions between two positions. Since Ricœur thought all philosophies are potentially and often actually mutually exclusive, he recommended we must do two things when approaching philosophy new to us: first, we should approach in a non-combative manner if possible, aware of our inability to fully articulate our disapproval; and secondly, we should be assertive in tackling the ideas of this new philosophy:

> . . . and acknowledge the opacity of my choice, the hypothetical character of my strategy and the irreducible polemical condition of philosophical conversation.[52]

It is vital to understand the oscillating provisionality that characterizes Ricœur's thought, and in uncomfortable ways forbids closure. This late definition is from 'Love and Justice':

> Here by dialectic I mean, on the one hand, the acknowledgement of the initial disproportionality between our two terms and, on the other hand, the search for practical mediations between them – mediations, let us quickly say, that are always fragile and provisory.[53]

These comments reflect a long-term commitment to dialectic, with persistent awareness of the need to avoid allowing the method to dominate the thought processes. Hegel was there as a warning, believing that form and content are one. In *Critique and Conviction* (1998: 76), Ricœur confesses that it is always difficult to know whether it is possible to develop a third position that is workable, 'capable of holding the road', whereas Derrida concluded that we cannot escape from the binaries that haunt our thought. Perhaps towards the end of his writing life, Ricœur became more conciliatory in his use of dialectic, citing as he did in *Memory, History, Forgetting* (2000/2004), one of his last major works, the possibility of dialectics of accommodation, harmonization or adjustment.[54]

Ricœur was neither monist nor dualist, but craved the possibility of creating a space in which to make open dialogue and debate possible. He sought the affirmative within the negative and wanted to demonstrate that both were integral to the human condition. His lifelong interest in theology and in his own living faith as a Protestant facilitated the development of a philosophy of affirmation and attestation; yet he wished above all to be understood by those who might not have formal faith so that his ideas could enrich the daily life of non-believers as well as believers. His lectures on negation show how his linguistic turn began earlier than usually thought to be the case, in the late 1950s with his interest in Plotinus' affirmative negative. This turn later became transformed from the likes of Plotinus and rendered accessible for use in the secular world, *The Rule of Metaphor* and, for ethics in the secular world, *Oneself As Another*. However, he retained in his own philosophy the powerful turn *within* and *inside* an argument, so that Plotinus' unity-in-disunity, an affirmative negative, could be transformed into a form of open dialectic and displace or at least challenge our fondness for axiologies based upon constructed positive: negative polarities.

CHAPTER SEVEN

Happiness – and you, what will you do?

Defy my own feelings, welcome A. enthusiastically supposing he comes to see me, amiably tolerate B. in my room, swallow all that is said at C.'s, whatever pain and trouble it may cost me, in long draughts.[1]

Life is both comic *and* tragic.[2] Do you know how to be happy? I will argue here that the negative is an essential component of happiness and that if we negate negation we negate our chances of happiness too. Finding a degree of happiness is for you to do, what I will do is to argue that living honestly with the negative is a necessary but not sufficient condition for achieving the happiness you desire. Depression is very real, existential distress can be overwhelming and I accept it all. Still I will insist that we should take care not to mistake these states with others *and yet* we must acknowledge their negative essence: Ricœur made a clear distinction between different forms of the negative: first, distinguishing between phenomena because they are different (this is not that); secondly, distinguishing between a sense of lack and loss and desire (defining ourselves by what we do not have); and thirdly, living with the knowledge that I am not the person I would like to be (I want the monist harmony of being at one with myself). These can become theoretical positions that we adopt in order to filter our perceptions, yet we may confuse them with each other, for example, I am not the person I want to be because I do not possess X, in stark contrast to the first Buddhist precepts of accepting desire and non-fulfilment. Such confusion can destroy our chances of any level of contentment by exaggerating the negatives already present in the human condition such as excessive reliance upon medication (see ADHD in Chapter 4), racism or sexism (see work with Muslim women in this chapter) and sterile pedagogy (see ELSA in Chapter 6).

Ricœur worked through several confusing yet simple, robust and surprisingly long lived models of negation: Parmenides argued for a unitary monist model, as did Plotinus and Spinoza; all is one (although Spinoza is difficult to categorize). Heraclitus argued for a both/and model of conflict and growth, unresolved dualism. Aristotle developed a dualist, either/or model. The dualist either/or model is the most popular, also adopted by Kant, Kierkegaard and Nietzsche, and by most of us, although some would deny it. Deleuze attempted to develop a more/less model, but was also a monist. Derrida challenged the oppositional but conceded that we think in binary ways.[3]

I draw three major attributes of the negative: first, negation is an integration of two related phenomena: one is a theoretical position, which I examine through Ricœur's early unpublished work on negation and the related phenomenon is an existential attitude, which I illustrate in this book with his early published work, as well as practical examples and parables. As death walks closer and even because of the suffering and the fear of pain that is part of having a mind and a body, we need to continue to act and to affirm our existence and our capacity to achieve something useful, good or beautiful.

The second attribute of the negative is that we can only hope to understand ourselves fully by trying to understand the other, whom we have identified as very different from us, which Ricœur developed in later work. I seek to address some of the others whom we negate and about whom we should, I believe, think more clearly and through whom we can understand ourselves better: women, children, the old, Eastern philosophy, Islam. If we do this, we will be more contented in the long term, yet it is painful as it involves accepting the existence of negative issues of many different sorts that we cannot resolve and would prefer to ignore. To decentre oneself, to 'unself', as Murdoch puts it, is painful, especially if it requires relinquishing a deeply held conviction, however unfounded or inaccurate the conviction may be, as Kant tells us. Sacrificing one's own happiness for the love of another can also be a form of happiness and may even approach some sense of the sublime in Kantian terms, because of the inalienable part played by the negative in the essence of that contentment. (And you may ask who I am to say 'we' – to which I reply that I belong to 'we' as I constantly struggle in my own mind against dualist thinking that takes various forms, including Kafkaesque raging (*I am not like these idiot 'friends', A, B and C*) and also racism and sexism.)

Thirdly, there are both active and passive aspects of negation: Ricœur describes the two main forms of negation as he saw them – willed or suffered, which come from Aristotle's analysis of human experience.[4] Willing is an active force, an act of negation. Suffering is negativity, a received passive act such as the suffering of the elderly in a hospital. Can we acknowledge the limits to our actions, limits that necessitate passivity on occasions? I also wish to push further than Ricœur on this and ask whether we can tell the difference

between willing and suffering . . . if not, then it may be that we mistake one
for the other and believe ourselves to be suffering some phenomenon that we
have in fact willed, as with Hegel's bad consciousness and Sartre's bad faith.

Theoretical negatives and positives

Ricœur did not pursue this line systematically, but I am particularly interested
in what outcomes these thinkers desired for their dialectical approach to the
positive and the negative, because it seems to be central to the way we think:
Heraclitus was a 'stuck' dialectical thinker, as his contraries did not resolve
themselves onto a higher level, as Hegel's did. Parmenides was a 'stuck'
monist, who denied the negative. Plato attempted to suggest a dualism
between truth and error, as well as between the sense and the world of ideas.
Aristotle was a scientific dualist, whose laws integrated binary dualisms (the
law of the double negative, of non-contradiction (a statement cannot be
both true and false), and the law of the excluded middle (something either
will be or not)). Plotinus was a monist, but he reached his unity by using
dialectical and metaphorical patterning.

Kant was a transcendental dualist, for whom human thought is
characterized by our inability to reconcile the way we perceive things and the
way they really are. Hegel was a dialectical monist, for whom the Spirit was
the ultimate and realizable goal. Sartre was a double dualist; dualist between
being in self (static, inert) and being for self (acting on the world) and also
dualist between consciousness as being in this world and consciousness
trying to transcend this world and attain ideal totality. Deleuze wished to
celebrate the intense essence of life through his model of difference, but it
seems to rely on denying the negative in an almost Parmenidean manner and
to lead to a dialectical monism.

Ricœur was, and here I will create a neologism, a 'dialectical manifolder'.
I deliberately use Kant's term, manifold, which is used to express multiplicity,
because it complements Hegelian dialectic: Ricœur saw himself, after Eric
Weil, as a post-Hegelian Kantian. His model is the least stable and the most
interesting, and bestows upon negation a central and strong role: I believe
Ricœur was able to use a binary model and develop it so that it became a
both/and, and also a *neither/nor*. Neither/nor sounds rather negative, yet
it is the model used by Eastern philosophy and Buddhism such as that of
Nagarjuna in order to open up a third way, a space for thinking new thoughts.
The nearest we come to that in classical Western philosophy is Plotinus, but
he endeavoured to attain the final unity, whereas Ricœur openly asserted his
interest in appealing to many intractable problems and the likelihood of failure,
as well as trying to appeal to both religious and non-religious thought.

The structure that we use for thinking will determine both how and what
we think, and what concerned Ricœur in the early 1950s was where the
different types of negative came from, what they were about and how they

would be resolved. At an existentialist level, he identified three forms of the negative: first, a purely factual one of differentiating between this and that, such as, I suggest, with Saussure's binary system for differentiating sound by creating minimal pairs. Secondly, he described the 'lessening of existence' – sorrow, regret, anxiety, need, which also included the ambiguous idea of nothingness as either meaning falling from grace or attaining perfect union with God, a contradiction he saw emerging through Kierkegaard. Thirdly, he identified the transcendental level of not being at one with oneself, because I am not the person I want to be. Only the first one is a straight binary. The other two are not. I suggest that we often conflate these three, perhaps unconsciously, in order to categorize the world clearly, and make decisions as to how to proceed and what to think. Yet if we do confuse these three, we risk creating trouble by too value-laden a use of positive and negative.

Theoretical happinesses

How have philosophers dealt with a putative relationship between negation and happiness? If we restrict ourselves to a brief summary of the major philosophers in Ricœur's study of negation, we have Aristotle, who eliminated the negative from his scientific model of the world as matter, and presented a four-stage framework for happiness based on heroic conduct and a sense of *eudaimonia*, a happiness related to nobility of spirit, and unrelated to worldly trappings. Plato was interested in a balance between reason, will and desire and saw the fair running of the state as vitally important to our well-being. Happiness for Hegel would be to submit one's will and desire to the great ineluctable thrust of history. For Kant, it is necessary to subsume one's desires within those of others and seek the happiness of those others by acting in ways that are universally acceptable, while also accepting the central negative, the *noumenon* that explains and channels our failure to understand. Kierkegaard saw submission to God's will as the only possible way to some form of contentment, whatever the cost. For Sartre, it is precisely those many others identified by Kant who deny me my happiness, stripping me of my autonomy by their gaze, such that any form of contentment would only be achievable by manning the barricades, both literally and metaphorically.

What is the idea of happiness? Is it correlative to well-being? I believe we must be absolutely sensitive to the complexity of happiness and the truth is that the theory of it will never match up to the reality, due to individual differences, different situations and our personal and cultural perceptions of its contrary, which we often call the negative. Most of us desire oneness, wholeness, and this is what we believe Parmenides offered us. Perhaps the moment before we lose consciousness when drifting off to sleep is the nearest we come to that sense of completeness. Sometimes everything seems to be in a state of equilibrium; the family is well, briefly there are no worries, there is no pain at present, the project is stable – but it does not last. These situations are those in which the *lack* of negative phenomena combines with the *presence* of positive features to be a cause for happiness in our daily lives, and this is intensely personal. In theological terms, we can see that 'lack' is evil, the lack of good, and 'loss' is the loss of perfection, the perfection of idealism or of God, these are then metaphysical conditions. We can differentiate between lack and loss, and desire and denial as anthropological positions; desire being a wanting that may be physical before it is anything else, and denial as an act of refusal, or negation (saying No!) or refusal to believe. We can also see all four (lack, loss, desire and denial) as profoundly unrelated to any theology, but in terms of understanding our cultural inheritance in Western countries and Ricœur's Protestant tradition, the fall from grace, loss of purity, loss of perfection and oneness with God function as negatives. Ricœur preferred the idea that we are fallible and capable of doing wrong, rather than inheriting sinfulness through original sin. However, for anyone who has caused pain or death to another, the idea of inevitability becomes familiar and sickening, because it has happened. It is possible for any of us to commit evil without intent. This is part of what Ricœur meant by the inescapability of the negative.

We also desire the positive happiness of pleasure: friendship, a good wine, a great joke, the ability to grasp a good idea and physical satisfaction. Whether we *believe* or not, that happiness is possible, the *idea* of happiness is bound up with our use of binaries, so we need to look at the relationship between negatives and happiness – some sense of happiness is implicit in positive–negative dichotomies, because one of them is by implication good and the other bad.[5] Ricœur recommends that through something like Aristotle's *praxis*, practical activity, we will strive for (although never attain) the fully good life of living well with and for others in just institutions. Ricœur offers narrative to give order to the teeming chaos of life and to incorporate a reworked form of Aristotle's *phronesis*; this is the practical wisdom that should be our guide, if we take control of it (rather than Heidegger's more descriptive use of *phronesis*). Yet narrative cannot ask the questions about the meaning of life, they must come from our belief systems, which in Ricœur's case were Protestantism and his post-Hegelian Kantian philosophy. Yet, against Protestant theology, Ricœur comes to the view that we must consider that we are fallible yet not fallen and accept consciousness as a task, not a given. Happiness as a fixed state is unattainable; yet, we derive purpose and pleasure from making the effort to find meaning that is ethical and to use that meaning to do good. Kafka saw it otherwise, or at least he presented us with parables that challenge the possibility of finding meaning or justice. Perhaps we should see Kafka's parables as often depicting the 'top down' inhuman state machine tormenting its citizens, as in the Doorkeeper in Chapter 5 who helps me to illustrate what we suffer if we refuse to challenge Kant – to try and understand and get justice. It is true that I am more interested in the sort of side to side loose use of the negative and positive that we develop for ourselves, just as much as the state doing it for us. However, I use Kafka here to show a frightening othering that takes its victims in an intensely personal way, just like the inventor-officer with his beloved machine.

THE PARABLE OF PUNISHING THE OTHER AS 'INFERIOR'

Existential Kafka and practical Kant

Franz Kafka (1883–1924) takes us 'In [to] The Penal Colony' with terrifying foreboding, it seems, of experiments on Jewish prisoners in the name of science and perfection such as were carried out in the Nazi concentration camps.[6] In this parable, a prisoner has revolted against inhumane treatment by lashing out at a staff member and his punishment is to be taught to respect his superiors. The officer is immensely proud of his beautiful machine and its sophistication and gradually the parable becomes both unbelievable and yet grotesquely realistic. We see it all through the eyes of a visiting explorer, who, like many of us, is more dispassionate than curious, increasingly disapproving yet disinclined to intervene to save the prisoner or petition the Commandant to have the practice stopped. Yet this is torture, slow, very painful and with every mechanical detail considered, from the sensible ways of ensuring that the sufferer does not bite his tongue or die before he has been tortured, to the elegant outlets for the blood to ensure that the machinery shall continue to function. What is this torture? We are impressed by the beauty of the terminology and the illusion of comfort and attention to aesthetic detail – the Designer is a tool for elegant writing, the Bed is covered with cotton wool and the Harrow is for inscribing the writing – upon the victim's skin. And not once but many times until he dies, after about 12 hours, the officer estimates from great experience with bureaucratic precision. The prisoner will have the words 'respect your superiors' inscribed on his skin.

And we are told of the officer-inventor's concerns about honest workmanship and bureaucracy, through discussion of reduced budgets and faulty mechanical parts. We become aware now of how alienated the explorer feels, despite being responsive to these apparently normal and indeed universal aspects of an honest craftsman who takes pride in doing his job well. He does not wish to be involved, and while being drawn through inertia into the officer's mad vision, he becomes more and more aware of his own limitations, yet only in a limited way, just as Kant tells us we think. This is a form of alienation that influenced Sartre and other existentialists, and really Kafka did not need to exaggerate this darkly negative side of life much, as he was witnessing the death throes of the Hapsburg empire becoming ever more vicious as it struggled to survive.

How shall we interpret this parable? Ricœur is very clear about the force of a parable, it contains very ordinary, normal, elements that are disrupted, often with shocking impact, in order to have some sort of heuristic effect: the vineyard owner sends servants to reason with rebellious workers; they kill each one and so then he sends his son. They kill him too. And you, what would you do? Do you intervene when injustice is done – do you even recognize it? Would your intervention do any good, or be useless, of enormous personal cost and to no avail, like that of the bereaved vineyard owner? The explorer in 'In The Penal Colony' is concerned and compassionate but he will not act and when he does it is too late and too little.

Given the work I do with minority groups, I can see Kafka's parable as a Foucauldian image of majority dislike of different others, often different-skinned minorities – we inscribe 'respect your superiors' onto their skin with our Sartrean looks of dislike and our spitting and our jostling. Spitting? Jostling? No, most of us are far too well mannered for that, but we ascribe sins to people who *look like* those who do wrong or have the same heritage and history as those who do wrong. Some accept what the media tell us about Muslims, some feel aggressive towards Jews because of Zionist policies against Muslims. We dimly fear the redneck boys who live on housing estates and chant racist taunts – well, some do chant, many don't. We feel better for knowing that there are them and there are us, and we negate those we believe are different from us in a way that makes us feel positive, positive in the sense of good. How does this happen? As we have seen from the ancients to the moderns, in order to feel happy, positive, we need to identify a negative: this involves taking our theoretical assumptions about binaries and superimposing them upon reality. Governments' rhetoric may even choose to enhance this feeling of an enemy within, inside society, but outside us, because we are good and need to be protected against evil. Kant will tell us that we are deluded, but we do it all the same.

Practical happiness in Kant

How can we square Kafka's exquisite bloodletting with Kant? For Kant, there should never, but probably will be, such horrific tales of man's inhumanity to man in the name of law and order and respect, as in Kafka's dystopian parables. We could even draw parallels between the officer-inventor who submits himself to his own machine as a final search for justice, and Kant's demand that we should develop actions and laws that we would be content to see enacted upon us as well as upon others. Kant accepted that we are not all moral and that we may choose not to obey the imperative. For Kant, there will also never be the unity of combined souls of the world – a corporate self such as that envisaged by Hegel in his Spirit, which for Hegel however may need to pass through such horrors as those to which Kafka alludes – wars, torture, injustice and terrible deaths. Kant does, however, in some way, anticipate the idea of the United Nations, in his essay 'Perpetual Peace'. And in Kant's second critique, *The Critique of Practical Reason*, Kant demands, incredibly it seems, that being good, being moral in Kant's way, *should* be seen to be theoretically compatible with happiness and there may be some accommodation possible – this is no longer a transcendental illusion but a practical one, based on practical reasoning, a working assumption. Kant defines

(*continued*)

contentment as a lack of lack, a negative condition where we are happy when we lack nothing. He demonstrates that this necessitates feeling completely free to follow the moral laws because these laws enable us to stop desiring more.[7] This happy conjunction may give us the *possibility* of a state of pure practical reason and Kant intended that this would displace Aristotle's *eudaimonia*, the definition of ethics as the search for happiness, which Kant rejects. We must seek to do good for its own sake, not for the sake of being happy. Kant distinguishes on the one hand that state of 0, homeostatic balance, which he calls a sort of intellectual contentment, in which one lacks nothing, and which cannot *produce* morality. On the other hand, he identifies the highest good, which is an impossible state in the real world, but one that we must categorically wish for, because it is true and pure reason at work in the moral sphere. This is a development from, yet still bears a family resemblance to his assertion in 'Negative Magnitudes' that 'aversion is just as much something positive as desire'.[8] In his essay 'Freedom in the Light of Hope' from the Conflict of Interpretations (1969/1974), Ricœur grasped and adapted Kant's productive imagination and emphasized the new antinomy that Kant introduces therein: wanting to be both happy and moral are incompatible and unrealizable goals, yet they can be assumed to be at least theoretically possible and are second best to the highest good, the supreme good, which is God incarnate.[9]

One of the unresolved issues of negativity is how to relate negation to happiness and the conditions of happiness – or should I say contentment, or even lack of sadness. . . . I propose that what we are actually doing is creating our own ideas of what is negative by the our loose use of dialectic dualism. It is often the ideas of someone who seems to think differently from us that threaten our own ideas, or rather that we believe to threaten our own ideas. What we could be using is a form of Ricœurian dialectical manifolding. If we feel able to face our own thoughts, we can use an analogous approach in addressing the possibility that there are those who think differently from us. We should also look honestly at some of the negatives we have created and that we love to hate. The negatives we create will provide us with what we want to dissociate ourselves from and which therefore enable us to set the limits to who we are, what we believe in and what makes us happy. We want to think that if we reject, negate certain phenomena, we will be happier than if we accepted them as part of our lives and thought. I agree with Ricœur that we should challenge this: we cannot escape the negative in its many forms and if we reject it we lose part of ourselves. To this end we often create dualisms in which we believe the 'negative' is to be shed and the 'positive' will make us happy, a privileging that Derrida discussed and believed we could never be rid of. I am interested here, at the end of this work on the negative, in juxtaposing Ricœur's work on negation with some current situations regarding happiness, well-being in which we find ourselves in the more economically developed world: health (mental and physical), educational achievement and ethnic diversity are my examples.

If we recognize these three aspects of negation and act to avoid confusion between them, we can attain some sort of contentment sometimes – whether that is happiness is another matter. If we therefore conclude that the negative has to be an integral part of that state of – possibly – happiness, this goes against the grain of much of the current policy and rhetoric about happiness quotients and questionnaires: they measure and calibrate and put costing on what makes us happy and our *levels* of happiness. Richard Layard offers to make happiness work for us, by basing his arguments on Jeremy Bentham's utilitarian approach: that happiness means creating the best conditions possible for the largest number of people possible. Although he is an economist, he also knows that this maxim is never uppermost in the mind of the money markets.[10] Equating happiness with pleasure is also a tendency in utilitarian thought, and an issue we should challenge, although it chimes well with our consumerist lives, in which we buy pleasure. Layard disagrees with John Stuart Mill, who challenged the Utilitarian theory of Bentham, his godfather, by asserting that there are different levels of happiness, some more and some less worthwhile and valuable than others, and which therefore require measurement. There is a marked tendency in such work to aspire to measuring causal effects when they are, at best, correlational. Layard applauds the use of certain drugs to make depressed people happier: 'before Prozac, the positive part of themselves had felt pulled down by the negative part, but now no longer'.[11] Yet he must know that the correlational effects are not necessarily causal – I may respond better to others, I may feel 'better', become easier to live with on Prozac, but these observed effects do not necessarily cause me to be happier, although they may dull the affective moods. In addition, Layard chastises people like me who are shocked at the epidemic of school children on Ritalin or the number of university undergraduates on antidepressants, inferring that because the means are available to make someone happier, they must be made easily available. It is our utilitarian duty to make available that which we have in our power to use to make others happy. My experience as an experienced child psychologist has shown me that these drugs do not necessarily help an individual to realize themselves, to achieve what they want or to be themselves. Great care must be taken as I believe that all such treatments are predicated on ideas of the normal that are becoming narrower and narrower and this extends beyond mood to cognitive functioning and social interaction; dyslexia, Asperger's and autism are very popular and overused diagnoses, and if they do offer solace to families, this is also an indictment of our cultures.

Ricœur drew a different conclusion to that of Kant and also of Layard – that the Aristotelian equation between happiness and the good cannot really be addressed except indirectly, by hoping to achieve the good life 'with and for others in just institutions'.[12] Layard would agree about just institutions and yet Ricœur's model is so much more sophisticated, not least because he makes us pay attention to the power of the negative, in its many forms the negative as possibility for urging us to live better. In this book, I take Ricœur's work out to the world through case studies and careful analysis of key texts and argue that there is, to my mind, a necessary but not sufficient condition for something like happiness: this condition is that we cannot be happy if we persist with the loose and varied use of the negative that helps us get through the day (such as casual racism and sexism) and yet we will probably not change. What this loose use also demonstrates is that, whether we like it or not, the negative is an essential component of our being – emotionally, intellectually, spiritually and aesthetically and if we negate many things *and* also deny the process of negation the honesty it deserves, then we do *not* end up with a double negative that gives us a positive – we end up frustrated and deluded. We should make the effort to differentiate between negation that is willed (e.g. racist attitudes) and negation that is suffered (e.g. racist abuse).[13]

Ricœur's philosophy is based upon the necessity for action, both willed and suffered and with language as a form of action to guide us in facing up to the negative that is an inevitable part of our being by thinking new thoughts while embodying the old. Ricœur believed we must undertake the task of attempting to recognize and accept our fallibility, finitude and splitness, while he also implored us to be ourselves in spite of, or because of the discrepancy between what we want and what we have, who we want to be and who we are, what we want to know and what we can understand.[14]

In order to tease out the relationship between happiness and negation, we need to look at negation in the real world, which is a very powerful impulse inextricably linked to happiness or any such state. We use it a great deal and we also deny doing so; for instance, when we condone the use of antidepressants by those who are probably simply growing up, and we fail to differentiate between those, who need comfort and company, and those in real need. Of course, these are sophisticated clinical judgements, yet the common response is to believe that everyone deserves to be happy and that they therefore should be happy and can be happy with drugs and indeed this comes close to positive psychology and Layard's almost suggesting that we think we have a duty to be happy. Perhaps this is partly a reminder that a double negative does not always make a positive. In linguistic and logical usage, a double negative customarily makes a positive, yet in existential terms if I deny that I am denying something, I am closer to suppression or repression than I am to a happy resolution. Hegel developed that, but maybe he overdid it, so that we risk ending up as master of none of these states of mind.

Hegel's negation: Jack of all trades

Ricœur concluded that there is an element of sensationalism or certainly exaggeration about the use of the negative, so he understood how Hegel overdid it, making the negative into a jack of all trades (and master of none?). Ricœur's book *From Text to Action*, containing essays written in the 1970s and early 1980s, and most specifically for us the essay 'Husserl and Hegel on Intersubjectivity', provides a definitive critique on Hegel, in which Ricœur deployed a technique that resembles that of Hegel in one respect – going backwards, that is, in this context, going progressively deeper into a person's thought.[15] I believe Ricœur's variation on the dialectical also differs from Hegel's in focusing on thinkers and their ideas, not on ideas as disembodied principles; insisting upon climbing inside each person's thought in order to critique it from within and then applying principles that emerge from the previous exercises.

For Hegel, the negative provides the vital counterbalance to a first principle or concept: for instance, the negative is the 'real' example that differs from the ideal and leads to a synthesis between real and ideal. Ricœur also understands why Husserl rejected the negative, with its Aristotelian and Hegelian hierarchification of nature, and returns to Husserl in order to see if he can strengthen the Husserlian model, weakened by Husserl's refusal of the negative. Thus, he played with the idea that if we combine Husserl and Weber, as a pair they can take on Hegel and defeat him. Husserl's abstractions make sense if yoked to Weber's sociological assertions, and Ricœur even saw in Husserl the major tenets of sociology. Husserl insists that I must be able to think of myself as someone else's 'other' – I must be my own alter ego, humans must understand that they see their world in a similar enough way as each other to be able to recognize it, and Husserl's human understands him/herself as analogically reflected in others, 'as if' s/he were the other.[16] Ricœur repeats his wish that Husserl had occupied himself with the negative, which would have enabled Husserl to explain phenomena more clearly, by describing things in terms of what they were not as well as what they are.[17]

I have given examples of how we create our own ideas of what is negative, and here are some more – it is very difficult to think the negative differently from how we do in our loose use of binaries, and we cannot alter the supreme and seductive utility of negation as a counterweight to the positive, in general conversation and writing. But we can try to think differently and not use it so lazily in moral issues.

NEGATING THE OTHER

The outcome of one strand of Ricœur's negation work, going back partly to Plato's conjecture that the other is a negative us whom we will never understand, has its flowering in his book *Oneself as Another* (1990). Here, he is returning to phenomenology and revisits themes on which he lectured in the 1950s, and the negative has now been subsumed within language work from his hermeneutical phase; each of us is fallible, and yet must use language and narrative to seek to act well, using memories of what we know and expectations of what we hope for in order to live better. He emphasizes the capable person, who says I can, and by the time in 2000 when he writes *Memory, History, Forgetting*, he has developed attestation – the statement that I am here, I will attest to my beliefs and my actions – an attempt to mediate between Descartes' privileged *cogito* and Nietzsche's damaged one. It is vital that the individual avoids being turned into an object and must use doubt and suspicion to doubt one's own motives and thoughts, and take responsibility for one's own actions.[18] Language is the key to thinking other, and can be dreadful: it was used in Rwanda to create murderous othering with the terms Hutu and Tutsi, terms that are purely linguistic creations according to Human Rights Watch.[19]

Wodak's work on linguistic othering of Jews

In another current example, close to home, Ruth Wodak (2011) used critical discourse analysis to analyse anti-Semitism in modern Austria. Wodak demonstrates how Haider, former Leader of the populist Freedom Party, mounted verbal attacks on prominent Jewish figures, using anti-Semitic allusions, in the form of jokes, word play and appeal to Jewish stereotypes. He most particularly applied these linguistic devices to issues about the characteristics of 'real' Austrian citizens, and contrasted that with Jewishness. In his 1967 essay 'Violence and Language', Ricœur invites us to assert that language and violence should be separate. Yet he shows us the paradox: language must be separate from violence and yet both are capable of moving into each other's territory. When we use language to discuss its violent potential that may bring possibilities of solving problems, or it may simply cause further difficulties. Yet Ricœur is not arguing, as Barthes did, that language can be fascist. The way Wodak saw Haider using the language of fascism resembles Ricœur's approach: he sees meaning in people, not language alone. There are huge issues in Europe that seem to be worsening, and some of the issues revolve around citizenship, identity and immigration. Ricœur, in his paper on 'Being a Stranger', describes what he sees as the excessive protectiveness of wealthy nations, when faced with requests by those less fortunate to enter and belong.[20] The randomness of being born in a particular country can harden into a perceived privilege and a right to be protected against putative dilution or contamination. If we face these issues, they can become very uncomfortable, but surely a combination of deontology (Kantian rights-based) and utilitarianism (greatest happiness of greatest number) forces us to consider them.

Muslims as the others

So if I am condemned to this existential disjuncture between my ideal self and my real self that seems rather Kantian, or on a really bad day, Sartrean, what would it feel like to be different?[21] Yet we do this 'othering' all the time: Robert Fisk once said that we behave as if the Muslims are invading us, when in fact it is the other way round, and has been for centuries, and this mistake is endorsed by certain governmental policies, such as the anti-terrorist PREVENT agenda in Britain. Of course, this is a typical colonizer's strategy and the British have done it for centuries to the Catholic Irish. This is a 'war on terror' policy that has the tragic tendency to define Islam by terror and terror by Islam, as identified by a British cross-party parliamentary report that found such thinking to be counterproductive.[22] Still, the negative impressions proliferate, such that I believe we can now define our own goodness by quasi-logical fallacious thinking like this:

Terrorists are Muslims.
Terrorists are evil.
I am not a Muslim.
So I am not evil.

What we can do is to use a technique similar to that developed by Ricœur and Kant in order to challenge our ideological positions, as in this current Western discourse about Islam and Muslims, which gives us a false comfort based on identifying and negating the other. It is difficult to know where to start, as we are provided with many reasons; political, social and religious, for refusing to respond amicably or even openly towards Islam. In other words, it is very possible to be caught in a vicious circle of not feeling able to consider Muslims as being like 'us', because definitional and ideological lines have already been drawn by publicity in the media of terrorist attacks and honour killings. In fact, Ricœur himself, in my opinion, was not particularly responsive here, although he was a fierce opponent of the French civil war in Algeria and sympathized with the plight of Muslim girls who wished to wear the hijab to school. He can help us to approach the reality of ignorance with his idea of humanism as a Kantian philosophy of limits, that reminds us that:

We do not know everything; we do not even know how work and speech, politics and culture, economic planning and free aesthetic creation are articulated. From time to time we detect the limited dialectics that we have already tried to extrapolate, but the total meaning escapes us.[23]

(continued)

Contentment may be achievable sometimes. If, for example, we adopt the stubborn Kantian humility of testing the limits of our own ignorance, we can perhaps see ourselves and Muslims differently, as different yet above all as similar. In 15 years of project work with Muslim groups in Britain, Pakistan, Algeria and Kenya, I have seen that we all face the same problems and all have to make decisions about personal safety, women's issues, child rearing, identity, education, being good and avoiding evil. The othering that takes place is of our own choosing. We represent the positive, the good, out in the light, honest and ready to be counted. The others represent the negative, and, as Kafka depicts in his parable 'Jackals and Arabs', they seem to deserve the hatred they get. Yet if we identify the negative in others, we should be able to see it in ourselves, because we will see ourselves reflected in the other. Instead of imposing negative attributes upon others, we should turn the negative upon ourselves, to question ourselves.

And you, what will you wear?

The headscarf, the hijab, is a rallying point for Western and Islamic feminism, as a sign of oppression or of emancipation.[24] It is seen as a badge of extremist tendencies, yet it is in fact also and often a cultural signal. If we apply Saussure's linguistic code of signifier, signified and referent, we can get a sense of how we create the symbols of evil. The referent is the object in itself, which in this case is a piece of cloth used as a head covering, for cultural and religious reasons. If the signifier is the term as used and recognized, this is hijab, the Arabic term for this head covering, and the signified is the meaning given to the term – in this case bi-valent meaning: agent of oppression and terror or an expression of faith and observance. There is thus an escalation from referent of cloth to signified of terror that should seem excessive and that we should be able to challenge by seeing the connection between, on the one hand, our desire to negate, to deny the validity of someone different from 'us', and on the other hand, our tacit knowledge that we have the other inside ourselves, our own desire to destroy with hatred. This would be an example of what Barthes, in his wonderful book Mythologies, describes as a second-order referent.[25] We cleverly project this desire to destroy on to the other person and seek to disown our impulse by that action of projection.

This process of projection is made all the more tragic because we focus on the woman, already the object in many cultures of cultural inscriptions as Foucault described it. She becomes, herself, a living breathing symbol of this perceived Islamist threat, which in world politics we the western powers are steadily making more and more real by our own actions. Yet it remains true that many, even Muslim scholars, do not know much about Muslim women, except what they wear. What Muslim women think about their faith is an issue that Shuruq Naguib is researching, through the ways in which Muslim women in Britain and Egypt explore the sacred texts upon which their communities put such emphasis.[26] They are living within a hermeneutical tradition that has been strictly managed, yet social, historical and religious changes are creating new possibilities for women to legitimate their own agency in order to reinterpret, subvert or challenge those texts that feminists like Mernissi consider oppressive. Sariya Contractor works in a different way from Shuruq

Naguib, less textual, more sociological and to the same end: to give voice to those British Muslim women about whom many have opinions and who are often not able to speak for themselves, sandwiched uncomfortably between the patriarchy of their culture and the judgements of their wider secular environment.[27]

THE NEGATIVE AS WILLED OR SUFFERED

The sickness of others

For over 30 years, health care professionals have been using Ricœur's work and I believe that this new research on negation has the potential to support such work in applied fields: issues such as empathy, diagnosis, training and other issues in the care of the sick.

There is a strong tradition in practice-based professions of applying Ricœur's work to professional practice. Within nursing and medicine, for example, there is a long tradition of applying Ricœur's ideas to practical problems in the field of nursing (Rawnsley 1990; Charalambous 2008). There is also indicative work by Marta (1997), Granger (2006) and Shapiro (2008) on medical training for informed consent, chronic heart disease treatment and doctors' empathy for patients, respectively.

Shapiro, a professor of family medicine whom I cited in Chapter 1, reports that she decided to use Ricœur's work when she realized that many young doctors have less empathy with patients by the time they end their medical training than when they started; she is concerned to address the perceived failings in medical training.[28] The increase in disillusion and cynicism in medical students seems, according to Shapiro, to be largely unaffected by the plethora of exercises intended to develop empathy and the capacity to identify with the other, such as getting trainee doctors to check in to hospital as if they were patients and accompanying patients on their medical appointments. In a search for understanding, she cites psychological models and also many modern thinkers from Goffman to Lacan. In medical training, she detects what she calls a modernist biomedical trend, wherein 'Understanding is translated as diagnosis and prognosis, and assistance becomes treatment and intervention'. The institutionalization that grips and constrains medical practitioners must play a part here.

Shapiro argues, most specifically, that Ricœur's writings (such as *Oneself As Another*) can influence trainee doctors by facilitating empathy, emphasizing their own vulnerability and helping them to face their own fear of disease and suffering; what she calls an ethics of imperfection. In *Oneself as Another*, Ricœur analyses the ways in which we can only really understand ourselves through seeing ourselves reflected in others, through using narrative, through fiction, through parable and dialectic and by attempting, for example, to moderate the relative

(continued)

insensitivity of the group to the needs of the individual, by modifying personal and group needs for recognition and tempering general rules for specific situations. This entails freeing oneself from an egotistical perspective, really considering oneself as being just one self among others. Indeed this resonates with the clinical and philosophical work of Declan Sheerin, a child psychiatrist, who analyses what he calls 'the sepulchre of narrative' and in his study of Ricœur and Deleuze he asks 'why narrate a self?' He notes that

> We cannot seem to avoid lack and loss in the heart of narrative. Indeed Ricœur firmly places it there.[29]

There are active attempts to teach or enhance empathy in medical training, as in the teaching programme of Samantha Pelican Monson (2009). This includes role-play, non-verbal manifestation of sympathy and writing about one's own suffering, all in an attempt to enhance empathetic understanding through narrative. Monson's teaching programme draws its impetus explicitly from Shapiro's work. Anjali Dhurandhar, in another project about empathy in medicine, makes more use of writing than Monson does, encouraging trainee doctors to imagine that they are the patients and to write about the experience. This requires an act of imagination, experiencing what the other experiences in one's imagination, some sort of imagined intimacy with the other's religion, or situation. Developing narratives that take a different point of view can be powerful, and Dhurandhar finds that medical students reported enhanced empathy for patients and for their classmates as a result of attending the writing courses. All of this resonates strongly with Ricœur's work on becoming oneself only through trying to understanding the other – in which we will fail, as Plato pointed out – and with his belief in narrative as a way of making sense of our lives, despite its tendency to be overdetermined by our assumptions and bigoted binaries. Ricœur established the groundwork for this approach by determining the various mechanisms of the negative as they affect personal relationships, as we see in Oneself as Another.

In a similar vein, Andreas Charalambous, working with nurses, finds Ricœur's work valuable for thinking about the interpretative potential in the diagnostic interview and subsequent treatment. Since the mid-2000s, Charalambous has explored the possibilities of using a Ricœurian hermeneutic phenomenology to challenge assumptions about nursing cancer patients and to provide cancer nurses with a basis for theorizing (2009). He argues that interpretation of Ricœur's texts can help to interpret 'the fresh text presenting itself in everyday experience'.[30] It seems to me that there must be aspirations towards reciprocity – ideally patients should know about these ways of thinking so they can understand the surgeon as well.

Smile, be positive or die

Ehrenreich tells us in *Smile or Die: How positive thinking fooled America and the world* that there are also powerful fashions for positive thinking that are now coming under critical scrutiny. At a very personal level, she challenges the credo: 'You must not whine or cry, because negative emotions and attitudes are not only a sign of psychological defeat, but also a sure way to make the cancer return or grow faster'. This is a good example of the need to seek a balance between willing and suffering – there will be negative moods and moments, as this is an integral part of human personality and should not be repressed or eliminated, seen by analogy with Aristotle who, at an epistemological level, eliminated the negative when defining terms. If the negative is excised, as a mood or a state of mind, we may lose our narrative identity, our capacity to tell our story and try to improve upon it.

Ricœur's work on narrative identity is also providing the impetus for new work: in Paris Olivier Taieb and his colleagues provide drug addicts with professional support based on the belief, taken directly from Ricœur, that narrative in the form of history, fiction and also specialist literature on addiction can help with recovery (2008). Addicts may be able to construct a new or reformed identity. Yet these are isolated cases of clinicians working in small teams and bringing their own insight into Ricœur's work to bear on their professional practice. It is worth asking whether this crossing over from idea to action can be strengthened as Shapiro asserts:

> An ethics of imperfection would likely draw heavily on the insights of philosophers such as Ricœur, whose philosophical theories could provide a foundation from which humane and empathetic behaviours might emerge, not just as checklist behaviours, but as deeply felt moral imperatives.[31]

Public discourse does not welcome this debate and indeed the concepts of choice, consumer autonomy and free will have become entangled with one another in a sclerotic refusal to give health warnings about obesity, alcohol and diabetes.

Conclusions

In his attempts to bring together the false positives and negatives that function as comforting axiology and that we use as shorthand to organize our values, Ricœur developed the concept of attestation: 'the assurance of being oneself acting and suffering'.[32] Attestation is the way in which I can testify that I am here, taking and receiving action, with Aristotelian resonances. Ricœur did not see this binary model as a simplification, insisting that it is a rejection of more than Descartes and Nietzsche, but a direct challenge to both certainty and despair, and one which is an assertion of our (imperfect) self. Before we reject this as simplistic and obvious, we would do well to consider whether we take agency seriously enough– do I act to demonstrate concern and try to make a difference? Often I do not, and you, what will you do? I demonstrated this in my book on the hermeneutics of suspicion and Ricœur's development of Hegelian dialectic constantly shows us the other, often negative side of arguments and presents us also with our difficulty in succeeding with intellectual searching and moral dilemmas.[33]

Increasingly, we see Ricœur combining a Hegelian dialectic of human activity with a Kantian refusal to believe that this dialectic can ever become an ideal synthesis of all the elements that are needed for leading a good, moral life. Thus for Ricœur, Kant's use of negation becomes more than it was, it becomes a guardian of the critical, truth-seeking functions. Yet Hegel and Kant can never become reconciled and that creates a tension within the process of using their ideas, which contributes to the need for an ever-present mediator.

I believe that Ricœur moved from a position in 1950 of analysing the Hegelian negative power of phenomena such as finitude, birth and death and lack or need, to a position of adopting the 'experiences of the negative (that) are intended to assure the "transitions" from one form to another'.[34] In this way, he moved from an event model to a process model, an active, fluid approach that can be implemented in our use of language as well as in physical actions. Moreover, when I take action, I take a risk.[35] Language is part of the risk that I take.

If we accept a Kantian statement such as the following; 'Limitation is nothing other than reality combined with negation',[36] then we can see how, for Kant, the relationship between thinking and perception is very complicated: the person, the I, is comprised of a manifold, a multiplicity of sense data, which are organized in thought according to categories that are provided by the understanding that I have. Kant's person, the 'I', attributes the connections within the categories to the real world, and presumes/assumes that there is an objective world and that this world is governed by a temporal sequence. The objective world and the temporal sequence are separate from me and must be faced by me and acknowledged before I can meet up with myself properly and have the self-identity I lacked initially. So, Ricœur takes Kant further to demonstrate how the person *develops* a sense of identity. Self-identity is not a given; it is a phenomenon in which we must actively engage in order that it becomes both real and worthwhile, while attempting to reconcile internal and external conflicts.

If I question my experiences critically, maybe I will be able to achieve something new and interesting or old and worth reviving. . . . My ethical position should be open to challenge and every day there is a new hope: yet if I relax and let my mind run in the comfortable careworn grooves of hate and narcissistic bumptiousness about other people's lives and loves and failures, such hopes evaporate. My thoughts and the reality I live are similar, as Hegel showed, in that I think thoughts that can then become forms of reality: if I think I see danger, I may be creating the idea of danger and a self-fulfilling prophesy – even where there is no danger. Also I should take care to harness the 'labour of the negative' because I can only understand the world by seeing how it is different from me – yet this creates negation that I need to accept and deal with, and above all, it challenges my ability to be happy, because I can never be at one with myself if I can never be at one with those around me, whoever they are.

In order to attain a state of attestation: 'this is me, this is what I stand for', Keats' negative capability can help, a way of being sensitive to what is out there, the potency of negation – it, negation, can counterfeit the appearance of happiness by giving me false security if I misuse it and it can help me to live more companionably with my own self-contradictory nature and in my riven world if I see it as a category mistake and also see the power of language to help me explore my own possible negative capabilities.

Why should we seek the negative actively? Because it is with us in everything we do and therefore facing it may help us to achieve some acceptable level of contentment. However, there are definitional problems – how can we face it if we don't know how to recognize it? There is great suffering in the world of course; we all suffer unnecessarily and in innocence in many ways. Yet we also deploy negation as a category mistake. In daily life, these difficulties are partly due to our very loose use of the term negative and the idea of the negative. Ricœur understood the negative as an empowering, positive force that presages in-completion and uncertainty, yet shows us who we are and helps us face the truths of famine, excess, despair and delight, in each of us as also in the wider world. We must use not-knowing, the provisionalities of ignorance and the desire to know more to reconsider and consider again the loose use we make of the negative, understanding it as part of the positivity that is each of us.

EPILOGUE

Overarching systems such as theology, politics or moral codes are used to try and resolve conflicts, ambiguities and problems in the world we inhabit, or rather the one we think we inhabit, and people use such systems in order to achieve a totalizing effect they call grace, or justice or the good. Such systems will fail, because it is not possible to explain everything or to radically eliminate conflict from our lives. Ricœur was highly sensitive to the fact that it seems to be part of the human condition to want to be able to understand up to the level of prediction and causal explanation. He noted this in all aspects of human life, especially philosophy, where the desire to use reason to resolve our problems is difficult to resist. The other major form of philosophy is one that seeks to understand and accept limits. I suggest that the negation lectures were part of his decision to play Hegel the totalizer off against Kant the limiter, in order to try and come to some form of reconciliation and to transcend both: we wish to be free to act and think as we wish, yet we are constrained by our own limitations. The problem contains then already a duality and Ricœur exploits this fully by developing various different techniques, which include dialectic, the use of negation and the judicious deployment of suspicion, so that we doubt ourselves as well as others.

The negation lectures start c.1952 and appear to end, about 1968–70, on a note that leads into and becomes a part of his middle period: in 1975, with his essay 'Biblical Hermeneutics' he makes use of the dualisms that are at the core of much of our thinking, and hopes to demonstrate how we place undue and unwarranted reliance upon reason as a problem-solving device. Aristotle's syllogistic reasoning and especially his laws of contradiction exemplify that and such an approach can also lead us to demote and underestimate the imaginative possibilities that language, poetry, myth or faith have to give us a different vision. Kant himself makes the imagination work very hard in different ways in both his *Critique of Pure Reason*, with its epistemological critique and his *Critique of Power of Judgement* with its aesthetic critique: he has to develop a model of the negative that is at the heart of a philosophy of limits and which explains the limitations of our ability to accurately perceive the real world in terms of really understanding. In this middle period of the 70s, Ricœur himself tried to further analyse the potential of human imagination, with and beyond Kant, and he uses linguistic devices to do so.

If an all-encompassing Hegelian concept of philosophy explains too much, a philosophy of limits explains too little, and in Western philosophy both rely upon binary forms of organization. In Kant, the binary of *phenomenon* and *noumenon* does not resolve itself in a higher form, but in Hegelian dialectic this resolution takes place, with a third state of synthesis that constantly brings reflection to a new, higher stage, but that ultimately goes too far. By going back to the beginnings of Western philosophy, Ricœur found many different forms of negative–positive and I believe he concluded that in order to avoid getting stuck like Kant or overstretching ourselves like Hegel, we should implement existing and potent linguistic structures such as those of metaphor that are defined by negative–positive tensions. This also reflects the 'linguistic turn' in philosophy that Ricœur himself incorporated, up to a certain extent, in his own use of language. The emphasis on language ultimately led to an incorporation of negation that tempers Hegel's overambitious ontological pretensions.

This sensitivity to binaries also shows later; for example in *Oneself As Another*, where we understand ourselves by being mirrored in another. This is the mature Ricœur's approach to the existential difficulties we face as fallible, limited humans with the potential to do good and evil. The human condition is thus based upon paradoxes and we have to evolve our own provisional clarity and attestation: an attempt to show what the human condition stands for and to use ethical positions to manage the potential for good that we create for ourselves in the space between possibilities.

There is a lot of frantic activity in philosophy, such as we see with Zizek for example, generating new work and stimulating ideas. I have a sense of wildly exuberant, repetitive and proliferating discussions, endless quantities of secondary literature that often strike a *fin de siècle* tone, the end of beyond. This can be seen as post-modern cynicism in Baudrillard and others and is presumably part of what Scruton objects to, with his 'arrest of the soul in the posture of negation'. Of course, I have indulged in it a little as well, with my conjuring of infantilizing education systems. However, when framed as philosophically fashionable, the negative is not necessarily leading us to a clearer idea of what to do next and we can see that Ricœur rescued negation from the post-modern theorists. He was interested in showing us that we are characterized by conflicts and limitations. These are to be acknowledged and investigated, in order that we can then attempt to resolve the contradictions: we will fail often, but we will have a clearer path from actually grappling with our desires and our inhibitions. This affirmation of the human capacity for action, in spite of and actually because of the negative, is an outstanding characteristic of the intention of Ricœur's philosophy.

Ricœur is highly distinctive in welcoming and embracing the full potential of language for grappling with the human condition. We can learn much from him and others and use techniques such as the linguistic turn of Ricœur or Keats' negative capability, to try and understand the other. Locke, Leibniz, Frege and many others by contrast desired the language of pure concepts and Locke even saw the metaphor as resembling pictures of beautiful ladies on the walls of men's clubs; nice but distracting. Parmenides would have agreed – ordinarily language is used for nothing but the Way of Opinion; distracting and inaccurate. Wittgenstein in his *Tractatus* drew the related conclusion that we cannot really expect to use language to depict thought accurately. Many philosophers, who have trouble with the negative, also have trouble with language and we see this in Aristotle and Spinoza. The difficulties arise not so much because of the grammar and the structure of the negative, but more because language itself interferes with the ultimate union of *being* by introducing messy stuff like metaphor. Ricœur celebrated these fecund possibilities in metaphor and added the power of parable, narrative and dialectic as useful structures for incorporating negation. So the labour of the negative is indeed the work of language, as Hegel decreed, but not language where *arkhe* and *telos*, foundation and ending, meaning and death are fused. This is language we make for ourselves in order to think freshly about the ethical issues that face us, and which we will continue to distort with our fondness for everyday loose use of dualisms. However these dualisms can be incorporated into our use of various tropes, so that we become more aware of them and imagine the possibilities of thinking differently.

My work involves me in dealing with the results of a particular form of totalizing thought process, a desire for complete conceptual mastery: our frequent desire to polarize the world we see into opposing 'types', one of which is privileged over the other: Male:female; pale:dark; mind:body; West:East. And I, what will I do? The next project will be to explore again and always the possible synergies among the less privileged of such binaries to see if we could possibly think differently, with sensitivity and love for what the other can bring, rather than an imposition of overdetermined structures. Such work involves acceptance of the role of limitrophe, never at one with oneself or the other. As researchers working on archives we feel like border troops: we are billeted at a distance from the legitimized action, the published works, using various approaches to piece together the working methods and possible impacts of unpublished yet clearly important and exciting materials. This in turn may help to think differently and beyond dualisms that are fixed yet deserve interrogation – not least of which, for archival research, is that fascinating one between the published and unpublished.

Negation draws our attention to a gap in existing ontologies, a gap that brings forth the necessity to think afresh. The meaning and the status of an archival collection should be neither over- nor under-estimated. With over 60,000 pages of material, much handwritten in a difficult script, it is tempting to believe that the Ricœur archives are simply a repository of the thinker's draft thoughts, and as such perhaps could furnish a hobby of sorting and numbering the handwritten or typed notes from reading, lectures, letters, reports, commentaries, private thoughts and book manuscripts. We can however, think completely differently about this phenomenon, in which a personal collection is bequeathed for the benefit of generations of philosophers yet to come. I suggest that we can think of the archives as something different, new and exciting: this can be achieved if we can encourage ourselves to think about establishing a conversation between us, the archives and the published works. The archives can doubtless shed light on published works, and the published works can also enlighten us about the archives, as Jean Leclercq indicates in his editorial about the Michel Henry archives at Louvain. Iterations and revisions can challenge us to think about the thought processes involved in developing a topic, changing it or abandoning it. A study of lecture notes can show us the influences upon the thinker as well as showing us how the work was presented to students. Ricœur's archive gives us more of the texture, the work against and with and from which his engagement with the negative grew.

The materiality of these papers cannot be denied, the ribbons and bows need to be untied, the papers rattle a little, the fountain pen and the ballpoint pen leave their different traces. In their delicacy and content, and as always with Ricœur, we find gestures to the future that remind us how transient, provisional and rich are our understandings of any body of knowledge.

NOTES

Prologue

1 This is a part of Paris with strong Protestant connections, including the huge bronze lion at the conflux of many roads at Denfert Rochereau – let this be a reminder about not lionizing Ricœur.

2 Foucault, M. (1972) *The Archaeology of Knowledge*.

3 Derrida, J. (1996) *Archive Fever*, p. 3, trans. E. Prenowitz. Chicago and London: Chicago University Press.

4 He is consistently neglected by most British philosophers, a sort of negation that relegates him by footnoting his major works while refusing to engage with his ideas to any significant degree. He is read by an increasing group of Americans and other Anglophone groups, with considerable interest in Latin America and several European countries.

5 For the Anglophone world, this *oeuvre* is mostly read in English, so, however well translated, it is still at one remove from the original.

6 Steedman, C. (2002) *The Archive and Cultural History*.

7 Osborne, T. (1999): 51–64 'The Ordinariness of the archive'.

8 Derrida, *Archive fever*, p. 3.

9 Scott-Baumann, A. (2009) *Ricœur and the Hermeneutics of Suspicion*; Groys (2012) *Under Suspicion*.

10 My thanks to Mme Goldenstein for her deep understanding for Ricœur's archives.

Introduction

1 Scruton, R. (1994): 460 *Modern Philosophy*. London: Sinclair-Stevenson.

2 Ricoeur *History and Truth,* 328.

3 Other issues of interest are those regarding his working practices, for which the negation papers provide a microcosm: he enjoyed adopting different intellectual positions simultaneously and accepted Kant's postulation that it may be impossible to reconcile contradictory positions. I can only look at that in passing in this book.

Chapter 1

1 Ricœur, *Freedom and Nature*, (1950): 139.

2 In *Symbolism of Evil*, 1960, Ricœur describes three major symbolic manifestations of sin, given that we find it difficult to visualize and describe sin: the stain, the fall and the deviation from the path.

3 Melamed, Y. (2012) in E. Forster and Y. Melamed (eds) *Spinoza and German Idealism*.

4 Kitaro, N. (1949/1987) *Nothingness and the Religious World View*.

5 The examples I will give of racism have perennial features, and will only become outdated when racism is eradicated or at least reduced.

6 Murdoch, *Existentialists and Mystics*, (1997), p. 146.

7 Murdoch, *Existentialists and Mystics*, (1997).

8 *Freedom and Nature*, pp. 316, 417, 445–7.

9 *Freedom and Nature*, (1950/1966): 23.

10 *Freedom and Nature*, (1950/1966): 316.

11 Ricoeur, Husserl. An Analysis of His Phenomenology (1967/1978): 79.

12 The Unity of the Voluntary and the Involuntary, in *The Philosophy of Paul Ricœur*, ed. Charles Reagan and David Stewart. Boston: Beacon Press, 1978.

13 Ibid., English version, p. 17.

14 *Freedom and Nature*, 228.

15 Around this time, Ricœur was presumably working on the essay that appeared in the second edition of *History and Truth*, 'Negativity and Primary Affirmation', first published in French in 1956. It is interesting to compare Ricœur's response with Deleuze's review of Hyppolite's book, from the previous year: perhaps Ricœur was conducting a conversation with Deleuze as he commented that Hegel's most serious problem is pushing negation as far as contradiction (as opposed to Plato, who pushed less hard on negation and chose difference and otherness as his version of negation). Deleuze had commented that Hegel's Logic contains absolute contradiction and thus pushes difference too far, and here we see, as we will do in Chapter 6 as well, how close many of Deleuze and Ricœur's ideas were. On the other hand, Deleuze also tried out his first construction of an aetiology of pure difference in this review of Hyppolite, which differentiates him from Ricœur.

16 Ricœur, *Husserl. An Analysis of His Phenomenology*. Evanston: Northwestern University Press, 1967, p. 206.

17 Ricœur, *From Text to Action*, p. 244.

18 Ricœur, *Time and Narrative*, 3, Derrida discusses these areas in *Spectres of Marx*.

19 Kempf translated 'Negative Magnitudes' into French, published 1972 and mentioned as a good work by Ricœur in his paper 'Kant et La Négation'. The five Kant lectures, focusing on 'Negative Magnitudes', are a relatively late addition to the lecture series on negation, as they were given in the Nanterre

period, although Ricœur worked on Kant's 'Negative Magnitudes' much earlier in *Fini et Infini* (1957–64) and was briefly introduced to them back in 1933.

20 Derrida, J. (1978/1987) Parergon in *The Truth in Painting*, trans. G. Bennington and I. McLeod. Chicago: Chicago University Press.

21 Scott-Baumann, A. (2010) 'Nausea under the net' in M. F. Roberts and A. Scott-Baumann (eds) *Iris Murdoch and the Moral Imagination*. Jefferson: McFarland.

22 Ricœur, *Husserl: An Analysis of His Phenomenology*. 'Existential Phenomenology', 210.

23 Ricœur Ibid., 211.

24 Ricœur wrote many major essays on Hegel, which include: 'Retour à Hegel' 1955, 'Hegel Aujourd'hui' 1974, *Freud and Philosophy, Conflict of Interpretations* 1969, *From Text To Action*, especially the essay 'Husserl and Hegel', and 'Renouncing Hegel?' in *Time and Narrative* 1985. Each one shows a progressive distancing from Hegel, yet in the full understanding of his omnipresence. In late texts (*Memory, History, Forgetting* and *The Course of Recognition*), Ricœur takes a more conciliatory tone, accepting Hegel as a key figure in the history of philosophy and not challenging his philosophy actively, yet showing a preference for young Hegel, who was less fixed in the dialectical to and fro.

25 Ricœur, *Freud and Philosophy*, p. 156.

26 *Ricœur* Ibid., p. 497.

27 Ricœur (1991) 'Love and Justice' in *Figuring the Sacred* 1995.

28 Ehrenreich, *Smile or Die. How Positive Thinking Fooled America and the World* 2010.

29 *Being Wrong: Adventures in the Margins of Error* by Kathryn Schulz (Independent 20.3.12).

30 Scott-Baumann, A. (2011) Unveiling Orientalism in reverse in *Islam and the Veil*.

31 Ehrenreich, *Smile or Die. How Positive Thinking Fooled America and the World*.

32 Bellini and Shea (2005).

Chapter 2

1 Three sections of the Negation lecture series that he called Part II and Part III have been typed out with the Greek terms inserted in biro. It seems likely, according to Mme Goldenstein, archivist, that these three lectures were based on notes taken by the Sorbonne students' co-operative, typed out by students, approved by Ricœur and then used by him subsequently; as he only ever refers to these three lectures, it seems plausible that they were the only ones singled out for this special treatment. Perhaps they constituted, for Ricœur, the reliable core of his negation work, given that most of his writing and thinking were strongly influenced by Aristotle. He referred to these typed sections by their

page numbers in a short paper from 20 years later, when he was working at Nanterre university, a paper called *Négation et réalité*, a reference that he makes to himself. AR/FR, BIB.IPT: Inv 1, dossier 96 « La Négation » Cours (c.1952-1970) feuillets 9260–9268

2   For a full grasp of these philosophical issues, I refer the reader to Olivier Abel, for biographical relationships within the philosophy to François Dosse and for a full grasp of the archival issues, I refer the reader to Catherine Goldenstein.

3   AR/FR, BIB.IPT: Inv 1, dossier 96 « La Négation » Cours (c.1952–70) feuillets 8749–70.

4   *Négativité et affirmation originaire* first appeared in *Aspects de la dialectique*, *Recherches de philosophie*, II, Desclée de Brouwer, 1956, pp. 101–124.

5   AR/FR, BIB.IPT: Inv 1, dossier 96 « La Négation » Cours (c.1952–70) feuillets 8809–13. This is English text by Ricœur; I have left the slight clumsiness of the repetition because I believe it is unwise to edit his words. Also I find it a useful expression of his constructive indecision, his Keatsian negative capability.

6   It is also possible that he was adversely influenced by the rather stridently Stalinist version of Marxism that dominated left-wing circles in Paris for some time in the 50s and 60s. Later we see Ricœur analysing Marx in some detail, for example, in the *Ideology and Utopia* lecture series in Chicago in 1975.

7   Ricœur (1967): 12 *Husserl. An Analysis of His Phenomenology*. Essays spanning 1949–57 published separately in French.

8   AR/FR, BIB.IPT: Inv 1, dossier 96 « La Négation» *The Origin of Negation and the Human Experience* (96C/005) course in English feuillets: 8809–13 Smallest paper. Handwritten in English in dark blue pen; mid-1950s; resembles work he prepared for early visit to Haverford College US – so presumably written after *Freedom and Nature* (1950).

9   Here, Ricœur told his students that he was not going to get to modern philosophy until the following year, even though in fact he comments on Sartre several times. There are several instances in other lecture series on the negative where he announces that he will delay analysis of modern philosophy, or crosses through a heading about modern philosophy.

10   AR/FR, BIB.IPT: Inv 1, dossier 20 La Négation. Petit cours. (1955) Feuillets 42783–829: 42803 *Finitude, Négativité, affirmation*. Leuven, [Conf 059].

11   Gabriel Marcel (1889–1973) See Iris Murdoch's delightful 1951 essay on him called 'The image of mind' in *Existentialists and Mystics* (1997). London: Chatto and Windus, pp. 125–9.

12   AR/FR, BIB.IPT: Inv 1, dossier 20 La Négation. Petit cours. (1955) Feuillets 42783–829: *Finitude, Négativité, affirmation*. Leuven, [Conf 059].

13   We will see again later this hubristic approach in Hegel as he reworks the negative in order to make it brilliantly shining and important, only to then seem to occlude its light by absorbing that very negative so that it is no longer the potent, illuminating and energetic force that he told us it was.

14   Husserl (1967): 210, 229.

15 I wonder whether they could they become part of western thinking or is this only possible in eastern philosophy with a 'third way' like that of Nagarjuna?

16 There is a set of lecture notes in the archives written by a student, Guy Basset on Ricœur lecturing about negation at Nanterre in 1968 that includes a detailed analysis of Aristotle and the *Physics*, a steady ingredient, yet also containing many new features that relate to structuralism.

17 AR/FR, BIB.IPT: Inv 1, dossier *Anthropology and Religion in the Philosophy of Existence* at Union Theological Seminary, USA, 1957–60?? A. 27. Feuillets 4057–4101. The original list contains no term for Marcel, and on p. 10 of the Union Anthropology lectures he adds a term for Marcel: unhope.

18 The phrase 'breaking as annihilation' reminds me of Bataille, but he attributes both to Sartre.

19 Husserl was of course later than Hegel, but Hegel's influence came to French reading of Husserl in the early twentieth century, at the time of Husserl. This destruction of phenomenology was possible because there is no negation in Husserl that can speak to Hegel's negation, and also because Hegel's negative introduced a dialectical logic that was different from the Leibnizian combinatorial logic that provided a background for Husserl's thought.

20 Ricœur, P. (1963/1981) Two encounters with Kierkegaard: 'Kierkegaard as evil'; 'Doing philosophy after Kierkegaard', in *Kierkegaard's Truth: The Disclosure of the Self* 1981, ed. J. S. Smith. New Haven and London: Yale University Press, pp. 313–42.

21 Here, Ricœur was deeply indebted to Jean Wahl and his work *Le malheur de la conscience dans la philosophie de Hegel*. Hence, the 'existential' Hegel. Wahl also introduced Kierkegaard and Jaspers to France.

22 Existential phenomenology in *Husserl: An Analysis of His Phenomenology*, p. 206: (1978: 78). This essay was written in 1957 and published in English in 1978.

23 This clearly requires further work, more access and a team of researchers!

24 Archives Ricœur: Fonds Ricœur- Bibliothèque de l'IPT – Paris Inventaire 1, dossier 96. La Négation **8749–8770:8752** [96A/002].

25 AR/FR, BIB.IPT: Inv 1, dossier A27 Cours/ 1957–60?? *Anthropology and Religion in the Philosophy of Existence* (1958), **4057–4101.**

26 In-itself is the inert non-conscious me, which is the bedrock of the for-itself yet must be negated by the active, dynamic and changeable for-itself which responds to situations and thereby introduces instability into both the in-itself and for-itself.

27 Ricœur, P. (1985) 'Irrationality and the plurality of philosophical systems', 1985 in *Dialectica* 39(4): 298–319.

28 AR/FR, BIB.IPT: Inv 1, dossier 96 « La Négation» (8601–994).

29 Roberts, M. F. and Scott-Baumann A. (2010) *Iris Murdoch and the Moral Imagination*.

30 AR/FR, BIB.IPT: Inv 1, dossier 96 « La Négation» (8603–4).

31 Ricœur, *History and Truth* (p. 305).

Chapter 3

1 Aristotle (1933) *Metaphysics Books 1-9 (Loeb Classics)*. This 'psychological' version of Aristotle's laws of contradiction appears at Aristotle Met IV 1005b23-24; the 'ontological' version in Aristotle Metaphysics IV, 1005b19-20; and the 'logical' version at Met IV 1011b13-14. Ricœur gave many lectures on Aristotle using the Physics particularly, in this negation series, seeking the potential, movement, energy that interested Aristotle. Doing justice to this work would be another major project.

2 AR/FR, Bib, IPT: Inv. I, d96 'La Négation' Cours. 91955-58. Feuillets 8749–70 96A/002: he called this chapter I in his archive on negation.

3 Heidegger, M. (1942–3/1998) *Parmenides* – in these lectures, Heidegger extols the Greek language, as in the word *aletheia*, truth.

4 Theaetetus 179c–180e; Plato (1990) Burnyeat; Theaetetus. Rolland de Renéville, Jacques (1962) *Essai sur le problème de L'Un-Multiple et de l'Attribution chez Platon et les Sophistes* Thèse principale pour le doctorat des lettres, L'université de Paris. Paris: Librairie philosophies J. Vrin. Ricœur annotated carefully and in some detail Renéville's text, especially the Theaetetus section (1962).

5 There has also been much other Franco-Greek activity with less emphasis on Heraclitus and Parmenides, yet very influential: in the 1960–70s, there was, for example, the so-called Paris School; Jean-Pierre Vernant (*Les origines de la Pensée Grecque* 1962), and also Pierre Lévêque and Pierre Vidal-Naquet, using structuralist arguments to analyse ancient Greece and to explore the Other through this framework. Simone de Beauvoir was influenced by their reworking of the Greek Other.

6 We also have the student workbook of Ricœur's lectures on *Platon et Aristote*, translated by David Pellauer in which Ricœur focuses upon Plato's dialogue Parmenides, whereas in the lectures I am studying, he concentrates more on the original; Parmenides' Poem.

7 Heraclitus *Fragment* XXII Kahn, 39.

8 AR/FR – Bib. IPT, Inv. 1, d96 'La négation' Cours. Feuillets 8749–70./8749 96A/002.

9 *Fragment*, 51; Kahn (2001).

10 Heraclitus' *Fragment*, 4; Kahn (2001).

11 Heraclitus' *Fragment*, 82; Kahn (2001).

12 I suggest that if, or when, the maidens cantered back to the city and found themselves, at some point, pregnant, even if not by Parmenides, they would surely understand that they were both themselves and not themselves; by carrying a foetus, they are both one individual and also two. The One can, indeed must often be, two. Aristotle attempted to deal with this sort of issue, in his strenuous refutation of his predecessors' outlandish ideas about women as carriers of seeds that conjoined with men's seeds to create a foetus; to think about women in a more balanced way we would need to consult Songe Möller for gender debates in her book *Philosophy Without Women* (2002), where

she argues that Parmenides rejects the girls who take him away from the city because they are female.

13 Diels, H. and Kranz, W. (1903–1910) *Die Fragmente der Vorsokratiker*. Werdmannsche: Buchhandlung.

14 Plotinus (1999): V, I, 8 *The Enneads*. London: Penguin. Here, Plotinus praises Plato for being more accurate in his dialogue than Parmenides himself! Plotinus prefers Plato's version of One in Many, which gives scope for Plotinus' monism to absorb the many.

15 Taylor, pp. 10–11.

16 Cornford, pp. 102–3, 107.

17 AR/FR – Bib. IPT, Inv. 1, d96 'La négation' Cours. Feuillets 8751/96A/002.

18 AR/FR – Bib. IPT, Inv. 1, d96 'La négation' Cours. Feuillets 8772–89 PR 96B/003.

19 AR/FR – Bib. IPT, Inv. 1, d96 'La négation' Cours. Feuillets 8772–89 PR 96B/003; AR/FR – Bib. IPT, Inv. 1, d96 'La négation' Cours. Feuillets 9290–300 96G/029 (28).

20 AR/FR – Bib. IPT, Inv. 1, d96 'La négation' Cours. Feuillets 8772–89 PR 96B/003; AR/FR – Bib. IPT, Inv. 1, d96 'La négation' Cours. Feuillets 9301–25 96G/030 (2, 6).

21 Kahn (2001): *fragment* 82.

22 AR/FR – Bib. IPT, Inv. 1, d96 'La négation' Cours. Feuillets 9301–25 96G/030, 6.

23 AR/FR – Bib. IPT, Inv. 1, d96 'La négation' Cours. Feuillets 9301–25 96G/030 15, 25.

24 AR/FR – Bib. IPT, Inv. 1, d96 'La négation' Cours. Feuillets 8772–89 PR 96B/003, 39.

25 AR/FR – Bib. IPT, Inv. 1, d96 'La négation' Cours. Feuillets 8772–89 96B003/34; Heraclitus in Kahn, *Fragment*, 60 and 88.

26 AR/FR – Bib. IPT, Inv. 1, d96 'La négation' Cours. Feuillets 9301–25 96G/030 5, 6.

27 AR/FR – Bib. IPT, Inv. 1, d96 'La négation' Cours. Feuillets 8902–94 96D 014, 2.

28 Parmenides fragments in Gallop, p. 65. Ricœur also makes these points in AR/FR – Bib. IPT, Inv. 1, d96 'La négation' Cours. Feuillets 8751 /96A/002, 6, 7.

29 Aristotle, *Metaphysics IV*, 1005b19-20; the psychological version appears at Met IV 1005b23-24 and the logical version at Met IV 1011b13-14.

30 AR/FR – Bib. IPT, Inv. 1, d96 'La négation' Cours. Feuillets 8772–89 PR 96B/003, 21.

31 AR/FR – Bib. IPT, Inv. 1, d96 'La négation' Cours. Feuillets 8902-8994 96D 014, 3.

32 AR/FR – Bib. IPT, Inv. 1, d96 'La négation' Cours. Feuillets 8772–8789 PR 96B/003, 34.

33　AR/FR – Bib. IPT, Inv. 1, d96 'La négation' Cours. Feuillets 9301–25 96G/030, 17.

34　Heidegger *Essais et conférences*, p. 249 ff.

35　*Fragment*, 10 and *Fragment*, 51; Kahn (2001).

36　AR/FR – Bib. IPT, Inv. 1, d96 'La négation' Cours. Feuillets 8772–89 PR 96B/003: 15; Heidegger *Essais et Conferences*, 260.

37　Sartre explores Heidegger's lack of dialectic, in his work on Heidegger in *Being and Nothingness* Sartre Etre et le Néant 54–5/18–19; 306/249 *Being and Nothingness*.

38　AR/FR –Bib. IPT, Inv. 1, d96 'La négation' Cours. Feuillets 9182–9206:9182.

39　AR/FR –Bib. IPT, Inv. 1, d96 'La négation' Cours. Feuillets 9290–9300 Heraclitus frag 10, 80 and frag 54.

40　AR/FR –Bib. IPT, Inv. 1, d96 'La négation' Cours. Feuillets 8772–8789.

41　*1955 Louvain, three lectures on* Finitude, Négativité, Affirmation, 2; Scott-Baumann, A. *Ricœur and the Hermeneutics of Suspicion* 2009: 38–44, 55, 98.

42　Plato, *Sophist*, trans. N. P. White. Indianapolis: Hackett: 249a.

43　Plato Sophist trans N. P. White Indianapolis: Hackett: 249b.

44　AR/FR – Bib. IPT, Inv. 1, d96 'La négation' Cours. Feuillets 8749–70 96A/002.

45　Ricœur differentiates between Plato's dialogue called Parmenides, and Parmenides' own poetry, by calling Plato's work *Le Parménide* and Parmenides' own work *'the poem'*.

46　*Fragment*, 2 Gallop.

47　Plato, *Sophist*, trans. N. P. White. Indianapolis: 250e; AR/FR – Bib. IPT, Inv. 1, d96 'La négation' Cours. Feuillets 8751 /96A/002, 3.

48　Sophist 257b and c; AR/FR – Bib. IPT, Inv. 1, d96 'La négation' Cours. Feuillets 8751, 3.

49　The issue comes up in Theaetetus. Rolland de Renéville, Jacques (1962) *Essai sur le problème de L'Un-Multiple et de l'Attribution chez Platon et les Sophistes*. Thèse principale pour le doctorat des lettres, L'université de Paris. Paris: Librairie philosophies J Vrin. Closely annotated sections by Ricœur, especially Theaetetus.

50　Hyppolite, J. (1953/1997) *Logic and Existence*, p. 145 fr./112 Eng.

51　Marcuse, H. (1964, 2002): 196 *One-Dimensional Man*.

52　Ricœur, Time and Narrative 3. See footnote 25, p. 333.

53　AR/FR – Bib. IPT, Inv. 1, d96 'La négation' Cours. Feuillets 8772–89 8789, 96B/003.

54　Ricœur read and referenced the Diels-Kranz translations 1934, *Fragmente der Vorsokratiker*. He went back to the original Greek in J. Zafiropulo (1950) *L'Ecole Eléate*. He compared translations by Cornford, Kranz, and Gigon with the Zafiropulo translation that comes from Kranz in Diels and annotated the differences.

55　AR/FR – Bib. IPT Paris, Inv.1, d 96 'La négation' Cours. Feuillets 8772–89, 8789, 96B/003.

56 AR/FR – Bib. IPT, Inv. 1, d96 'La négation' Cours. Feuillets 8809–13 96C/003 written in English for delivery in USA, probably early 50s, sounds as if it came after *Freedom and Nature* and before the three Louvain lectures.

57 1955 Louvain, three lectures on *Finitude, Négativité, Affirmation.*

58 Ricœur's next challenge, in these lectures on negation is Aristotle's *Physics.* This would merit a study of its own. Aristotle struggled with the belief that matter is the key to understanding and has no negative (there was no anti-matter yet in human science). Aristotle refused to acknowledge the idea of negation in nature, yet brought the possibility of *movement* that creates something, from nothing something may come, and facilitated the development of dialectical models of debate, despite his personal rejection of dialectical thinkers. However, we could and really should also consider the Rig Veda and the Upanishads, which were debating these issues 2,000 years earlier.

59 Ricœur (1995/1998): ch 7. *Conflict and Conviction.*

Chapter 4

1 Hegel, (2010) *The Science of Logic.* Cambridge: Cambridge University Press.

2 Hegel, (2010) *Encylopaedia of the Philosophical Sciences in Basic Outline, Part 1: Logic,* Cambridge: Cambridge University Press.

3 *Négation et Realité* AR/FR –Bib. IPT Paris, Inv.1, d 96 'La négation' Cours. Feuillets 9260–9268.

4 Hegel's Logic (1873/1975), p. 112.

5 Paul Ricœur, 'Le lieu de la dialectique', in *Dialectics. Dialectiques,* ed. Ch. Perelman (The Hague: M. Nijhoff, 1975).

6 Kojève, A. *Introduction to the Reading of Hegel*; desire for recognition, p. 192, struggle for recognition, p. 225, work, p. 189, speech, p. 212, and finally death, p. 246; death and freedom are two aspects of the same thing, p. 247.

7 Kojève was a major figure in the planning of the European Common Market, after World War II.

8 Kolb, D. (1986) *The Critique of Pure Modernity.* Chicago: University of Chicago Press, 218.

9 There are British Hegelians, of whom Bradley is probably the best known.

10 Hegel's Logics: The Science of logic/Encyclopaedia Logic follow the same structure, but the Logic in the Encyclopaedia is shorter and much easier to understand than the Science of Logic. There are the same forms of negation in each. There are three main areas in the Logic that Hegel develops, with dialectic as the methodological underpinning for everything and several meanings of the negative, which I develop in Chapters 6 and 7: 'The highest mode of the nothing for itself would be freedom, but this freedom is the mode of negativity that has deepened itself so as to reach the highest intensity. Thus it is itself affirmation, and even absolute affirmation' Enc 1 i.e. Enzyklopedie der philosophischen Wissenschaft im Grundrisse 1 para 87, cf L, 160/146 (1817–1839) Hegel's Logic, trans. M. Wallace (Oxford: Clarendon Press, 1975), p. 75.

11 Ricœur, (1950/66) *Freedom and Nature: The Voluntary and the Involuntary*. Evanston: Northwestern University Press.

12 Ricœur, (1960/65) *Fallible Man*. New York: Fordham University Press; *Histroy and Truth* 1955/1965 Evanston, Illinois: Northwestern University Press.

13 Ref Ric's notes on Hyppolite on *Logic and Existence* boite 24, dossier 8, p. 182.

14 Ricœur, (1965/70) *Freud and Philosophy: An Essay on Interpretation*. Yale: Yale University Press.

15 Ricœur (1955): 1383 *Retour à Hegel* Esprit 23/8, 1378–91.

16 Ricœur *Time and Narrative* 3 (1985/1988): 193–207.

17 Ricœur, (2000/09) *Memory, History, Forgetting*. Chicago: Chicago University Press.

18 Ricœur, (2004/07) *The Course of Recognition*. Harvard: Harvard University Press.

19 Ricœur *Conflict of Interpretations* 1969/74: 412.

20 Ricœur *Conflict of Interpretation* 1969/1974: 413 and Hegel Preface to Philosophy of Right, Paragraph 4.

21 Ricœur *Conflict of Interpretation* 1969/1974: 414.

22 Ricœur, *Husserl* 1967: 207 Evanston.

23 AR/FR –Bib. IPT, Inv. 1,d27 Cours. 'Anthropology and Religion in the philosophy of existence' 1958 Feuillets 4057-4101.

24 Ricœur 1963/1981: 313–42. Two encounters with Kierkegaard: 'Kierkegaard and Evil' and 'Doing Philosophy After Kierkegaard'; In *Kierkegaard's Truth: The Disclosure of the Self*, ed. J Smith. Newhaven and London: Yale University Press.

25 Kierkegaard, (1981) *The Concept of Anxiety*. Princeton: Princeton University Press.

26 Kierkegaard, (1983a) *The Sickness unto Death*. Princeton: Princeton University Press.

27 Kierkegaard, (1983b) *Fear and Trembling*. Princeton: Princeton University Press.

28 Ricœur 1963/1981: 320. Two encounters with Kierkegaard.

29 Kierkegaard, (1988) *Either/or*. Princeton: Princeton University Press.

30 Ricœur 1963/1981: 324. Two encounters with Kierkegaard.

31 Smith 1981: 324 in *Kierkegaard's Truth*.

32 Ibid.

33 Ricœur 1969/1974: 415 *Conflict of Interpretations*; I imagine that the as yet unpublished Ricœur lectures on Imagination are his development of creative imagination beyond Kant's limiting of it.

34 'Hegel et la négation' box 24/ folder 90 p. 2; Ricœur, P 1975, 'Le 'Lieu' de la dialectique' in *Dialectics/Dialectiques* offprint Entretiens Varna 1973. P. 104.

35 Hegel, (1977) *Phenomenology of Spirit*, Oxford, Clarendon Press.

36 See Ricœur, *Time and Narrative*, vol. 3, pp. 192–206.

37 Judith Butler, (1987) *Subjects of Desire: Hegelian Reflections in Twentieth Century France*. New York: Columbia University Press.

38 Ricœur (1956/65): 328 'Negativity and Primary Affirmation', in *History and Truth*. Evanston: Northwestern University Studies.

39 Hegel (2010): 437, *The Science of Logic*.

40 Ricœur (1986) *Lectures on Ideology and Utopia*.

41 Kao, W., in Roberts and Scott-Baumann (2010).

42 Ricœur (1975/1977): 337, *The Rule of Metaphor*.

43 The multiple meanings of *Aufhebung* make it very difficult to pin down. English translations use sublation. The French have struggled with this greatly. Hyppolite in 1939 used *dépasser* and *supprimer*, Wahl, in 1966 invented *sur-primer*, Barquin in 1975 used *abroger*, Doz in 1976 used *enlever*, Vieillard-Baron in 1977 used *mettre en grange*, Denis in 1984 used *conserve*, et *dépasse*, Tilliette in 1973 used *dépasser*, *surpasser*, Martineau in 1984 used assumer, Derrida in 1975 used relever, as did Nancy in 1973, Gauthier in 1967 used sursumer, as did Labarriere and Jarczyle in 1972 and 1993 and Lefevbre in 1999 used abolir/abolition. A Koyre played a significant role here, before his pupil Kojève. Cassin B 2004 *Vocabulaire Européen des philosophes. Dictionnaire des intraduisibles*. Paris: Seuil Le Robert.

44 Ricœur (1965): 322, *History and Truth*.

45 Husserl (2012) *Logical Investigations*.

46 Ricœur, (1991) *From Text to Action*, Evanston, Northwestern University Press.

47 AR/FR – Bib. IPT, Inv. 1, d27 Cours La Négation 8677, 96D/014.

48 AR/FR – Bib. IPT, Inv. 1, d96 'La négation' Cours. Feuillets 9301–25 96G/030.

49 Kant, E. (1781/1998): A167, B209 *Critique of Pure Reason*.

50 AR/FR – Bib. IPT, Inv. 1, d27 Cours. 'Anthropology and Religion in the philosophy of existence' 1958. Feuillets 4057–101, 17.

51 AR/FR – Bib. IPT, Inv. 1, d96 'La négation' Cours. Feuillets 9301–25 96G/030.

52 Ricœur (1955/1965) *History and Truth* 1965: 328.

53 Ricœur, P. (1985): 309 'Irrationality and the plurality of philosophical systems'. *Dialectica* 39(4): 298–319.

Chapter 5

1 Kafka (1919) *Before The Law*.

2 Ricœur, 'Kant et la négation', Cours, p. 8478. See note below for full reference.

3 Archives Ricœur, Fonds Ricœur, Bibliothèque de l'IPT – Paris, inventaire 1, dossier 96, La négation, Cours. (c. 1952–68) feuillets 8450–840.

4 There is a history to Ricœur's interest in the Kant essay: he took a lecture course called *Kant et le problème de la négation* as a young scholar in the early 1930s, when he presumably read 'Negative Magnitudes' in German and was introduced to it by, among others, his tutor Dalbiez. We have a comment in his 1933 lecture notes *Kant et le problème de la négation* where he has written that in 1763 Kant discovered the synthetic character of mathematics in

opposition to Leibniz and Hume, yet the student Ricœur/his tutor wondered how it could be possible for Kant to argue synthetically, when he had not yet developed *a priori* thinking. (8483).

5 Kant, (2002) 'Attempt to Introduce the Concept of Negative Magnitudes into Philosophy', in *Theoretical Philosophy 1755-1770*. Cambridge: Cambridge University Press, 207–41.

6 Kant (1998) *Critique of Pure Reason*. Cambridge: Cambridge University Press.

7 David-Ménard, M. (2005) *Deleuze et la psychanalyse* Monique David-Ménard describes how desire is often perceived in psychoanalysis; desire as a lack, a negative that will be impossible to fulfil, involving sexual dysfunction and impulses deemed to be socially inappropriate: denial, guilt, malfunction, repression, resistance – not on Kant's list, yet undeniably part of our being since Freud explained us to ourselves. David-Ménard writes extensively on Kant's role, as she sees it, as a transformative force with great potential value for psychoanalysis, and she engages with Deleuze, Guattari and Lacan to create a different narrative for the negative. Her views are interesting as a foil to those of Ricœur upon the same Kant essay. Ricœur is much more critical of Kant's essay on 'Negative Magnitudes' than David-Ménard is, and yet he also attributes great importance to it because of the contribution it makes to the way in which our humanity is influenced by the way we desire and seek to master understanding.

8 David Walford, Preface to Kant, *Theoretical Philosophy 1755-1770*, pp. xv–xxii.

9 Kant, 'Negative Magnitudes', p. 209.

10 Ibid., p. 225.

11 The 'Negative Magnitudes' essay is one of four interesting essays by Kant from the so-called pre-critical period 1762–64, and of which *False Subtleties* and 'Negative Magnitudes' really show Kant's thinking about the problem of causal laws. He challenges traditional metaphysics with its belief that human reason gives us a direct insight into how things really are – in fact he is beginning to argue in *False Subtleties*, and continues this much later in the *Transcendental Dialectic* of the first critique, that we make judgements about what we perceive and develop them into inferences (which he called syllogisms). These are vitally important and yet they also demonstrate that we cannot really understand the world or God or the human soul, because our thought processes are also characterized by illusions produced by our perceptions. Much later he will argue that we combine practical wisdom with belief in order to adduce 'facts' that we cannot prove but that seem both reasonable and necessary, such as the existence of God or the rightness of justice.

12 Kant, 'Negative Magnitudes', p. 211.

13 Kant, *Essai pour introduire en philosophie le concept de grandeurs negatives*, trad. et introduction Roger Kempf. Paris, Vrin, 1949 (reprint 1991).

14 Mme Granier and her husband were both colleagues of Ricœur's at Nanterre. I have not found these lectures, only the plan for them.

15 AR/FR, Bib. IPT: Inv. 1, d96 La Négation, Cours. (c. 1952–68) 8868–874 feuillet: 8874.

16   Ricœur, (1950/66) *Freedom and Nature: The Voluntary and the Involuntary*. Evanston: Northwestern University Press.

17   Ricœur, *Freedom and Nature*, p. 17.

18   Ricœur Ibid., p. 19.

19   Sartre, J. P. (1939/2008) *Sketch for a Theory of the Emotions*. London: Routledge.

20   Ricœur, *Freedom and Nature*, pp. 316–7.

21   Ricœur, *Fallible Man*. New York: Fordham University Press.

22   Ricœur Ibid., p. 11.

23   (*Fallible Man*, p. 73, fn 24).

24   Ricœur, *Freedom and Nature*, p. 317.

25   Ricœur, (2007) *Husserl: An Analysis of His Phenomenology*. Evanston: Northwestern University Press, pp. 210–11.

26   Ricœur, (1960) *The Symbolism of Evil*. New York: Harper and Row, p. 11.

27   Ricœur, (1965/70) *Freud and Philosophy: An Essay on Interpretation*. Yale: Yale University Press.

28   Ricœur, (1969/2000) *The Conflict of Interpretations*. London: Continuum.

29   Neither Kant nor Ricœur saw this in the same way that, say, Anthony Burgess did, great wordsmith and moralist, whom I introduce here for comparison. He is famous for *Clockwork Orange*, yet he wrote many sophisticated novels, of which MF (MF is the name of the novel) interests me as it analyses Levi Strauss on structuralism and incest. The gap between Burgess and his Roman Catholic religious upbringing yawns much wider than the discrepancies between Kant and the formal faith of his time or Ricœur and his Protestant upbringing. Kant and Ricœur, like Burgess, based their imagination upon the religious conviction that we have 'fallen' from a hypothetical state of pure grace and goodness. Burgess refuses to explore these areas explicitly, yet Ricœur does.

30   Kant is a great inspiration for Ricœur in other domains too, namely, in his practical philosophy. In the eighth study of *Oneself as Another*, Ricœur finds a tension in the several formulations of the categorical imperative, in that they command both respect for the person and for the (moral) law. However, Ricœur argues, sometimes we can have conflict between different (moral) laws, between duties stemming from different orders, as is the case in the moral dilemma of the *Antigone*. In these cases, he argues, the person should always be over and above the law because, ultimately, love has to correct and perfect the justice which, by itself, can only be blind. See Ricœur, (1990/95) *Oneself as Another*. Chicago: Chicago University Press.

31   AR/FR, Bib. IPT: Inv. 1, d96 La Négation, Cours. (c. 1952–68) feuillet 8450.

32   Kant, *Critique of Pure Reason*, B111 (p. 215).

33   AR/FR, Bib. IPT: Inv. 1, d96 La Négation, Cours. (c. 1952–68) feuillet 8452.

34   AR/FR, Bib. IPT: Inv. 1, d96 La Négation, Cours. (c. 1952–68) feuillet 8458.

35   AR/FR, Bib. IPT: Inv. 1, d96 La Négation, Cours. (c. 1952–68) feuillet 8459.

36 AR/FR, Bib. IPT: Inv. 1, d96 La Négation, Cours. (c. 1952–68) feuillet 8459.

37 AR/FR, Bib. IPT: Inv. 1, d96 La Négation, Cours. (c. 1952–68) feuillet 8472.

38 AR/FR, Bib. IPT: Inv. 1, d96 La Négation, Cours. (c. 1952–68) feuillet 8473.

39 Ricœur discussed on p. 8473 that he sees in Kant the tendency for negation to operate more to provide evidence (probative) than to stand in judgement (Judicatory, as he describes Eric Weil's term).

40 AR/FR, Bib. IPT: Inv. 1, d96 La Négation, Cours. (c. 1952–68) feuillet 8478.

41 AR/FR, Bib. IPT: Inv. 1, d96 La Négation, Cours. (c. 1952–68) feuillets 8479–80.

42 Marco Giovannelli, *Reality and Negation – Kant's Principle of Anticipations of Perception. An Investigation of Its Impact on the Post-Kantian Debate.* Dordrecht: Springer Verlag, 2010.

43 Kant (1781) *Critique of Pure Reason*, A172.

44 Ricœur, *Fallible Man*, p. 137.

45 Scott-Baumann, A., in *Iris Murdoch and The Moral Imagination*, 2010.

46 AR/FR, Bib. IPT: Inv. 1, d96 La Négation, Cours. (c. 1952–68) feuillet 8461.

47 AR/FR, Bib. IPT: Inv. 1, d96 La Négation, Cours. (c. 1952–68) feuillet 8472.

48 Kant, E. (1763) in *1755-1770 Theoretical Philosophy*, Kant's interest in the negative shows in other early texts, for example, even earlier than 'Negative Magnitudes', in 1755, 'Concerning the Principle of Contradiction', asserting the impossibility of the Aristotelian law of contradictions:

49 Kant (1781) *Critique of Pure Reason*, A575-6/B602/3.

50 Kant (1781) *Critique of Pure Reason*, CPR B307.

51 Ricœur, *Fallible Man*, p. 27.

52 AR/FR, Bib. IPT: Inv. 1, d96 La Négation, Cours. (c. 1952–68) feuillet 8471.

53 Kant (1781) *Critique of Pure Reason*, CPR B312.

54 Ricœur (1960) *Fallible Man*, pp. 133–34.

55 AR/FR, Bib. IPT: Inv. 1, d96 La Négation, Cours. (c. 1952–68) feuillet 8468 and Kant, CPR B275-6).

56 Ricœur, *Fallible Man*, p. 137.

57 AR/FR, Bib. IPT: Inv. 1, d96 La Négation, Cours. (c. 1952–68) feuillet 8450.

58 AR/FR, Bib. IPT: Inv. 1, d96 La Négation, Cours. (c. 1952–68) feuillet 8476.

59 Kant (1781) *Critique of Pure Reason*, A255.

60 Kant (1781) *Critique of Pure Reason*, B307.

61 1990 Reprinted in 2008. Ricœur, (2008) *Amour et Justice*. Paris: Seuil.

62 Ricœur, (1995) *Figuring the Sacred*. Fortress Press, p. 320.

63 Kafka, F., (1995) 'Before the Law', in *The Metamorphosis and Other Stories*, trans. W. and E. Muir. New York: Schocken, pp. 148–50; Derrida, J. (1982) 'Before the Law', in *Acts of Literature*, ed. D. Attridge. London: Routledge, pp. 182–320.

64 Ricœur (1975) *Biblical Hermeneutics'* in Semeia.

65 Ricœur, 'Le lieu de la dialectique' in *Dialectics. Dialectiques,* ed. Ch. Perelman. The Hague: M. Nijhoff, (1975), p. 102.

Chapter 6

1   François Dosse, (2007/2010) *Gilles Deleuze and Félix Guattari: Intersecting Lives*. New York: Columbia University Press.

2   Dosse. Ibid., 151, 516–17; Mongin, O. (2004) 'L'excès et la dette'. Cahier l'Herne. Paris: Herne, 271–83.

3   AR/FR – Bib. IPT, Inv. 1, d27 Cours. 'Anthropology and Religion in the philosophy of existence' 1958, Feuillets 4057–101.

4   Ricœur (1967): 208, *Husserl. An Analysis.*

5   Ricœur, *Time and Narrative*, 3 (1985/88): 240.

6   Deleuze, G. (1968/2004): 259–60, *Difference and Repetition.*

7   Deleuze, G. (1968/2004) *Difference and Repetition.*

8   Dosse, F. (2007/2010) *Gilles Deleuze and Felix Guattari. Intersecting Lives.*

9   N. B. Foucault expounded about Marx, Freud, Nietzsche as the masters of suspicion in 1967 (see Dosse, Deleuze, p. 132 and p. 545, Cahiers de Royaumont, no. 6, Paris, Minuit, 1967 and reprinted in Foucault *Dits et Ecrits* (Paris: Gallimard, 1994, 1: 564–79), yet Ricœur first named them before Foucault in 1960 at Bonneval, with an essay called *The Conscious and the Unconscious.* See *Ricœur and the hermeneutics of suspicion* pp. 43–4, although it was not published until 1966 in French in the *Conflict of Interpretations.* Did Ricœur often get there first?

10 Scott-Baumann, A. (2009) *Ricœur and the Hermeneutics of Suspicion.*

11 *Basic Writings of Nietzsche* (2000): 726.

12 Ibid, 163.

13 Dosse (2007/2010), 129ff. Deleuze had published a book on Kant in 1963 in which he analysed the three major texts of Kant and showed the centrality of the *Critique of Judgment,* and his love-hate relationship with the cool rationality of Kant lasted throughout his life: he wrote a preface to Tomlinson's and Habberjam's translation of his *Kant's Critical Philosophy.* In this preface, he summarizes some of the main points from his lecture series on Kant of 1978.

14 Dosse, F. (2007/2010): 133 *Gilles Deleuze and Felix Guattari. Intersecting Lives.*

15 Scott-Baumann, A. (2009) *Ricœur and the Hermeneutics of Suspicion.*

16 Ainscow, M. and Tweddle, D. (1984) *Early Learning Skills Analysis.* New York and London: Wiley.

17 For me as a linguist this has huge implications for world citizenship, and Ricœur wrote well in his three essays *On Translation,* which I discuss in Scott-Baumann (2010) and address in the context of Arabic in Scott-Baumann and Contractor (2011b).

18 Deleuze, G. (1965): ch. 3, 'Nietzsche', in *Pure Immanence.*

19 Deleuze, G. (1965) 'Nietzsche' in *Pure Immanence.*

20 Duns Scotus with his *haecceitas,* thisness, was also a great inspiration to G. M. Hopkins.

21 Deleuze, G. (1968/2004): 258–9, *Difference and Repetition.*

22 Deleuze, G. (1954/2004): 36, *Desert Islands and Other Texts.*

23 Deleuze, G. (1954/ 2004): 37, *Desert Islands and Other Texts.*

24 Deleuze, G. (1968/2004): 67, *Difference and Repetition.*

25 Jean Wahl, as a Hegelian, was wary of this move.

26 Deleuze, G. (1968/2004): 257, *Difference and Repetition.*

27 Ibid.

28 Ricœur (1950): 450, *Freedom and Nature.*

29 Ricœur (1956/65): 328, *History and Truth.*

30 Roberts, M. F. and Scott-Baumann, A. (2010) *Iris Murdoch and the Moral Imagination.* Jefferson: McFarland.

31 Scott-Baumann, A. (2010) 'Nausea under the Net', in Roberts, M. F. and Scott-Baumann, A. (eds) *Iris Murdoch and the Moral Imagination.* Jefferson: McFarland; Scott-Baumann, A. (2012) 'Ricœur and Murdoch: The Idea and the Practice of Metaphor and Parable'. *Il Protagora* XXXIX (17): 67–79.

32 Murdoch, I. (1953/1987) *Sartre. Romantic Rationalist.* London: Chatto and Windus, pp. 111–12.

33 *Sartre. Romantic Rationalist,* 91ff; *Being and Nothingness,* 626ff.

34 Badiou, A. (1988/2005) *Being and Event*; Badiou, A. (2008) 'We need a popular discipline: Contemporary Politics and the crisis of the negative' in *Critical Inquiry* 34.

35 Murdoch used her philosophical knowledge to investigate the human condition, addressing, for example, Plato in *The Unicorn,* Sartre in *Under The Net,* Heidegger in *The Time of The Angels,* Nietzsche in *The Sea, The Sea* and Freud in *The Severed Head.* She also used parables such as The Good Samaritan for heuristic effect.

36 Ricœur (1956/1965): 328, *History and Truth.*

37 Ricœur (1975): 144–5 'Biblical hermeneutics' in *Semeia*; Ricœur (1975/77): 24 *Rule of Metaphor.*

38 Ricœur (1975): 143 'Biblical hermeneutics' in *Semeia.*

39 Henry, P. (1991) *The Place of Plotinus in the History of Thought in Plotinus Enneads,* trans. S. MacKenna. London: Penguin.

40 AR/FR – Bib. IPT, Inv. 1, d96 'La négation' Cours. Feuillets 9236–58: 9243 96F/025.

41 Ibid.

42 AR/FR – Bib. IPT, Inv. 1, d96 'La négation' Cours. Feuillets 9236–58: 9246–7

43 AR/FR – Bib. IPT, Inv. 1, d96 'La négation' Cours. Feuillets 9236–58: 9207–35: 9211 96F/025.

44 AR/FR – Bib. IPT, Inv. 1, d27 Cours. 'Anthropology and Religion in the philosophy of existence' 1958, Feuillets 4057–101, 17–18. As described in Chapter 2, in these eight lectures given in the United States of America in 1958, Ricœur listed the eight protagonists of what he described then as a modern philosophy of negation: Hegel, Kierkegaard, Nietzsche, Marx, Jaspers, Marcel, Heidegger and Sartre.

45 We have evidence of Ricœur working in some detail on Hegel's Logic: in the late 1960s there are nine pages in the archives on *Hegel et la négation*. At this point, we have to assume, by inference, that Ricœur was engaging fully with the *Encyclopaedia Logic*, not with the *Science of Logic*, which is much longer. He was reading the *Encyclopaedia Logic* in German *Hegel et la négation* – boite 24, folder 90, 8.1: 1. This imperious demand from Hegel is impossible to countenance, yet Ricœur argued that we have to accept it if we want to read him. This may explain partly why, in Ricœur's sequence of lectures about negation, he focused mainly upon the *Phenomenology of Spirit* and very little upon the *Encyclopaedia Logic*. This appears to be similar in his lectures as catalogued in the archives, where it is also clear that he lectured mainly about the *Phenomenology of Spirit*, to a lesser extent about Hegel's *Philosophies of Religion* and of *Law* and hardly at all on Hegel's Logic.

46 Ricœur (2000/2004): 605, *Memory, History, Forgetting*.

47 Plotinus (1991) *Enneads*, trans. S. MacKenna, p. 404.

48 Murdoch (1997) *Existentialists and Mystics*, pp. 130–1; Sartre she saw as a dualist of two different stripes; the dualism between being in self (static, inert) and being for self (acting on the world) and also the dualism of the consciousness trying to attain ideal totality. Ibid., p. 135.

49 Ricœur (1956/1965):190, *History and Truth*.

50 Scott-Baumann, A. and Norris, C. (2004) *Derrida and Indian Thought: Prospects for an East/West Dialogue?* E-journal Consciousness, *Literature and the Arts*, vol. 5: 2.

51 Ricœur, 'Le lieu de la dialectique': 102.

52 Ricœur, 'Irrationality and the plurality of philosophical systems'. 1985 in *Dialectica*, vol. 39(4): 298–319.

53 Ricœur (1995): 315 *Figuring the Sacred*.

54 Ricœur (2000/2004): 13 *Memory, History, Forgetting*.

Chapter 7

1 The sudden walk Kafka, F. (1919/1995): 19, in *The Metamorphosis and Other Stories*.

2 Do you know which sort of cheese will entice a bear out of a tree? Camembert; Do you know how many polar bears are left in the arctic?

3 See Scott-Baumann, A. and Norris, C. (2004).

4 1950, in *Freedom and Nature*, and he returns in 1993 to the agent and patient as well: The Moral, Ricœur, P. (1994): 13–24, 'The Moral, the ethical and the political'.

5 See H. Cixous for an excellent example of a challenge: *The laugh of the Medusa*.

6 Kafka in fact wrote it before the Great War at a time when those who spoke out against the Hapsburg Empire could be imprisoned and tortured.

7 Kant, E. (1788/1999): 5.117 *Critique of Practical Reason*.

8 Kant, E. (1763): 2.196 'Attempt to Introduce the Concept of 'Negative Magnitudes' into Philosophy'.

9 There is also something else taking place; a twisting turning semi-circular motion is happening as Kant moves towards his final critique: aversion is *becoming* desire, desire to capture the sublime and be captivated by it, despite the sublime's imperfections and the negative impulse at its heart, as we will see in Kant's Third Critique. This will create problems for us in aesthetic matters, perhaps more than in morals and happiness, yet aesthetics affect the human condition significantly, so it is worth analysing. In Kant's *Critique of Judgement*, his third Critique, the beautiful is harmonious, peaceful and proportionate, the result of a complex yet happily balanced process. Yet the sublime, which is even more gorgeous and also closer to God, is out of kilter, exquisitely imperfect, containing within itself the negative of imperfection and thus continuing to offer the negative as a positive impulse. The sublime is achieved through conflict, it is disproportionate within itself, and this is a process that is faulty, producing a failure that is exquisite and sublime *because* it does not respond freely to the conformity to law that the imagination seeks and finds in harmony. Even if this is Kant describing an idea rather than a phenomenon, I believe that his sublime provides another way of considering the negative: the harmony of the beautiful is replaced in the sublime by discordance that seems almost to take us back to Heraclitus, with movement made possible. The sublime has these discordant, exhilarating characteristics that lead to conflict and that in their turn lead to reason, because the free play of the imagination will still result in a resolution that is not possible under the rules of the antinomies of the *Critique of Pure Reason*. There must be some form of end, of conclusion; teleological thinking and the controlled chaos with the negative within the Sublime can provide this, not least by giving reason a reason to exert itself, and an arena.

10 Layard, R. (2005) *Happiness. Lessons from a New Science*. London: Penguin.

11 Layard (2005): 218.

12 Ricœur, *Oneself as Another* (1990/1992): 172.

13 Searching for negation in the Pre-Socratics, Plato, Aristotle and finally in Plotinus, Ricœur found a strong intimation of how our subjective natures, the way we experience life from our own point of view, creates a reaction between *nothingness*, the apophatic way to God (and *non-being* in the Aristotelian sense of potential; *vision*, the capacity to 'see' God and *metaphor* which shows us the possibilities and the limits of our attempted vision of God and how to get beyond them. Ricœur looked at these to see if they would help him to challenge Hegel, and also, as well as developing his own religious faith, he hoped to demonstrate that 'secular' thinking can benefit from his work.

14 P. 112, Interview with F. Ewald, 20 June 2000, Magazine litteraire in Appendix M. C. Dowling, *Ricœur on Time and Narrative*. Notre Dame: University of Notre Dame Press 'Of course we can use negatives to assert a positive . . . Ricœur: I deeply admire the formula that Simone Weil described as the four refusals or negations': not to believe that anything is exempt from fate or chance, never to admire force that derives from mere power, never to hate your enemies and never to humiliate those who suffer from misfortune. These are

not simply negations or refusals, but principles that impose a certain moral structure on existence, a starting point from which we may go about inventing a positive form of life'.

15 Ricœur, P. (1986/1991) *From Text To Action: Essays in Hermeneutics* II: 227–45.

16 Yet Husserl was not able to convince us by conjuring up a real sense of self and other. So to this Ricœur added Weber's corollaries that human agents must be able to recognize the actions of others; that sociology looks at human behaviour that is other-oriented and that humans need order and actions that are meaningful. Here, Ricœur saw the potential for a phenomenology of intersubjectivity that could challenge Hegel's *Phenomenology of Spirit*.

17 Ricœur, P. (1986/1991) *From Text To Action: Essays in Hermeneutics* II: 236.

18 Ricœur (1996) 'From metaphysics to moral philosophy'. *Philosophy Today* 40(4): 443–58, 447–8. 'The philosophy of action is, in its analytic phase, a semantics of action sentences, and, in its reflective phase, an investigation of ways of speaking of oneself as an agent, ways of recognizing oneself verbally as the author of one's acts; narration is speaking par excellence, discourse and text; and moral imputation is spoken through the features of a special kind of attribution, an 'ascription' joining imputed action to the responsible agent.'

19 http://www.hrw.org/reports/1999/rwanda/Geno1-3-09.htm.

20 Ricœur (2010), 'Being a Stranger', trans. A. Scott-Baumann, in *Theory Culture and Society*, vol. 27, no. 5 pp. 37–48; The work of Paul Weller on discrimination on grounds of religion is important (Weller et al 2013) *http://www.religionandsociety.org.uk/uploads/docs/2013_01/1359118897_Weller_Phase_3_Large_Grant_Block.pdf.*

21 The first thing to be clear about here is that 'Muslims' fall into many different categories and subgroups and, like all human groups, such as Catholics and Protestants, may not get on with each other and may (and do) seek to do each other harm. In Britain, I work with Sunnis (deobandi and Barelvi) and Shias and sufis (the last group cross various denominational boundaries). However, I will simplify with the term 'Muslim' and the term 'Islam' as a way into this discussion, and indeed, despite my years of working with Muslims, I am still a white western liberal feminist woman. Many Muslim groups would see me as alien, but I am concerned here with our responsibilities to our fellow citizens and my desire to challenge Islamophobia in the media and in the general loose use of negative views. I believe we can accept that all sectors of British society want to be safe, and endorse attempts by the central government to foil terror plots and to reduce likelihood of terrorist attacks and of radicalization of British citizens. Please see bibliography for some of my work in this area.

22 House of Commons Communities and Local Government Committee (2010) *Preventing Violent Extremism: Sixth Report of Session 2009–10*. London: The Stationery Office.

23 Ricœur, P. (1974): 85–6 *Political and Social Essays*.

24 It is a clear example of the importance of understanding Ricœur when we look at how these symbols arise, how a piece of cloth comes to represent terror and evil. At the same time as he was working on negation intensively in the

1950s and 60s, Ricœur was also analysing guilt and sin: he found that it is difficult for us to represent sin directly to ourselves, and that it is part of a complex web of meaning tangled up in guilt. He used Saussure to consider the relationship between signs, symbols and reality.

25 Barthes, R. (1957) *Mythologies*. Paris: Seuil.

26 *Politics, Philosophy and Religion*, Lancaster University.

27 Dr Sariya Contractor, Derby University.

28 Bellini, L. M. and Shea, J. A. (2005) *Mood Change and Empathy Decline Persist during Three Years of Medical Training.*

29 Sheerin, D. (2009) Deleuze and Ricœur. Freud fascinates with his various approaches to the negative, described in his 1925 essay on Negation and discussed in O'Neil and Akhtar.

30 Charalambous, A. (2008) *Ricœur's Hermeneutical Phenomenology: An Implication for Nursing Research*; Charalambous, A., Papadopoulos, I. R. and Beadsmoore, A. (2009) *Towards a Theory of Quality Nursing care for Patients with Cancer through Hermeneutic Phenomenology*; Charalambous, A. (2010): 8, *Interpreting Patients as a means of Clinical Practice: Introducing Nursing Hermeneutics.*

31 Shapiro, J. (2008) Walking a mile in their patients' shoes: empathy and othering in medical students' education in *Philosophy, Ethics and Humanities in Medicine*. 3:10, http://www.peh-med.com/content/3/1/10.

32 Ricœur (1990/1992): 22 *Oneself as Another.*

33 Scott-Baumann (2009) *Ricœur and the Hermeneutics of Suspicion.*

34 Reagan, C. and Stewart, D. (eds) (1978): 79, *The Philosophy of Paul Ricœur.*

35 This is ever more true, as foretold by Ricœur in 'Universal Civilisation and National Cultures' (in *History and Truth*) and 'Violence and Language' (in *Political and Social Essays*).

36 Kant, E. (1781/1998): B111, *Critique of Pure Reason.*

BIBLIOGRAPHY

Ainscow, M. and Tweddle, D. (1984) *Early Learning Skills Analysis (ELSA)*. New York, London: Wiley.

Allen, R. E. (1983) *Plato's Parmenides. Translation and Analysis*. Oxford: Basil Blackwell.

American Psychiatric Association (2000) *Diagnostic and Statistical Manual for Mental Disorders (DSM-IV-TR)*, 4th edn, Text revision. Washington DC, APA.

Aristotle (1933) *Metaphysics Books 1-9 (Loeb Classics)*, trans. H. Tredennick. Cambridge, MA: Harvard University Press.

— (2006) *Metaphysics Books 10-14*, trans. H. Tredennick and G. Cyril Armstrong. Cambridge, MA: Harvard University Press.

Austin, J. L. (1979) Performative Utterances in *Philosophical Papers*, 3rd edn, ed. J. O. Urmston and G. J. Warnock. Oxford: Oxford University Press.

Badiou, A. (1988/2005) *Being and Event*. New York, London: Continuum.

— (2008) 'We need a popular discipline: Contemporary Politics and the crisis of the negative'. *Critical Inquiry* 34 (Summer 2008): 645–59.

Barthes, R (1957) *Mythologies* Paris: Seuil.

Beiser, F. (2005) *Hegel*. London: Routledge.

Bellini, L. M. and Shea, J. A. (2005) 'Mood change and empathy decline persist during three years of medical training'. *Academic Medicine* 80: 164–7.

Butler, J.(1987) *Subjects of Desire: Hegelian Reflections in Twentieth Century France*, New York, Columbia University Press.

Burgess, A. (1971) *MF*. London: Jonathan Cape.

Burgess, A. (2001) 'Oedipus Wrecks', in *This Man and Music*. New York: Applause Theatre and Cinema Books (first published McGraw-Hill, 1983).

Burnet, J. (1908) *Early Greek philosophy* London: Adam and Charles.

Cannadine, D. (2013) *The Undivided Past: history beyond our differences* London: Allen Lane.

Cassin, B. (2004) *Vocabulaire Européen des philosophes. Dictionnaire des intraduisibles*. Paris: Seuil Le Robert.

Changeux, J-P. et Ricœur, P. (2000) *What Makes Us Think?* Princeton and Oxford: Princeton University Press.

Charalambous, A. (2008) 'Ricœur's hermeneutical phenomenology: An implication for nursing research. *Scandinavian Journal of Caring Sciences* 22(4): 637–542.

— (2010) 'Interpreting patients as a means of clinical practice: Introducing nursing hermeneutics'. *International Journal of Nursing Studies*. doi:10.1016/ijnurstu.2010.02.011. www.elsevier.com/ijns.

Charalambous, A., Papadopoulos, I. R. and Beardsmoore, A. (2009) 'Towards a theory of quality nursing care for patients with cancer through hermeneutic phenomenology'. *Eur J Oncol Nursing* 13(5): 350–60.

Clark, S. H. (1990) *Paul Ricœur*. London: Routledge.

Cornford (1939) *Plato and Parmenides*. London: Kegan Paul.

David-Menard, M. (2005) *Deleuze et la psychanalyse*. Paris: PUF.

Deleuze, G. (1954/2004) 'Jean Hyppolite's *Logic and Existence*'. *Desert Islands and Other Texts 1953-74*, ed. D. Lapoujade and trans. M. Taormina. New York: Semiotext (e) MIT Press.

—(1962/2010) *Nietzsche and Philosophy*. London: Continuum.

—(1968/2004) *Difference and Repetition*. London: Continuum.

—(1983/1984) *Kant's Critical Philosophy*. London: Continuum.

—(2005) *Nietzsche in Pure Immanence*, trans. A. Boyman. New York: Zone Books.

—(2012) *Foucault*, trans. Sean Hand. London: Continuum Bloomsbury.

Deleuze, G. and Guattari, F. (1972/2011) *Anti-Oedipus*. London: Continuum.

Derrida, J. (1978/1987) *The Truth in Painting*, trans. G. Bennington and I. McLeod. Chicago: Chicago University Press.

—(1982) 'Before the law', in D. Attridge (ed.), *Acts of Literature*. London: Routledge, pp. 182–320.

—(1996) *Archive Fever*, p. 3, trans. E. Prenowitz. Chicago and London: Chicago University Press.

Diehl, C. (2011) 'Negative and intensive magnitudes in Kant's pre-critical philosophy' http://www.academia.edu/660211/Negative_and_Intensive_ Magnitudes_in_Kants_Pre-Critical_Philosophy.

Diels, H. and Kranz, W. (1951–54) *Die Fragmente der Vorsokratiker*, 7th edn. 3 vols. Berlin: Weidmann Verlag.

Dosse, F. Paul (2008) *Ricœur Les sens d'une Vie*. Paris: La Découverte.

Dosse, F. (2007/2010) *Gilles Deleuze and Felix Guattari. Intersecting Lives*, trans. D. Glassman. New York: Columbia University Press.

Dhurandhar, A. (2009) Writing the Other: An Exercise in Empathy in *Journal for Learning Through The Arts* 5(1) http://escholarship.org/uc/item/8K29v4tf.

Ecclestone, K. and Hayes, D. (2009) *The Dangerous Rise of Therapeutic Education* New York and Abingdon: Routledge.

Ehrenreich, B. (2009) *Smile or Die. How Positive Thinking Fooled America and the World*. London: Granta.

Forster, E. and Melamed, Y., eds (2012) *Spinoza and German Idealism*. Cambridge: Cambridge University Press.

Foucault, M. (1972) *The Archaeology of Knowledge*, trans. A. M. Sheridan Smith. London: Routledge.

Gallop, D. (2000) *Parmenides of Elea. Fragments*. Toronto: University of Toronto Press.

Ganeri, J. (2011) *The Lost Age of Reason Philosophy in Early Modern India 1450-1700*. Oxford: Oxford University Press.

Gillespie, S. (2008) *The Mathematics of Novelty: Badiou's Minimalist Metaphysics*. Melbourne: re.press.

Granger, B. B., et al. (2006) 'Caring for Patients with chronic heart failure: the trajectory model'. *Eur. Journal of Cardiovascular Nursing* 5(3): Epub.

Gregor, M. (1995): 215–32. 'The Live Metaphor', in L. Hahn (ed.), *The Philosophy of Paul Ricœur*. Chicago and La Salle: Open Court.

Groys, B. (2012) *Under Suspicion: Phenomenology of Media*. New York: Columbia University Press.

Hall, W. D. (2007) *Paul Ricœur and the Poetic Imperative*. New York: State University of New York Press.

Heraclitus. *The Fragments of Heraclitus' Poem*, http://www.ou.edu/logos/heraclitus.

Hegel, G. W. (1831/1969) *Science of Logic*, trans. A. V. Miller. New York: Humanities Books.

—(1873/1975) *Logic*, trans. W. Wallace. Oxford: Oxford University Press.

Heidegger, M. (1942–43/1998) *Parmenides*, trans. A. Schuwer and R. Rojcewicz. Bloomington and Indiananpolis: Indiana University Press.

Heidegger, M. (1954/48). *Essais et conférences* trans A Préau Les Essais LXC Paris: Gallimard.

Henry, P. (1991) 'The place of Plotinus in the history of thought', in Plotinus *Enneads*, trans. S. MacKenna. London: Penguin.

Honneth, A. (2000) *La Lutte pour la reconnaissance*, trans. P. Rusch. Paris: Cerf.

Houlgate, S. (2005) *The Opening of Hegel's Logic*. West Lafayette: Indiana Purdue University Press.

House of Commons Communities and Local Government Committee (2010) *Preventing Violent Extremism: Sixth Report of Session 2009–10*. London: The Stationery Office.

Hughes, J. (2010) *Deleuze's Difference and Repetition*. London: Continuum.

Husserl (2012) *Logical Investigations*. London: Routledge.

Hyppolite, J. (1953/1997) *Logic and Existence*, trans. L. Lawlor and A. Sen. Albany: State University of New York Press.

Inwood, M. (1992) *Hegel Dictionary*. London: Blackwell.

Kafka, F. (1919/1995) 'Before the Law and In the Penal Colony', in *The Metamorphosis and other Stories*, trans. W. and E. Muir. New York: Schocken, pp. 148–50.

Kahn, C. (2001) *The Art and Thought of Heraclitus*. Cambridge: Cambridge University Press.

Kant, E. (1763a/2002) 'Attempt to Introduce the Concept of Negative Magnitudes into Philosophy', in *1755-1770 Theoretical Philosophy*, trans. David Walford in collab. with R. Meerbote. Cambridge: Cambridge University Press.

—(1763b) *Essai pour introduire en philosophie le concept de grandeur négative*, trans. R. Kempf, 1949. Paris: Librairie philosophique J Vrin.

—(1781) *Critique de la Raison Pure* 3ieme édition, trans. A. Tremesaygues et B. Pacaud. Paris: Presses Universitaires de France.

—(1781/1998) *Critique of Pure Reason*, trans. P. Guyer and A. Wood. Cambridge: Cambridge University Press.

—(1788/1999) *Critique of Practical Reason* in Practical Philosophy. Cambridge: Cambridge University Press.

—(1790/2000) *Critique of Power of Judgement*. Cambridge: Cambridge University Press.

Kao, W. H. (2010) 'Domination, Resistance, and Anglo-Irish Landlordism in *The Servants and the Snow*', in M. F. Roberts and A. Scott-Baumann eds, *Iris Murdoch and the Moral Imagination*. Jefferson: McFarland.

Kirk, G. S. (1954) *Heraclitus: The Cosmic Fragments*. Cambridge: Cambridge University Press.

Kirk, G. S. and Raven, J. E. (1957) *The Presocratic Philosophers*. Cambridge: Cambridge University Press.

Kitaro, N. (1949/1987) *Nothingness and the Religious World View*. Honolulu: University of Hawaii Press.

Kofman, S. (1989/1998) *Socrates, Fictions of a Philosopher*, trans. Catherine Porter. London: Athlone.

Kojève, A. (1947/1980) *Introduction to the Reading of Hegel*. Cornell: Cornell University Press.

LaCocque, A. and Ricœur, P. (1998/1998) *Thinking Biblically*, trans. D. Pellauer. Chicago: Chicago University Press.

Layard, R. (2005) *Happiness. Lessons from a New Science*. London: Penguin.

Leclercq, J. (2012) Editorial *Revue Internationale Michel Henry* No. 2. Michel Henry Textes Inédits sur l'expérience d'autrui. UCL Presses Universitaires de Louvain, pp. 9–10.

Marcelo, G. (2010) 'From conflict to conciliation and back again: Some notes on Ricœur's dialectic' *Revista Filosofica de Coimbra* 38: 341–66.

Marcovich, M. (1967) *Heraclitus* Merida: University Press.

Marcuse, H. (1964, 2002) *One-Dimensional Man. Studies in the Ideology of Advanced Industrial Society*. New York, London: Routledge.

Marta, J. (1997):198–212 'Towards a bioethics for the twentieth Century: A Ricœurian post-structuralist narrative hermeneutic approach to informed consent', in H. L. Nelson (ed.) *Stories and their Limits: Narrative Approaches to Bioethics*. New York: Routledge.

Mongin, O. (2004) 'L'excès et la dette', in *Cahier l'Herne* Paris: Herne, pp. 271–83.

Monson, S. P. (2009) STFM *Empathy*-1.pp http://fmdrl.org/index.cfm.

Murdoch, I. (1953/1987) *Sartre. Romantic Rationalist*. London: Chatto and Windus.

—(1954/2002) *Under The Net*. London: Vintage Books.

—(1970/1989) 'The Servants and the Snow', in *Three Plays*. London: Chatto and Windus.

—(1997) *Existentialists and Mystics*. London: Chatto and Windus.

Nietzsche, F. (2000) *Basic Writings of Nietzsche*, trans. W. Kauffmann. New York: The Modern Library.

Nordmann, A. *Establishing Commensurability Intercalation, Global Meaning and the Unity of Science*. Accessed 24/8/12, http://www.philosophie.tu-darmstadt.de/media/institut_fuer_philosophie/diesunddas/nordmann/estcommensurability.pdf.

Noys, B. (2010) *The Persistence of the Negative: A Critique of Contemporary Continental Theory*. Edinburgh: Edinburgh University Press.

O'Neil, M. K. and Akhtar, S., eds (1993) *On Freud's 'Negation'*. London: Karnac Books.

Osborne, T. (1999) 'The Ordinariness of the archive'. *History of Human Sciences* 12(2): 51–64.

Owens, J. (1951) *The Doctrine of Being in the Aristotelian Metaphysics*. Toronto: Pontifical Institute of Medieval Studies.

Pinkard, T. (1996) *Hegel's Phenomenology. The Sociality of Reason*. Cambridge: Cambridge University Press.

Pippin (2008) *Hegel's Practical Philosophy: Rational Agency as Ethical Life*. Cambridge: Cambridge University Press.

Plato (1990) *Theaetetus*, ed. M. Burnyeat and trans. M. J. Levett. Indianapolis: Hackett.

—(1993) *Sophist*, trans. N. P. White. Indianapolis: Hackett.

Poem of Parmenides, http://philoctetes.free.fr/parmenidesunicode.htm.

Plotinus (1991) *Enneads*, trans. S. MacKenna. London: Penguin.

Rawnsley, M. (1998) 'Ontology, epistemology and methodology: A clarification'. *Nursing Science Quarterly* 11: 2–4.

Reagan, C. and Stewart, D., eds (1978) *The Philosophy of Paul Ricœur*. Boston: Beacon Books.

Redfield, J. (1975) *Nature and Culture in the Iliad: The Tragedy of Hector*. Chicago: University of Chicago Press.

Remschmidt, H. (2005) *Eur Journal Adolescent Psychiatry* 14: 127–37. D01 10.1007/5 00787-015-0139.

Ricœur, P. (1948) *Gabriel Marcel et Karl Jaspers. Philosophie du mystère et philosophie du paradoxe*. Paris: Temps Présent.

—Ricœur (1950/1966) *Freedom and Nature. The Voluntary and the Involuntary*, trans. E. Kohak. Evanston, IL: Northwestern University Press.

—Ricœur (1950/1967) *Husserl: An Analysis of His Phenomenology*, trans. E. G. Ballard and L. E. Embree. Evanston: Northwestern Press.

—Ricœur (1950/1996) *A Key to Edmund Husserl's Ideas 1*, trans. B. Harris and J. B. Spurlock, ed. P. Vandevelde. Milwaukee: Marquette University Press.

Ricoeur P. (1953-4/ 2013) *Being, Essence and Substance in Plato and Aristotle* transl. D Pellauer Cambridge Polity.

—Ricœur (1955) *Philosophie et Ontologie Retour à Hegel*. Esprit no. 8.

—Ricœur (1955, 1964/1965) *History and Truth*, trans. C. A. Kelbley. Evanston, IL: Northwestern University Press.

—(1960/1965, 1986) *Fallible Man*, revised trans. C. A. Kelbley (FM). New York: Fordham University Press.

—(1960/1967) *The Symbolism of Evil*, trans. E. Buchanan. Boston: Beacon Press.

—Ricœur (1963/1981) Two encounters with Kierkegaard: 'Kierkegaard as evil'; 'Doing philosophy after Kierkegaard', in J. S. Smith (ed.), *Kierkegaard's Truth: The Disclosure of the Self*. New Haven and London: Yale University Press, pp. 313–42.

Ricœur (1966/70) *Freud and Philosophy: An Essay on Interpretation*, trans. D. Savage. New Haven and London: Yale University Press.

—Ricœur (1969/1974) *The Conflict of Interpretations*, trans. D. Ihde. Evanston: Northwestern University Press.

—Ricœur (1974) *Political and Social Essays*, ed. D. Stewart and J. Bien. Athens: Ohio State University Press.

—Ricœur (1975a) 'Biblical Hermeneutics'. *Semeia* 4: 29–148.

—Ricœur (1975b) 'Le "Lieu" de la dialectique', in *Dialectics/Dialectiques*, offprint Entretiens Varna 1973.

—Ricœur (1975/1977) *The Rule of Metaphor: Multi-disciplinary Studies of the Creation of Meaning in Language*, trans. R. Czerny. Toronto and Buffalo: University of Toronto Press.

—Ricœur (1976) 'Ideology, Utopia and Faith'. *The Centre for Hermeneutical Studies* 17.

—Ricœur (1983/1984, 1985/1985, 1985/1988) *Time and Narrative*, vols. 1–3. Chicago: University of Chicago Press.

—Ricœur (1985) 'Irrationality and the plurality of philosophical systems'. *Dialectica* 39(4): 298–319.

—(1986) Engl./Fr 1997 *Lectures on Ideology and Utopia*. New York: Columbia University Press.

—(1986/1991) *From Text to Action: Essays in Hermeneutics II*, trans. K. Blamey and J. B. Thompson. London: The Athlone Press.

—Ricœur (1986/2007) *Evil, a Challenge to Philosophy and Theology*, trans. J. Bowden. London: Continuum.

—Ricœur (1990/1992) *Oneself As Another*, trans. K. Blamey. Chicago: Chicago University Press.

—Ricœur (1994) The Moral, the Ethical and the Political, trans. A. Scott-Baumann, in G. S. Johnson and D. Stiver (eds), *Paul Ricœur and the Task of Political Philosophy*. New York, Toronto: Lexington Books, pp. 13–24.

—Ricœur (1995) *Figuring The Sacred. Religion, Narrative and Imagination*, trans. D. Pellauer. Minneapolis: Fortress Press.

Ricœur (1996) 'Being a Stranger' trans A. Scott-Baumann in *Theory Culture and Society* Sept 2010, vol 27(5), pp. 37–48.

—(1999) *Lectures 1*. Paris: Éditions du Seuil.

—Ricœur (2000/2004) *Memory, History, Forgetting*. Chicago: Chicago University Press.

—Ricœur Interview with F Ewald, in M. C. Dowling, (2011) *Ricoeur on Time and Narrative*. Notre Dame: University of Notre Dame Press.

—Ricœur (2001/2007) *Reflections on The Just*. Chicago: University of Chicago Press.

—(2004/2005) *The Course of Recognition*, trans. D. Pellauer. Cambridge, MA: Harvard University Press.

—Ricœur (2004/2006) *On Translation*, trans. E. Brennan. London: Routledge.

—Ricœur(2007a) *Autour de la Psychoanalyse*, ed. C. Goldenstein and J-L. Schlegel. Paris: Seuil.

—Ricœur (2007b) *Vivant jusqu'à la mort*. Préface O. Abel, postface C. Goldenstein. Paris: Seuil.

—Ricœur (2008) *Amour et Justice*. Paris: Seuil.

Ritivoi, A. D. (2006) *Paul Ricœur: Tradition and Innovation in Rhetorical Theory*. Albany: State University of New York Press.

Rolland de Renéville, Jacques 1962 *Essai sur le problème de L'Un-Multiple et de l'Attribution chez Platon et les Sophistes* Thèse principale pour le doctorat des lettres, L'université de Paris. Paris: Librairie philosophie J Vrin.

Roberts, M. F. and Scott-Baumann, A. (2010) *Iris Murdoch and the Moral Imagination*. Jefferson: McFarland.

Robinson, R. (1953) *Plato's Earlier Dialectic*. Oxford: Clarendon press.

Ross, W. D. (1936) *Aristotle's Physics: A Revised Text with Introduction and Commentary*. New York: Clarendon Press.

Sartre, J-P. (1938/2000) *Nausea*. London: Penguin.

Sartre, J-P. 1938/2008 *Sketch for a Theory of the Emotions* London: Routledge.

—(1943/2008) *Being and Nothingness*, trans. H. Barnes. London and New York: Routledge.

Saussure, F. de (2011) *Course in General Linguistics*. Transl. W. Baskin. New York: Columbia University Press.

—(2002/2006) *Writings in General Linguistics*. Oxford: Oxford University Press.

Schilpp, P. A., ed. (1981) *The Philosophy of Jean-Paul Sartre*. La Salle Il: Open Court.

Scott-Baumann, A. (2003a) 'Reconstructive hermeneutical philosophy: Return ticket to the human condition'. *Journal of Philosophy and Social Criticism* 29(6): 705–29.

—(2003b) 'Teacher education for Muslim women: Intercultural relationships, method and philosophy'. *Ethnicities* 3(2). pp. 243–61.

—(2003c) 'Citizenship and Postmodernity'. *Intercultural Education* 14/4.

—(2006) 'Ethics, Ricœur and philosophy: Ethical teacher workshops'. *International Journal of Research and Method in Education* 29(1): 55–70.

—(2007) Collaborative partnerships as sustainable pedagogy: Working with British Muslims', in C. Roberts and J. Roberts (eds), *Greener by Degrees: Exploring Sustainability through Higher Education Curricula*. Geography Discipline Network (GDN) University of Gloucestershire. http://www.glos.ac.uk/shareddata/dms/FF071DBEBCD42A039FF8B1E4A2EE4606.

—(2009) *Ricœur and the Hermeneutics of Suspicion*. New York, London: Continuum.

—(2010a) *Muslim Faith Leader Training Review* with Dr Mukadam. Department for Communities and Local Government, http://www.communities.gov.uk/publications/communities/trainingmuslimleaderspractice.

—(2010b) 'Nausea under the net', in Roberts, M. F. and Scott-Baumann, A. (eds), *Iris Murdoch and the Moral Imagination*. Jefferson: McFarland.

—(2010c) 'Ricœur's translation model as a mutual labour of understanding' in *Theory Culture and Society*, special section on Ricœur under editorship of Prof Stephen Clark (September 2010, vol. 27, no. 5).

—(2011a) 'Enhancing the visibility of Muslim women in Islamic Studies with S. Contractor' *Perspectives 2: Teaching Islamic Studies in Higher Education*. Higher Education Academy. http://www.islamicstudiesnetwork.ac.uk/islamicstudiesnetwork/resources/display?id=/resources/alldetails/islamicstudies/Perspectives_issue_2_June_2011.

Scott-Baumann, A. and Contractor, S. (2011b) *Arabic Language and the Study of Islam: Who Studies Arabic and Why and How can these Skills be Used at University and Beyond?* https://www.llas.ac.uk/sites/default/files/nodes/6359/Final_ASB_SC_HEA_Arabic_Project_May_2012.doc.

—(2011c) Developing Islamic higher education for a secular university sector: Orientalism in reverse?', in I Niehaus et al. (eds), *Muslim Schools and Education in Europe and South Africa*. Munster. New York: Waxmann.

—(2011d) 'Unveiling Orientalism in reverse', in T. Gabriel (ed.), *Islam and the Veil*. New York, London: Continuum.

—(2012) 'Ricœur and Murdoch: The idea and the practice of metaphor and parable'. *Il Protagora* XXXIX(17): 67–79.

Scott-Baumann, A. and Norris, C. (2004) 'Derrida and Indian thought: Prospects for an East: West dialogue?'. *Consciousness, Literature and the Arts*, http://blackboard.lincoln.ac.uk/bbcswebdav/users/dmeyerdinkgrafe/archive/norris.html.

Scruton, R. (1994) *Modern Philosophy*. London: Sinclair-Stevenson.

Shapiro, J. (2008) Walking a mile in their patients' shoes: Empathy and othering in medical students' education in *Philosophy, Ethics and Humanities in Medicine*.3:10 http://www.peh-med.com/content/3/1/10.

Sheerin, D. (2009) *Deleuze and Ricœur. Disavowed Infinites and the Narrative Self.* London: Continuum.

Siddiqui, A. (2007) *Islam at Universities in England: Meeting the needs and Investing in the Future*. www.dfes.gov.uk/hegateway/uploads/DrSiddiquiReport. pdf.

Skinner, Q. (2002) *Visions of Politics*, Volume 1: *Regarding Method*. Cambridge: Cambridge University Press.

Smith, J. (1981) Kierkegaard's Truth. Newhaven and London: Yale University Press.

Songe-Möller, V. (2003) *Philosophy without Women*, trans. P. Cripps. London: Continuum.

Steedman, C. (2002) *The Archive and Cultural History*. New Jersey: Rutgers University Press.

Taieb, O., Rivah-Lévy A., Moro, M. R. and Baubet, T. (2008) 'Is Ricœur's notion of narrative identity useful in understanding recovery in drug addiction?'. *Qualitative Health Research* 18(7): 990–1000.

Taylor, A. E. (1934) *Plato's Parmenides*. London: Clarendon Press.

Tenneman, W. (1792–95) *System der Platonischen Philosophie* Leipzig.

Vernant, J-P. (1962/2007) *Les origines de la Pensée Grecque*. Paris: PUF.

Wahl, J. (1930) *Etude sure le Parménide de Platon*. Paris: Rieder.

Weiss, P. (1964) *The Persecution and Assassination of Jean-Paul Marat as Performed by the Inmates of the Asylum of Charenton Under the Direction of the Marquis de Sade*. London: John Calder.

Weller, P., Purdam, K., Ghanea, N. and Contractor, S. (2013) *Religion or Belief, Discrimination and Equality* London: Bloomsbury.

Wheelwright, P. (1961) *Heraclitus* Princeton NJ: Princeton University Press.

Wodak, R. (2011) 'Suppression of the Nazi Past, Coded language and discourses of silence: Applying the Discourse-Historical approach to Post-War anti-Semitism in Austria', in W. Steinmetz (ed.), *Political Language in the Age of Extremes*, German Historical Institute, Oxford: University Press, pp. 351–80.

Wundt, M. (1935) *Platons Parmenides*. Stuttgart, Berlin: Kohlhammer.

Zizek, J. (2008) *In Defence of Lost Causes*. London: Verso.

INDEX

2014.06.09   34.95 (32.35)